SMART\

A BEGINNER'S GUIDE

DEXTER J BOOTH

PITMAN PUBLISHING
128 Long Acre, London WC2E 9AN

A Division of Longman Group UK Limited

© Dexter J. Booth 1990

First published in Great Britain 1990

British Library Cataloguing in Publication Data

Booth, Dexter J.
   Smartware: a beginner's guide.
   1. Microcomputer systems. Software packages
   I. Title
   005,36

ISBN 0-273-03185-6

All rights reserved. No part of this publication may be reproduced, stored in a retrieval system, or transmitted, in any form or by any means, electronic, mechanical, photocopying, recording and/or otherwise without either the prior written permission of the Publishers or a licence permitting restricted copying in the United Kingdom issued by the Copyright Licensing Agency Ltd, 33–34 Alfred Place, London WC1E 7DP. This book may not be lent, resold, hired out or otherwise disposed of by way of trade in any form of binding or cover other than that in which it is published, without the prior consent of the publishers.

> SmartWare is a registered trademark of Informix Software Ltd.

ISBN 0 273 03185 6

Printed and bound in Great Britain by
Biddles Ltd, Guildford and King's Lynn

CONTENTS

Preface	1
Acknowledgements	2
Section 1: The SMART System: An Overview	3

Chapter 1: The SMART System

Objectives	5
Introduction	5
Entering the SMART System	5
The Introductory Screen	6
The Five Modules	7
The System Commands	8
Activating Commands	9
The F10 Function Key	9
Moving into the Modules	10
The HELP Facility	11
The SMART Documentation	14

Chapter 2: The Time-Manager

Objectives	17
Introduction	17
Opening the Diary	17
The Time-Manager Display	18
Using the Diary	19
Displaying the Week and the Month	23
The SMART Commands	25
The Other Time-Manager Commands	25

Chapter 3: The Data-Manager

Objectives	29
Introduction	29
Files and Databases	29
Entering The Data-Manager	30
Creating a File	32
Key Fields	36
Entering Data into Records	40
Creating a Customised Screen	42
Entering Data into a Customised Screen	43
Update	45

Find	45
Save, Load and Unload	45
Browse	46
Order	46
File-Specs	47
Recap And Review	48

Chapter 4: The Spreadsheet

Objectives	51
Introduction	51
The Screen Display	52
Entry Mode and Command Mode	53
Cursor and Sheet Control	55
Information Entry	55
Constructing a Worksheet	57
Enter Text	57
Enter Numbers	58
Enter Formulas	58
Copy	59
Insert	60
Width	62
Justify	62
Spillover	62
Save, Unload and Load	63
Recap and Review	63

Chapter 5: The Wordprocessor

Objectives	67
Introduction	67
Laying out the Page	70
The Document	71
Editing	72
Insert	73
Delete	73
Undelete	73
Move	74
Fonts	75
Save, Unload and Load	76
Printing the Document	76
Recap and Review	77

Section 2: The Data-Manager 79

Chapter 1: An Amplified Review

Objectives	81
Introduction	81
Data Management and the Components of a Database	81
Database Features	82
An Interactive Database	83
The Data-Manager Display	83
HELP	84
Selecting Command and Quick-Keys	84
Viewing Files	84
Active and Inactive Records	85
Entering Information	86
F5 and F6	86
Key Fields	88
Browsing a File	88
Unload, Save and Activate	89
Exiting the Data-Manager	89

Chapter 2: Ordering Records

Objectives	91
Introduction	91
Browse and Order	91
How a Key Field Works	92
Sort	92
Query	94
Query options	96
Special Query Clauses	98

Chapter 3: Creating Files

Objectives	99
Introduction	99
The SUPPLIER File	99
Entry Status	102
The STOCK File	103
The Customer Order File	105

Chapter 4: Lookups

Objectives	109
Introduction	109
Lookups	109
Defining a Lookup	110

Using a Lookup	114
Closing Down	115
Stock Items	115

Chapter 5: Relations

Objectives	117
Introduction	117
Loading the two Files	117
Relating the two Files	118
The Relationship	120
Intersect	121

Chapter 6: Transactions

Objectives	125
Introduction	125
Transactions	125
Defining the Transaction	126
Executing the Transaction	128

Chapter 7: Reports

Objectives	129
Introduction	129
Table Reports	129
Breakpoints	134
Grand Total	134
Form Report	137

Chapter 8: The Remember Mode

Objectives	143
Introduction	143
Order Entry	143

Chapter 9: Additional Commands

Objectives	149
Introduction	149
Find	149
Scroll	149
Utilities	150
Link, Unlink	150
Border	150
Display	150

File	151
Macro	151
Parameters	151
Read, Write and Send	151

Section 3: The Spreadsheet — 153

Chapter 1: An Amplified Review

Objectives	155
Introduction	155
Data Management and the Role of the Spreadsheet	155
Spreadsheet Features	155
The Spreadsheet Display	156
HELP	157
Selecting Commands and Quick-Keys	157
The Two Modes of operation	157
Moving Around the Worksheet	158
Special Commands in Entry Mode	158
Special Commands in Command Mode	159
Exiting the Spreadsheet	159

Chapter 2: Creating A Worksheet

Objectives	161
Introduction	161
Loading a Worksheet	161
Inserting a Column	162
Cell References	163
Copying Formulas	163
Absolute Cell References	164
Relative Cell References	164
The Prize Worksheet	165
Moving a Block of Cells	167
Pointing	167
Sorting	168

Chapter 3: The Matrix Command

Objectives	171
Introduction	171
The PRICE Worksheet	171
Changing The Prices	172

Chapter 4: The Appearance of the Worksheet

Objectives	175
Introduction	175
Insert, Move, Width, Colnumbers, Rownumbers, Border	175
Formatting a Worksheet	176
Reformat	176
Titles	176
Display and Paint	177

Chapter 5: Printing the Worksheet

Objectives	179
Introduction	179
Printing Text	179
Printing Formulas	180
Fonts	180
Font Design	180

Chapter 6: Worksheet Maintenance

Objectives	181
Introduction	181
Unauthorised Access	181
Lock and Unlock	182
Newname and Name	182
File	182
Directory and Index	182

Chapter 7: Windows and Multiple Worksheets

Objectives	183
Introduction	183
The COST List	183
The Profit Worksheet	185
What ... If ... Projections	187
The Profit Projection System	188

Chapter 8: Graphs

Objectives	191
Introduction	191
The Bar Chart	191
Graphics View	196
Printing a Graph	196
The Pie Chart	197

Chapter 9: The Graphics Edit Mode

Objectives	199
Introduction	199
Graphics Pictures	199
Movement of the Cursor	200
Lines	201
Text	201
Set	201
Editing Existing Graph Files	201

Chapter 10: Reports

Objectives	203
Introduction	203
Report Headings and Body	204
Load the Worksheet	204
The Report Definition	204
Printing the Report	206
Further Report options	207

Chapter 11: The Remember Mode

Objectives	209
Introduction	209
Directly Written Programs	209
The Remember Mode	209
PROFITS	209

Chapter 12: Additional Commands

Objectives	213
Introduction	213
Blank	213
Find	213
Sort	213
Fill	214
Index	214
Macros	214
Parameters	214
Write, Send and Read	214

Section 4: The Wordprocessor — 215

Chapter 1: Editing A Document

Objectives	217
Introduction	217
The Document LETTER	217
Replace	218
Scroll	219
Find/Goto	220
Bold, Underscore and Font	220
Footnotes	221
Split	222
Graphics	224
Compute	225

Chapter 2: Document Layout and Handling

Objectives	227
Introduction	227
Reformat	227
Tabs	228
Border, Paint and Ruler	229
Newname	229
Margin	230
Justify	230
Text-Sort	232
Document Handling	232
Marker	232
Password	233
Directory	234
Index	234
File	234

Chapter 3: Spellchecking a Document

Objectives	235
Introduction	235
Dictionary	235
Dictionary Custom	236
Dictionary Hyphenation	237

Chapter 4: Printing a Document

Objectives	239
Introduction	239
Print	239

Print Template	240
Print Options	241
Additional Options	242

Chapter 5: Handling Multiple Documents

Objectives	243
Introduction	243
Windows	243
Zoom	244
Transferring Information Between Documents	244
Close	245

Chapter 6: The Mail-Merge Facility

Objectives	247
Introduction	247
Text-File	247
Merge	248

Chapter 7: The Remember Mode

Objectives	251
Introduction	251
Directly Written Programs	251
The Remember Mode	251
Graphics Insert and Mail-Merge	252
Executing the Project	253

Section 5: Integration — 255

Chapter 1: Integration

Objectives	257
Introduction	257
Information Transfer	257
File Types	258
Transmitting Information	259

Chapter 2: Write and Read

Write - the Format	261
Write and Read	261
Write	262
The Summary Definition Screen	264
Read	265

Chapter 3: Send and Xlate

Objectives	267
Introduction	267
Send - the Format	267
Send	267
Xlate	268

Section 6: Project Processing   269

Chapter 1: Introduction to Project Processing

Objectives	271
Introduction	271
The SMART Programming Language	271
Project Files	271
Project File Extensions	272

Chapter 2: Creating Projects

Objectives	273
Introduction	273
The Remember Command	273
The Project Editor	274
Moving Around the Project Editor Window	275
Editing a Project	275
Exiting the Project Editor	276
The SMART Wordprocessor as a Project Editor	276

Chapter 3: Project Variables

Objectives	279
Introduction	279
Variables	279
Standard Project Variables	279
User Defined Project Variables	280
Parameter Variables	280
Assigning Data to Variables	280

Chapter 4: Project Commands

Objectives	283
Introduction	283
Display Commands	283
Control Commands	283
Decision Commands	284

Sub-Routine Commands	284
Variable Assignment Commands	285
Screen Commands	285
Project Execution Commands	285
Special Data-Manager Commands	286
Special Spreadsheet Commands	286

Chapter 5: Project Data Files

Objectives	287
Introduction	287
Fopen	287
Fwrite	288
Fread	288
Fclose	288
Fseek	289

Chapter 6: Project Menus

Objectives	291
Introduction	291
SMART Colors	291
Menu Commands	292

Chapter 7: Principles of Project Processing

Objectives	295
Introduction	295
The Information System Life Cycle	295
The Terms of Reference	295
Designing the System	296
The System Structure	296
Top Down Design	296
Developing the System	299
Phase 6: Pseudocoding the Modules	304
System Projects	305
Data-Manager Projects	305
Spreadsheet Projects	307
Wordprocessor Projects	308
Phase 7: Constructing the Final System	310

Chapter 8: The System Main Menu

Objectives	311
Introduction	311
The Main System Menu	311

Chapter 9: The Data-Manager

Objectives	315
Introduction	315
The Data-Manager Menu	315
ORDERS	317
WEEKLY	319
Transfer of Information	321
TOMAIN	322

Chapter 10: The Spreadsheet

Objectives	323
Introduction	323
WEEKSA	323
MONTHSA	325

Chapter 11: The Wordprocessor

Objectives	327
Introduction	327
EDIT	327
PRINT	328

Chapter 12: Implementation and Maintenance

Objectives	331
Introduction	331
Implementation	331
Maintenance	332

Section 7: The Communications Module   333

Chapter 1: Computer Communications

Objectives	335
Introduction	335
Computer to Computer Communications	335
Talking to Each Other	335
Terminal Emulation	336
File Transfer	336
The SMART Communications Module	336

Chapter 2: The SMART Communications Module

Objectives	339
Introduction	339
The Status Screen	339
The Terminal Screen	341
Establishing the Communications Settings	342

Chapter 3: Establishing Contact as Originator

Objectives	343
Introduction	343
Making a Call	343
Entering Commands	344
Capture Mode	344
Transmitting Files	345
Hangup	345

Chapter 4: Establishing Contact in Answer Mode

Objectives	347
Introduction	347
Answer Mode	347
Remote Command Mode	347
Restricted Commands	348

Chapter 5: The SMART Communications

Objectives	349
Introduction	349
Setting Communications Parameters	349
Miscellaneous Commands	350

Index   351

Preface

This book has been written with the novice SMART user in mind. The SMART Integrated Software Suite is a software package that is designed to be operated on a variety of expertise levels. To accommodate this design the software is accompanied by a set of four comprehensive manuals that describe the operation of the SMART System in fine detail. To cater for the first time user each manual contains a User Guide Section in which the command structure is demonstrated by example.

So why this book? When I saw the look in the eyes of so many users when presented with the set of four tomes I realised that a single, small book which used the same principle of teaching by example would go a long way to alleviate the apprehensions.

Anyone faced with a new piece of software asks two questions:

> What does it do?
> How does it do it?

This book answers those questions in a progressive manner to lead the user gently into using the SMART System.

Section 1 covers all aspects of the SMART System in broad outline at the most elementary level possible. The following six Sections then look at each Module in turn and develop the ideas introduced in the first Section. Throughout the book new concepts are introduced by example and all the examples relate to a single situation - the Sales Department of a mythical company called ABC Supplies.

Please note that though this book is entitled **SmartWare** the name **SMART** is used throughout because this is the name by which the software is popularly known. The name SmartWare is a precursor to **SmartWare II** which has recently been introduced. SmartWare II has a modified command structure and a re-styled Data-Manager but in most other respects it is similar to the original SmartWare.

I hope that you enjoy reading this book every bit as much as I enjoyed writing it. The SMART System is a remarkable piece of software and must surely serve as a benchmark for future developments in the field.

Dexter J Booth
Huddersfield 1989

Acknowledgements

This book is dedicated to everyone at Concorde Informatics Limited of Huddersfield for a most enjoyable year spent with them learning how to use this system. Particularly, Mike Fretwell, without whose humour and patience this book would never have been written. I should also like to express my gratitude to Innovative Software Limited and Informix Limited for all their assistance during the preparation and writing of this book.

Section 1 : The SMART System : An Overview

This Section provides an introduction to the SMART System. The first Chapter describes the general features of the SMART System. It shows that there are five modules to the System and demonstrates how each module is accessed. The following four Chapters look at each of the modules in turn.

Chapter 2 describes in full the operation of the Time-Manager. In doing so it demonstrates the basic philosophy behind the operation of the SMART System, namely the fact that the entirety is command driven.

Chapter 3 deals with the Data-Manager and details the creation of files and screens. It further describes the subsequent manipulation of the information within the files at an introductory level.

Chapter 4 looks at the Spreadsheet and introduces the two modes of operation - the Entry Mode and the Command Mode. By constructing a simple Worksheet the elements of spreadsheet manipulation are demonstrated.

Chapter 5 considers the Wordprocessor. Again there are two modes of operation and a short memo is constructed within this module to introduce the ideas of text manipulation.

The fifth module, namely Communications, is not dealt with in this Section. Rather, it is left to the last Section where it is discussed extensively.

There are five Chapters in this Section. They are:

- **The SMART System**
- **The Time-Manager**
- **The Data-Manager**
- **The Spreadsheet**
- **The Wordprocessor**

Chapter 1 : The SMART System

Objectives

When you have read this Chapter you will be able to:

- Enter the SMART System from DOS
- Recognise the Introductory Screen
- Recognise and access the five modules of the SMART System
- Appreciate that every component of the SMART System is operated by using a set of commands
- Recognise and activate the System commands available
- Move from one module to another
- Use the on-line HELP facility
- Identify the components of the SMART Documentation

Introduction

The **SMART System** is a comprehensive, integrated software package that combines a **Time-Manager**, a **Data-Manager**, a **Spreadsheet**, a **Wordprocessor** and a **Communications** Module. Whilst each module of the SMART System can be used as a stand-alone package the real power of the System can only be realized when each of the modules is being used as part of a single, integrated whole.

The SMART System is purchased on a collection of floppy diskettes and is then installed onto a hard disk by following the **Installation Procedure** that is fully described in a booklet that accompanies the software. We shall assume that the SMART System has been so installed and is ready for use.

In addition to the System software, the SMART System also includes four large and comprehensive manuals. We shall look at the contents of these manuals at the end of this Chapter. For now, we must first enter the SMART System.

Entering the SMART System

It is assumed that your SMART System is resident on the hard disk in a sub-directory called

6   *Chapter 1: The SMART System*

C:\SMART

and that there is an executable file called SMART also resident on the hard disk in the SMART sub-directory that when called will automatically boot up the SMART System.

From DOS enter the SMART sub-directory and enter the word **SMART** followed by **enter**. The SMART suite of programs will then become activated resulting in the **Introductory Screen**.

The Introductory Screen

The **Introductory Screen** is your first view of the SMART System and it appears as follows:

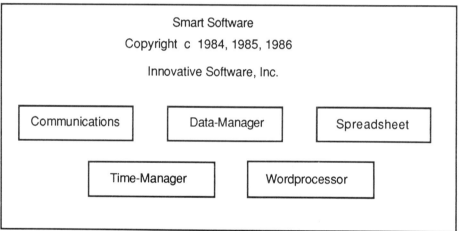

This screen display consists of four distinct areas:

> The Display Window
> The Control Area
> The Status Line
> The Autohelp Line

The Display Window

The uppermost area of the screen is called the **Display Window** and it is here that the consequences of the interaction between the user and the computer are displayed. At the moment the display shows the five modules that are available within the SMART System.

The Control Area

The Control Area consists of the two lines below the Display Window and it is here that the various commands and occasional prompts to the user are displayed. As you see at the moment it consists of two lines of words. These words are called **commands**, the first one of which is **highlighted**. The commands are preceded by the words **Command list 1**. There are other lists and we shall look at these shortly. When commands are displayed in this manner the system is said to be in **Command Mode** - this means that the commands displayed are currently available for use. We shall look at how to activate these commands in a little while.

The Status Line

This line, just below the control area, displays the status of the SMART Module being used. At present there is no module being used so it just displays the date and the time. What is meant by status we shall see as we consider each module separately.

The Autohelp Line

This displays a single line of **HELP** information relating to the command that is highlighted in the command area above. It displays a brief description of the command - we shall see later how to obtain more extensive HELP information. At the moment of entry into the SMART System the command **Communications** is highlighted and so the **Autohelp** line displays a brief description of this command.

The Five Modules

The names of the five modules within the SMART System are displayed in the Display Window of the Introductory Screen. They are:

> **Communications**
> **Data-Manager**
> **Spreadsheet**
> **Time-Manager**
> **Wordprocessor**

Each module is designed to either stand alone or act in conjunction with any other module as part of an integrated whole. For instance, information created within the Data-Manager can be sent to and processed within the Spreadsheet without ever having to leave the SMART System. This facility is fundamental to the concept of **integration** embodied within SMART.

We shall look at each of these modules in turn in the next four Chapters, but before doing so we shall take a closer look at the commands in the Command Area just below the Display Window.

The System Commands

At the the moment the SMART System is at the **System Level**. At this level there are three lists of Commands. We can move from one list to another by:

>Pressing / to go to the next list.
>Pressing \ to go to the previous list.
>Pressing the number 1, 2 or 3 to select the appropriate list.

Try it and you will see the following:

Command list 1:   Communications Data-Manager Learn Spreadsheet
                       Time-Manager Wordprocessor

Command list 2:   Autohelp Beep Confidence Directory File G-Calculator
                       Help Macro Text-Editor

Command list 3:   Configure Display Execute Font-Design Printer-Setup
                       Remember

Each one of these words represents a command that will instruct the SMART System to perform some operation. For example, move to Command list 2 and you will see that the command **Autohelp** is highlighted. At the bottom of the screen is the autohelp line and it now reads:

AUTOHELP - remove/restore help line at bottom of screen (toggle)

Now press the space bar once and the command **Beep** is highlighted. The autohelp line now reads;

BEEP - set error beeper on/off (toggle)

Every time you press the space bar the highlight moves on to the next command and the autohelp line gives a brief **help** description of what that command does. Do not worry if the explanation is too brief because there is always a more detailed explanation available as we shall soon see. Try this with each of the Command lists in turn.

Activating Commands

Now move back to **Command list 2** and highlight the command Autohelp. Because this command is highlighted it is now available for use. We activate the command by pressing enter. Do it. What happened? If you are not sure keep pressing enter until you are sure.

The Autohelp command turns the autohelp line display on and off - it is a toggle switch as the description states.

Now that was pretty painless and we have learned something.

- There are three lists of commands.
- Each command can be selected by moving to the appropriate Command list and pressing the space bar until the command is highlighted.
- The command is then activated by pressing enter.
- An activated command performs some operation within the SMART System.

The F10 Function Key

The **F10 Function Key** is used throughout the SMART System to finish or exit from whatever you are doing. Press **F10** now and the following display appears at the bottom of the screen:

Select option: Quit Spreadsheet Wordprocessor Data-Manager
Time-Manager Communications
exit main-menu
EXIT - exit main-menu

On the third line below the Display Window - the Status line - is the phrase:

exit main-menu

and that is the command that pressing the **F10** key has activated. The Introductory Screen with its three lists of commands is referred to as the **main-menu** and by pressing the **F10** key you have told the System that you wish to **exit** from this main-menu. You are then faced with a number of options displayed in the Command Area. Since **Quit** is highlighted we shall activate it by pressing **enter**. Do it.

So now you are back in **DOS**, having left the SMART System. Re-enter the SMART System and again you are confronted by the Introductory Screen displaying the **Command list 1**.

Moving into the Modules

An alternative way of activating a command is to move to the Command list displaying that command and then simply pressing the initial letter of the command - you will notice that on each list no two commands start with the same letter and that the commands are listed in alphabetical order. On Command list 1 the command Communications is highlighted but we wish to activate the **Data-Manager** so press **D**. After a few moments the screen display changes to;

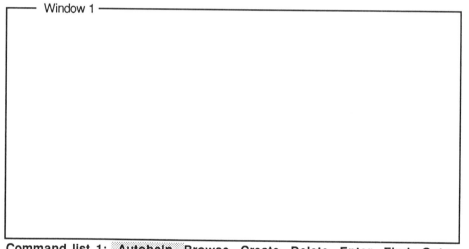

Command list 1: **Autohelp** Browse Create Delete Enter Find Goto
                Help Print Query Report Scroll Update
File: (none)   Window: 1
AUTOHELP - remove/restore help line at bottom of screen (toggle)

You are now in the **Data-Manager** Module of the SMART System. Easy isn't it? We shall not spend any more time here, press **F10** and the following options are displayed:

Select option: Quit Main-Menu Spreadsheet Wordprocessor Time-Manager
                      Communications

Select the **Main-Menu** by pressing **M**. Now we are back at the Introductory Screen. Why not experiment and move to all the other modules in turn. Notice that when you want to leave a module you can move to a further module without going back to the Introductory Screen.

Did you notice that all the modules have a similar appearance? The Display Window may have been different but underneath it every module displays a set of commands, a status line and an autohelp line. You will have found that the Spreadsheet and Wordprocessor modules did not display a Command list when you entered them. However, if, when you have entered them, you then press the **Esc** key the Command lists will appear. Try it.

This similarity of appearance is no accident, it is all part of the unified, integrated nature of the modules. Every module is operated by using commands that are available within that module and are displayed in the module's command area. The commands in each module are all activated in the same manner - by pressing the appropriate initial letter of the command - and many of the commands are similar. For example, the command Help appears in all of the modules as well as on Command list 2 of the Main-Menu. This similarity of screen display, commands and method of activating the commands makes it possible to become familiar with the SMART System very quickly.

To illustrate this we shall look at the HELP facility offered by the System.

The HELP Facility

Within the SMART System main menu and every Module there is a HELP facility that can be activated to provide an explanation of all the commands that are available. The manner in which this facility is accessed is the same no matter where you are in the System.

Move to the Introductory Screen and Command list 2 of the Main-Menu and select the command Help by pressing H. The following display then appears:

```
┌─────────────────────────────────────────────────────────────────┐
│                         Smart Software                          │
│                   Copyright c 1984, 1985, 1986                  │
│                                                                 │
│                      Innovative Software, Inc.                  │
│                                                                 │
│     ┌──────────────────┐  ┌──────────────┐  ┌───────────────┐   │
│     │  Communications  │  │ Data-Manager │  │  Spreadsheet  │   │
│     └──────────────────┘  └──────────────┘  └───────────────┘   │
│                                                                 │
├─────────────────────────────────────────────────────────────────┤
│   HELP  -  help information                                     │
│                                                                 │
│   Pressing the F1 key displays help information about the command│
│   that is currently highlighted or the activity you are currently performing.│
└─────────────────────────────────────────────────────────────────┘
```

Related topics: Autohelp
F1 Large help F2 Print help F3 Help Index F10 Finished Cursor keys

HELP - help Information

Large help is obtained by pressing F1 so do so. The screen then fills with information. As you see the information on this screen is incomplete. Press **PgDn** and the remainder will appear. Try it.

> **HELP Information**
>
> Pressing the F1 key displays help information about the command that is currently highlighted or the activity you are currently performing. A help box appears in the lower portion of the window, displaying the first four lines of on-line information available for the topic. The cursor keys (PgUp, PgDn and the up and down arrows) scroll the display of help information.
>
> If the help information extends over more than four lines you can press the F1 key again to enlarge the help box so that it fills the window.
>
> For most topics, a list of related topics appears at the bottom of the screen. You can obtain help information for these topics by moving the highlighter to the desired topic (use the space bar) and pressing the Enter key, just as if you were selecting a command.
>
> F3 displays an index of help topics. You can view the help info

Related topics: Autohelp
F2 Print help   F3 Help index   F10 Finished   Cursor keys

HELP - help information

> ➤   AUTOHELP - remove/restore help line at bottom of screen   (toggle)
>   BEEP - set error beeper on/off (toggle)
>   COMMANDS - description of commands used in project files
>   COMMUNICATIONS - access the Communications module
>   CONFIDENCE - change level of confidence
>   CONFIGURE - change configuration settings
>   DATA-MANAGER - access the Database Manager
>   DIRECTORY - list the files on a disk drive or directory
>   DISPLAY - alter display mode to black/white, color or graphics
>   EXECUTE - execute a project file
>   FILE - copy, erase, or rename a file; change the default data path
>   FONT-DESIGN - create or modify screen and printer fonts
>   G-CALCULATOR - general calculator
>   HELP - help information
>   LEARN - access the Tutorials
>   MACRO - clear, define, load, remove, save or view macros
>   PRINTER-SETUP - modify printer parameters or initialize printers
>   REMEMBER - create a new project file or modify an existing file
>   SPREADSHEET - access the Spreadsheet module

We shall now look at the **Help Index** which, as you can see, can be accessed by pressing the **F3** key - do it and the index appears.

The arrow is currently pointing at AUTOHELP. Use the cursor keys to point it at CONFIDENCE and press **F1** for help on that topic. The following appears:

```
                         Smart Software
                  Copyright c 1984, 1985, 1986

                      Innovative Software, Inc.
```

CONFIDENCE - change level of confidence

There are five Confidence levels (1 through 5). The first three levels provide command selection from menus. Level 1 offers basic commands. Level 2 offers the confidence level 1 commands plus more advanced commands. Levels 3-5 make all commands available .

Confidence levels 4 and 5 are non-menu prompting modes. Confidence level 4 allows you to select commands by typing the command name; Confidence level 5 provides automatic command recognition.

F2 Print help   F3 Help index   F10 Finished   Cursor keys

HELP - help information

Don't worry if this does not mean much to you at the moment, we shall be saying more about Confidence Levels in the next Chapter.

This procedure for obtaining help is the same no matter where you are within the SMART System. The only differences that occur are in the Help Index. Within any particular module only those commands appropriate to that module are contained in the Help Index. Why not move to each of the modules in turn and access the on-line HELP facility from within each.

The SMART Documentation

The SMART System Documentation consists of four individual loose leaf manuals:

> The Smart System Manual
> The Smart Data-Base Manual
> The Smart Spreadsheet Manual
> The Smart Wordprocessor Manual

Each Manual is also accompanied by its own pocket-sized Quick Reference Guide.

The SMART System Manual

There are five Sections to this manual :

System Commands

The various Commands that appear in the three Command lists that accompany the Introductory Screen are described in full. Also described is the Time-Manager which is the subject of the next Chapter.

Communications Reference Guide

This Section describes all the features of the Communications Module. We shall be looking at the Communications module in the last Section.

Project Processing

Project Processing consists of programming the SMART System to perform tasks automatically. This Section deals with this aspect of SMART in full. We have not previously mentioned this side of SMART handling as it is not appropriate here. Instead it is the subject of the penultimate Section.

Formula Reference

All the formulas that are available to SMART are reviewed in this Section. We shall be saying more about this feature as we progress.

Glossary

The last Section of this Manual is a complete glossary of terms for the entire SMART System.

The remaining three manuals each follow a similar pattern. Rather than deal with each manual separately we shall simply describe the pattern.

The SMART Module Manuals

Each manual has two Sections :
>Reference Guide
>Users Guide

Reference Guide

The Reference Guide describes all the features that are specific to that Module. It describes in detail both concepts that are specific to the particular Module and the action of each of the Commands available. It is completely comprehensive containing also a description of all the error messages that can occur.

Users Guide

This Section contains a tutorial that takes the user through all aspects of the Module. It is annotated and explains every step by example.

Chapter 2 : The Time Manager

Objectives

When you have completed this Chapter you will be able to:

- Use the Time-Manager as a diary
- Appreciate the use of commands within the SMART System

Introduction

The SMART Time-Manager is an Electronic Diary and Appointment Book that keeps a track of tasks to be performed and meetings to attend. As with any diary it arrives with a number of dated, blank pages each of which can be used to display information. We start by opening the diary.

Opening The Diary

We open the diary by selecting the **Time-Manager** command from the Command list 1 on the Introductory Screen. This is done either by moving the highlight with the space bar to **Time-Manager** and pressing enter or by simply pressing **T**. After a moment the following display will appear.

18   *Chapter 2: The Time Manager*

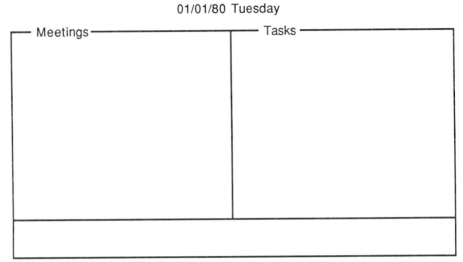

Command list 1: Autohelp Beep Display Edit Find Goto Help Insert
                Load Output Purge Remove Use
Today: 01/01/80   File: stm.dtm   Time: 12:00:55
AUTOHELP - remove/restore help line at bottom of screen (toggle)

The Time-Manager Display

The screen is now displaying the first page of the diary. As you will see from the top of the screen the date is Tuesday 1st January 1980. This is the default date that any PC will assume when it is switched on. If your PC has an internal, battery-driven calendar then the date that will appear should be today's date. Alternatively, you may have entered today's date into your PC when it was first switched on. In this case also today's date will appear. If the date is not today's date, don't worry as we shall sort that out later. Below the date is the Display Window which is displaying a blank diary page that is split into two. The left hand side you will see is reserved for meetings and the right hand side for tasks.

Below the blank page are four lines of information.

> **Lines 1 and 2**   These two lines form the Command Area and contain the commands that allow us to use the diary. There is only one list of commands in the Time-Manager.

> **Line 3**   This is the status line that provides information relevant to the status of the diary. The date and the current time are shown. Again, the time may be correct or not depending upon whether your PC's internal clock has been set either automatically or by you when you first switched your computer on. In the middle of the status line is the file name stm.dtm. This is the name of the disk file in which the diary is stored.

Line 4 This bottom line contains a help display of the currently highlighted command. By pressing the space bar you will be able to move the highlight from one command to the next. Try it and you will see a brief description of each relevant command appear on this line.

Using the Diary

Having familiarised ourselves with the screen display we shall now insert a meeting and a task.

Select the Command **Goto** by either highlighting it and pressing enter or simply by pressing **G** on the keyboard. This command is instructing the diary to go to a specific date. You are now asked to enter the required date by the prompt **Date:** appearing in the command area. Type in the following date:

21/07/69

followed by enter and immediately this date appears at the top of the screen. The Display Window is now available for entering meetings and tasks for Sunday 21st of July 69. We shall now enter a meeting into the diary.

Select the **Insert** Command and enter the following sequence of commands:

PROMPT	ENTER
	I: Insert
Select option: Meeting Task	**M:** Meeting

After pressing **I** and you are requested to choose between inserting a meeting or a task. We wish to insert a meeting. Select **Meeting** by pressing **M** and the following display appears at the bottom of the screen.

```
┌── Meeting Parameters : ─────────────────────┐
│                                             │
│ Date: 21/07/69                              │
│ Time:                                       │
│ Short Description:                          │
│                                             │
└─────────────────────────────────────────────┘
```

F10 when finished or ESC to cancel

You are now being requested to edit the Date (if that is necessary), enter the Time of the meeting and give a Short Description of the meeting.

Chapter 2: The Time Manager

Press the down arrow thereby leaving the date as displayed.

Enter the time **9:00** followed by enter.

Enter the short description : **Rendezvous**

When you have entered this description press **enter**. Immediately, the following display appears:

```
┌─ Edit Description: ─────────────────────────────────┐
│                                                     │
│                                                     │
│                                                     │
└─────────────────────────────────────────────────────┘
```
F10 when finished or ESC to cancel

You are being requested to give a more detailed description of the meeting. In this space type the following text:

Meeting with Edwin Aldrin to discuss the final arrangements to be made for the lunar landing

(At the end of the first line of text press **enter** to start the second line.) This completes the details of the meeting so press **F10** as you are finished.

You will now see that your 9:00 Meeting is displayed in the Window and at the bottom is the long description of what the meeting is about.

```
                        21/07/69 Sunday
┌── Meetings ─────────────────┬── Tasks ──────────────────┐
│ 9:00 Rendezvous             │                           │
│                             │                           │
│                             │                           │
│                             │                           │
│                             │                           │
│                             │                           │
├─────────────────────────────┴───────────────────────────┤
│ Meeting with Edwin Aldrin to discuss the final arrangements to be made │
│ for the lunar landing                                   │
└─────────────────────────────────────────────────────────┘
```

Command list 1: Autohelp Beep Display Edit Find Goto Help Insert
                        Load Output Purge Remove Use
Today: 01/01/80   File: stm.dtm   Time: 12:30:45

Insert - insert a new meeting or task into a day

To review: Meetings are inserted by selecting the command **Insert** followed by the option **Meeting**. Every meeting has associated with it a **Date**, a **Time**, a **Short Description** and an **Expanded Description**. When these are completed the meeting has been successfully entered into the diary.

The other type of entry into the diary is the task and, as we shall now demonstrate, this follows a similar pattern.

Select **Insert** from the Command list followed by **Task** from the option list. Immediately, the following appears at the bottom of the screen:

```
┌── Task Parameters : ────────────────────────────────┐
│                                                     │
│ Date: 21/07/69                                      │
│ Priority:                                           │
│ Short Description:                                  │
│                                                     │
└─────────────────────────────────────────────────────┘
```

F10 when finished or ESC to cancel

As with the meeting entry you are being requested to edit the Date, Enter the Priority of the task and give a Short Description of the task.

Press the down arrow thereby leaving the date as displayed.

The Priority will give the order in which tasks are to be listed on the screen. Enter the priority 1.

Enter the short description : **Leave lunar module**.

When you have entered this description the following display appears:

```
┌─ Edit Description: ──────────────────────────────────┐
│                                                      │
│                                                      │
│                                                      │
└──────────────────────────────────────────────────────┘
```

F10 when finished or ESC to cancel

In this space type the following:

Leave the lunar module when all preparations have been made and utter the immortal words - 'One step for a man, a giant leap for mankind'

This completes the details of this task so press **F10** as you are finished.

Your screen should now look as follows:

To move the highlight from the task to the meeting press the right arrow key. As the highlight moves so the description at the bottom of the Display Window changes - try it.

```
                    21/07/69  Sunday
┌─── Meetings ──────────────┬──── Tasks ────────────────┐
│                           │                           │
│   9:00 Rendezvous         │   1: Leave lunar module   │
│                           │                           │
│                           │                           │
│                           │                           │
│                           │                           │
│                           │                           │
├───────────────────────────┴───────────────────────────┤
│ Leave the lunar module when all preparations have been made and utter the
│ immortal words - 'One step for a man, a giant leap for mankind'
└───────────────────────────────────────────────────────┘
```

Command list 1: Autohelp Beep Display Edit Find Goto Help Insert
                    Load Output Purge Remove Use

Today: 01/01/80   File: stm.dtm   Time: 12:30:45

Insert - insert a new meeting or task into a day

Displaying the Week and the Month

The screen is currently showing the day of Sunday 21st of July 1969 when Neil Armstrong became the first person to step on the moon's surface. We can also display the week and the month that contains this day. First we shall look at the week.

Select the command **Display** and enter the following sequence of commands:

PROMPT   **ENTER**

                                                    D: Display
Select option: Day   Week   Month   W: Week

This causes the following to appear:

Chapter 2: The Time Manager

Week of 21/07/69

time	sun 21	mon 22	tue 23	wed 24	thu 25	fri 26	sat 27
- 07:00	-	-	-	-	-	-	-
08:00	-	-	-	-	-	-	-
09:00	▓	-	-	-	-	-	-
10:00	-	-	-	-	-	-	-
11:00	-	-	-	-	-	-	-
12:00	-	-	-	-	-	-	-
13:00	-	-	-	-	-	-	-
14:00	-	-	-	-	-	-	-
15:00	-	-	-	-	-	-	-
16:00	-	-	-	-	-	-	-
17:00	-	-	-	-	-	-	-
18:00	-	-	-	-	-	-	-
+19:00	-	-	-	-	-	-	-
tasks	▓	-	-	-	-	-	-

Today: 01/01/80   **File: stm.dtm**   **Time: 13:04:56**

This display of the week shows that on Sunday 21/07/69 you have a meeting between 8:00 and 9:00 and at the bottom a marker shows that you also have a task to perform.

To display the month we must first remove the week display. We do this by pressing **Esc** - the escape key - (the **Esc** key is always used to return you to the state the System was in before you started to enter a sequence of commands). This returns the screen to the day's display. Now press **D** to select **Display** again but this time press **M** to select the option **Month**. The following display appears:

July 2069

Sunday	Monday	Tuesday	Wednesday	Thursday	Friday	Saturday
	1	2	3	4	5	6
7	8	9	10	11	12	13
14	15	16	17	18	19	20
21 ▪	22	23	24	25	26	27
28	29	30	31			

Today: 01/01/80   **File: stm.dtm**   **Time: 13:25:01**

The display of the month shows that on Sunday 21st July 2069 (oops, wrong century! - it is not possible to set a date on a PC before 01/01/1980) you have either a meeting or a task or both. Press **Esc** to return to the Diary Page Display.

The SMART Commands

We have seen how to move from day to day through the diary. We have seen how to insert meetings and tasks and how to view them by the day, the week and the month. The underlying principle behind all this has been the use of the commands displayed in the Command Area - each command being selected by typing the first letter of the command. When certain commands have been selected a further option has to be made, again done by typing the first letter of the particular option desired. All commands and options are listed in alphabetical order. This method of instructing the Time-Manager is used throughout the SMART System as we shall see as we progress.

The Other Time-Manager Commands

To complete this description of the Time-Manager we list and describe the remaining commands available. Try each of them in turn.

Autohelp:

This command is used to remove or restore the help line at the bottom of the screen.

Beep:

If an incorrect key is depressed then a beep will sound. This may be found to be irritating so by selecting the **Beep** command this sound can be turned on or off.

Edit:

Edit permits a highlighted meeting or task to have its parameters edited. This could be used, for example, to edit the date and so move the meeting or task to another day.

Find: Options : First Last Next Previous

Find will display the first, the last, the next or the previous day to the day currently displayed on the screen.

Help:

The On-Line HELP is there to assist you with any problems you may have concerning a command. Pressing **H** for **Help** tells you that if a command is highlighted then pressing **F1** will describe what the command does and how it is used. Pressing **F2** will cause this information to be printed out and pressing **F3** will list all the commands available, each with a short description.

Load:

It is possible to have more than one diary, each one being stored on disk under its own name. If **L** is selected for **Load** then you are prompted to enter a filename with the prompt

>   **Enter time filename:**

followed by
>   **Save changes made in stm.dtm (y/n):**

Press **Y** for **Yes**. If you have entered a filename that does not exist then the prompt line produces the message

>   **<file name> does not exist, create it (y/n)?**

Selecting **Y** for **Yes** here will cause a new, empty diary to be created under that filename.

Output: *Options: Day Week Month*

Output is the command for printing information that is contained within the diary. Selecting Output produces the request to choose either the current Day, Week or Month. After making your selection you are prompted:

Options: Short Long

This refers to a Short or a Long output. A Short output just lists the meetings and tasks whereas a Long output also prints the Extended Description that accompanies each meeting or task.

Purge: *Options : Day Week Month*

Purge will clear information out of the diary. When Purge is selected you are faced with the choice of one of three options - Day, Week or Month. Whichever option you choose all information relating to that Day, Week or Month will be cleared from the diary.

Remove:

Removes the currently selected meeting or task from the diary. The currently selected item is the one that is highlighted. This is similar to the Purge command except that it only operates on a single task or meeting.

Use:

This command permits the currently selected task or meeting to be used as a template to copy meetings and tasks to other days in the diary. For example, if you have a Board Meeting every Friday at Noon this meeting can be copied to every Friday by using this command.

Chapter 3 : The Data-Manager

Objectives

When you have completed this Chapter you will be able to :

- Understand the component parts of a data file
- Construct a file by creating both a record template and a customized screen
- Designate a field to be a key field
- Enter data into the file
- Update the data in the file
- Browse the file
- Order the file into key order
- Review the file specifications

Introduction

The SMART Data-Manager is a facility for managing and manipulating data and information contained within a number of files -it is called a **Database Management System - DBMS** for short. To make this description more easily understood we must first understand exactly what is meant by both a file and a database.

Files and Databases

A database consists of a collection of **files**. A file consists of a collection of **records**. A record consists of a collection of **fields**. A typical example of a file is a **card index of names and addresses**. Each card within a card index is a record in the file. Within each record there are entries called **fields**. Typical fields are **name, address, telephone number** and **post-code**. A collection of such card indexes is called a **database**.

Chapter 3: The Data Manager

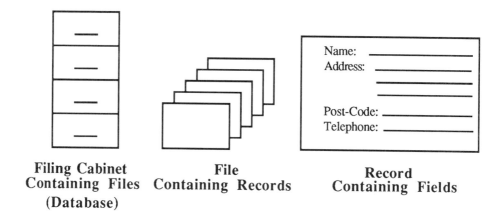

Filing Cabinet　　　　　File　　　　　　　Record
Containing Files　Containing Records　Containing Fields
(Database)

What the SMART Data-Manager allows you to do, amongst other things, is to:

- Design a record template by defining a number of fields
- Build up the file by entering information into the records
- Link files together to create a database

In this way data can be stored, manipulated and used for whatever purposes desired.

Entering The Data-Manager

We enter the Data-Manager from the Introductory Screen by typing in the letter **D**. After a moment the following display appears:

Command list 1: Autohelp Beep Create Delete Enter Find Goto Help
Print Query Report Scroll Update
Files: (none)   Window 1
AUTOHELP - remove/restore help line at bottom of screen (toggle)

Just like the **Time-Manager** we see a Display Window. Below the Display Window are two lines of commands in the **Control Area**. The line below the Control Area is the **status line** which tells us that there is **no file in memory** and that we are looking at Window 1. The bottom line is the **Autohelp** Line.

Unlike the Time-Manager, the Data-Manager has **five** command lists and we can view each one in turn simply by typing in the appropriate number from **1** to **5**. Try it, type in the number **2** and you will see the Control Area display change to:

Command list 2: File-Specs Key Lookup Order Relate Sort Transactions
    Utilities

Range through the other lists and you will see;:
Command list 3: Border Close Link Paint Split Unlink Zoom

Command list 4: Activate Directory File Index Load Read Save Unload Write

Command list 5: Beep Confidence Display Execute F-Calculator
    Input-Screen Macro Parameters Remember Send Text-Editor

That's a whole lot of commands and at first sight they can be rather daunting. But don't worry, you will be surprised at how quickly you come to know how to use them. However, to ease your burden in these early stages there is a very useful facility for reducing their number. Move to Command list 5 by pressing the number **5**. Move the highlight to the Confidence command by pressing the **space bar**. Now press **enter** and the following prompt appears in the Control Area:
  Enter the new confidence level:

There are five confidence levels and the Data-Manager is currently at confidence level 3. Type in the number **1** and press **enter**. Immediately the Command list 5 changes to:

Command list 5: Confidence Execute F-Calculator Parameters Text-Editor

A reduction from 11 commands to just 5. If you range through the other Command lists you will see that they too have fewer commands in them. Confidence level 1 is the novice command level and is there to make the initial task of learning how to use the Data-Manager less daunting.

Move to Command list 1.

Command list 1: Autohelp Browse Create Delete Enter Find Help Print Update

Creating a File

Data management is all about manipulating information contained in files so the first thing we need to do is to create a file. We are going to set up a file for a company called **ABC Supplies** who require to have their customers on file. We shall create a file of names and addresses. To do this we select the **Create** command in Command list 1. To select this command we can either press the space bar until **Create** is highlighted and press **enter** or we can simply press C. When we do this we are confronted with the following sequence of prompts:

PROMPT	ENTER
	C: Create
Select option: File Screen:	F: File

This option is asking whether we wish to create a file or a screen display. We select **File** by pressing **F**.

Enter the new filename:	CUSTOMER

The file must have a name so that it can be stored on the disk under that name. We shall call this file **CUSTOMER**. Make note that we can only use up to eight characters for the file name and they can be either upper case or lower case.

Select option: Fixed-Length Variable-Length:	F: Fixed-Length

For now just select **Fixed-Length** by pressing **F**. The differences between these two options will be explained in a later Chapter.

SmartWare: A Beginner's Guide Section 1 33

Select option: No-Password   Password: **No-Password**

The file can be password protected but we shall not do this at the moment. Press **N** for **No-Password**. Notice that as you have been selecting options they have been accumulating on the second line of the Control Area. At the moment this should read as;

> **create file CUSTOMER fixed-length no-password**

The next prompt reads:

Select option: New   Matching   Similar: **N: New**

This is going to be a new file so we shall select **New** by pressing **N**.

After a few moments the screen changes to the File Creation display.

Fld No	Title	Type	Length	Running Total

Creating file

```
F3 Calc fld  F7 Insert  F10 Exit   PgUp Prev page   Home First entry
F4 Del calc  F8 Delete  Esc Abandon PgDn Next page  End  Last entry
Title can be up to 16 characters long
```

CREATE - creates a new file or screen

It is into this display that the specifications of the record fields will be entered. Do not concern yourself with the descriptions in the Control Area for now. We shall proceed to define the fields.

Type in the word **Name** followed by **enter** and you will see it appear at the top of the Title column. The number 1 automatically appears in the first column. This is the first field in the record. In the third line below the Display Window you will now see

34   *Chapter 3: The Data Manager*

A Alphanumeric N Numeric D Date

This prompt is asking you what type of data this field is going to contain. Names are composed of alphabetic characters so we press **A** for **Alphanumeric** - (A - Z, 0 - 9) - and the A appears in the third column. The other options will be explained as they are needed. The third line prompt now changes to

Length can be from 1 to 50 characters, 1000 characters left

This is telling you that any one field can contain up to 50 characters and any one record can contain up to a total of 1000 characters. We shall require up to **24** characters for the name so enter **24** at the keyboard and press **enter** to complete the definition of the first field.

The cursor then flips to the second line in readiness for the next field to be defined. Continue in this manner until the screen looks like the following:

```
┌─ Creating file ─────────────────────────────────────────────────┐
│   Fld No      Title           Type    Length   Running Total    │
│                                                                 │
│     1         Name             A       24                       │
│     2         Address1         A       20                       │
│     3         Address2         A       20                       │
│     4         Address3         A       20                       │
│     5         Post Code        A       10                       │
│     6         Telephone        A       12                       │
│     7         FAX              A       12                       │
│     8         Salesperson      A       17                       │
│     9         LastMonthSales   A                                │
│                                                                 │
└─────────────────────────────────────────────────────────────────┘
```

F3 Calc fld F7 Insert F10 Exit   PgUp Prev page   Home First entry
F4 Del calc F8 Delete Esc Abandon PgDn Next page End Last entry
A Alpha I Inv name N Num C Counter D Date T Time S SSN P Phone

CREATE - creates a new file or screen

Any particular customer of ABC Supplies will be serviced by a particular Salesperson so that name must also appear on the customer's record. Also appearing on the customer's record will be the sales figures for the last month and this month. At the moment we are entering last month's field. This field is a **numeric** field so select **N** for **Numeric**. When you do this the following prompt appears:

Enter numeric precision (0-8)

SmartWare: A Beginner's Guide Section 1 35

This prompt is asking you how many decimal places you wish the field to contain. We are talking money so there should be **two** decimal places. Enter **2**. The length of the number depends upon the possible value of a total month's sales. We shall assume that ABC Supplies have customers that only buy up to a maximum of a thousand pounds or so. The length will then be **7** so change the default **4** to **7** by overtyping - make note that the decimal point also takes up one space in the number.

Finally you are asked:

Keep running total of this (y/n)

The values in this field for all the records can be held in a running total if we wish. We do not so wish - enter N. When all the fields have been defined your screen should look like this

Creating file

Fld No	Title	Type	Length	Running Total
1	Name	A	24	
2	Address1	A	20	
3	Address2	A	20	
4	Address3	A	20	
5	Post Code	A	10	
6	Telephone	A	12	
7	FAX	A	12	
8	Salesperson	A	17	
9	LastMonthSales	N2	7	N
10	ThisMonthSales	N2	7	N

F3 Calc fld F7 Insert F10 Exit   PgUp Prev page   Home First entry
F4 Del calc F8 Delete Esc Abandon PgDn Next page End Last entry
Title can be up to 16 characters long

CREATE - creates a new file or screen

If you have made any mistakes then you can amend them by overtyping. Move the cursor around using the cursor control keys. If you wish to take a complete field out of the definition, place the cursor on the line containing its description and press **F8**. To make a space to insert a field move the cursor to where you need the space and press **F7**. To illustrate this we recognise that our record does not have a **record number** in it. Though it is not necessary it is always useful to number the records in a file explicitly. We shall do this by inserting a field for this purpose. Move the cursor to the **N** of **Name** - the first field. Now press **F7** and a space appears above this field which has been automatically re-numbered as **2**. On the top line of the screen type in **Number** and designate the field to be a **Numeric** field with precision 0, length 6 and no running total. As you see the length is automatically set at 6.

Your final field definition screen now looks as follows;

```
┌ Creating file ─────────────────────────────────────────────────
│       Fld No  │ Title         │ Type │ Length │ Running Total
│       1       │ Number        │ N0   │ 6      │
│       2       │ Name          │ A    │ 24     │
│       3       │ Address1      │ A    │ 20     │
│       4       │ Address2      │ A    │ 20     │
│       5       │ Address3      │ A    │ 20     │
│       6       │ Post Code     │ A    │ 10     │
│       7       │ Telephone     │ A    │ 12     │
│       8       │ FAX           │ A    │ 12     │
│       9       │ Salesperson   │ A    │ 17     │
│       10      │ LastMonthSales│ N2   │ 7      │ N
│       11      │ ThisMonthSales│ N2   │ 7      │ N
```

F3 Calc fld F7 Insert F10 Exit   PgUp Prev page   Home First entry
F4 Del calc F8 Delete Esc Abandon PgDn Next page End Last entry
A Alpha I Inv name N Num C Counter D Date T Time S SSN P Phone

CREATE - creates a new file or screen

You have just completed the definition of what is called the **Data Dictionary** for the CUSTOMER file. Press **F10** to exit the definition. You will then be faced with the following prompt:

Are you finished defining the file (y/n)

Press **Y** for Yes. A message then appears

Saving new file definition

as the computer saves the file definition to disk. This is followed by

Do you want to define a key field (y/n)

Before we respond to this prompt we must be sure of what a key field is.

Key Fields

Imagine that you have a box full of cards, each card containing a name and an address. In what **order** are you going to want the cards stored? You will naturally want to order them so that the names on successive cards are all in alphabetical order. If, instead of cards, the names and addresses are on computer records you will still wish to order the names in alphabetical order. To do this you would designate the **name field** to be a **key field**. Then you could **order the records against that key field**. This is what a key field is - a field that is specially selected to allow all the records in the file to be ordered against that field. In our file we shall want to be able to order the records in record **Number** order, in customer **Name** order and also **Salesperson** order so we are going to want **three** key fields.

In response to the key field prompt press **Y** and the following display appears:

```
┌─ Creating file ─────────────────────────────────────────────────────┐
│        Fld No    Title           Type      Length    Running Total  │
│                                                                     │
│          1       Number          NO          6                      │
│          2       Name            A          24                      │
│          3       Address1        A          20                      │
│          4       Address2        A          20                      │
│          5       Address3        A          20                      │
│          6       Post Code       A          10                      │
│          7       Telephone       A          12                      │
│          8       FAX             A          12                      │
│          9       Salesperson     A          17                      │
├─ Available Fields ──────────────────────────────────────────────────┤
│    ──▶ 1 Number            2 Name            3 Address1             │
│        4 Address2          5 Address3        6 Post Code            │
│        7 Telephone         8 FAX             9 Salesperson          │
│       10 LastMonthSales                                             │
└─────────────────────────────────────────────────────────────────────┘
```
[-
F6 will select the current field

CREATE - creates a new file or screen

We wish to make field 1 into a key field and the arrow is already pointing at this field. Press **F6** followed by **enter**. Immediately the following display appears:

38   *Chapter 3: The Data Manager*

```
┌ Creating file ─────────────────────────────────────────────────────┐
│              Fld No │ Title         │ Type │ Length │ Running Total │
│                   1 │ Number        │ N0   │   6    │               │
│                   2 │ Name          │ A    │  24    │               │
│                   3 │ Address1      │ A    │  20    │               │
│                   4 │ Address2      │ A    │  20    │               │
│                   5 │ Address3      │ A    │  20    │               │
│                   6 │ Post Code     │ A    │  10    │               │
│                   7 │ Telephone     │ A    │  12    │               │
│                   8 │ FAX           │ A    │  12    │               │
│                   9 │ Salesperson   │ A    │  17    │               │
│                  10 │ LastMonthSales│ N2   │   7    │       N       │
├─────────────────────┴───────────────┴──────┴────────┴───────────────┤
│        Field Title          Asc/Descending        Length in key     │
│        Number                   --> A                   6           │
└─────────────────────────────────────────────────────────────────────┘
 F1   Help        F10   Finished        Esc   Abandon
```

CREATE - creates a new file or screen

You are being asked whether you wish the key to order from **A to Z - Ascending** - or from **Z to A - Descending**. Select **A** for Ascending followed by **F10** for **Finished**. The following prompt will then appear;

Do you want to define another key field (y/n)

Press **Y** for Yes. The next key field will be **Name** so follow the previous procedure to make this field a key field (use the cursor keys to point the arrow at **Name**). The final key field will be the **Salesperson** so use the cursor keys to place the arrow so that it is pointing at field 9

```
┌─ Creating file ─────────────────────────────────────────────┐
│       Fld No │ Title       │ Type │ Length │ Running Total │
│       1      │ Number      │ NO   │   6    │               │
│       2      │ Name        │ A    │  24    │               │
│       3      │ Address1    │ A    │  20    │               │
│       4      │ Address2    │ A    │  20    │               │
│       5      │ Address3    │ A    │  20    │               │
│       6      │ Post Code   │ A    │  10    │               │
│       7      │ Telephone   │ A    │  12    │               │
│       8      │ FAX         │ A    │  12    │               │
│       9      │ Salesperson │ A    │  17    │               │
├─ Available Fields ──────────────────────────────────────────┤
│    k   1 Number        k   2 Name          3 Address1       │
│        4 Address2          5 Address3      6 Post Code      │
│        7 Telephone         8 FAX         ▶ 9 Salesperson    │
│        10 LastMonthSales                                    │
└─────────────────────────────────────────────────────────────┘
```

[9;2]
F6 will select the current field

CREATE - creates a new file or screen

Press **F6** and then type in **2]** to leave the display as shown. Here we have designated field 9 to be a **major** key field with field 2 as a **minor** key. This means that when we sort on field 9 - **Salesperson** - those records containing the same **Salesperson** will be grouped together and each group ordered in the **minor** field - customer **Name**. The fact that we have chosen field 2 to be a minor field to the major field 9 has nothing at all to do with the fact that field 2 is a major key field in its own right.

Again we choose the key to be Ascending - select **A**. Finally, to the reappearance of the prompt

Do you wish to define another key field (y/n)

the response is **N** as our file definition is now complete. The computer then saves all this information to the disk and finishes with the following display:

40 *Chapter 3: The Data Manager*

**Command list 1: Autohelp Beep Create Delete Enter Find Goto Help
Print Query Report Scroll Update**
Files: (none)   Window 1
AUTOHELP - remove/restore help line at bottom of screen (toggle)

This is the **record template** - it is called the **Standard Screen** - into which information will be entered for each customer. Notice the status line now contains the name of the file - CUSTOMER. Page: 1 refers to the first page of the record template - there is only one - and REC: EOF (0) refers to the fact that the record being viewed is the only one and that it is empty. The initials **EOF** stand for End Of File.

Entering Data into Records

To enter data into the record template select **Enter** from Command list 1 by pressing **E**. Straight lines now appear alongside the field names and the cursor is flashing against the field name **Number**. The record is now ready to have information entered into it. Type in the following:

```
┌─ Window 1 ─────────────────────────────────────────────┐
│ Number  1-----                                         │
│ Name  Dexter J Booth-----------------                  │
│ Address1 The Polytechnic----------                     │
│ Address2 Queensgate---------------                     │
│ Address3 HUDDERSFIELD--------                          │
│ Post-Code HD1 3DH------                                │
│ Telephone 0484 422288---                               │
│ FAX 0484 51615                                         │
│ Salesperson Angela-----------------                    │
│ LastMonthSales 123.45--                                │
│ ThisMonthSales 246.90--                                │
└────────────────────────────────────────────────────────┘
```
Insert ON   F3 Prev fld F5 Not used F7 Fld delete F9 Repeat fld
F2 - Date   F4 Next fld F6 Next rec F8 Fld reform   F10 Finished
File: CUSTOMER   Window 1   Page: 1 Rec: EOF (1)   Act: Y
ENTER - add new records to the current file

As you complete the entry for the last field in a record the screen automatically flips to the next record, so don't worry if you find yourself suddenly looking at a blank screen. All it means is that you did not stop before you pressed **enter** for the last field. Notice that on the status line, after EOF is the record number 1. Do not concern yourself at the moment with the meaning of **Act: Y** on the status line, this will be explained later.

You will also notice that in the Control Area there are a number of prompts to help you fill in the record. They all mean exactly what they say. Try them, it is by far the best way of sorting out exactly what they do - experience is worth a thousand words. Why not put a number of different records into the file. For Salespersons use only the following names

> **Angela**
> **Brian**
> **Clara**
> **David**
> **Erica**
> **Felix**

The reason for just using these names will become clear as we progress through the book.

When you are through entering records into the file press **F10** to exit from the entry mode. You will then be asked the question

> **Do you wish to update keys now (y/n)**

Answer **Y** to this question and you will see the message

42   *Chapter 3: The Data Manager*

Sorting . . .

What is happening here is that the **key files** are being created that will permit you to order the records against either of the three keys. We take a closer look at this a little in a later Chapter.

Creating a Customised Screen

The screen into which you have just been entering data is called the Standard Screen associated with the file CUSTOMER. It is a pretty boring screen as it simply lists the fields one under another. To add some interest to the game we can design our own screen. You will remember that when we set about creating the file we selected **Create** in command list 1 and we were then given the option of **File** or **Screen**. We chose **File** but now we choose **Screen**.

Go to command list 1 and enter the following sequence of commands:

PROMPT	ENTER
	C: Create
Select option: File Screen	S: Screen
Enter the screen name	CUSTOMER
Select option: No-Password Password	N: No-Password
Select option: New Matching Similar	N: New

```
F1  Help       F5  Prior field      F7  Insert field      F9  Clear page
                F6  Next field       F8  Delete field      F10 Exit
Field 1 Number        Length 6            Pg: 1  Ln: 1  Ps: 1        IO:#
CREATE - Creates a new file or screen
```

It is into the top area of the display that we shall now design our customised screen.

The position of the cursor is described on the status line by **Ln:1 Ps:1** which tells us that the cursor flashing at top left is located on line 1 and column (Ps for position) 1. The cursor can be moved about by using the cursor control keys - try it.

The fields are entered into the screen at the point where the cursor is located. Press **F7** and the field name appears followed by a line that is as long as the field is defined to be.

The field that is currently available for entry is described at the beginning of the status line. Here you see that field 1 - called **Name** - is currently available. Why not play around with these controls just to see how they work It does not matter if the screen you end up with is not the screen you want because any field can be taken off the screen using **F8** and the entire screen can be cleared using **F9**. Notice that each record can occupy more than one page - you can move from page to page using **PgUp** and **PgDn**.

The following screen is a suggestion:

```
    Name     ----------------------       Number     -----------

    Address1  --------------------
    Address2  --------------------
    Address3  --------------------       Salesperson  ----------------
                                         LastMonthSales  ----------
    Post Code  ---------------            ThisMonthSales  ----------
    Telephone  -----------------
         FAX   -----------------


F1  Help       F5  Prior field     F7  Insert field     F9  Clear page
               F6  Next field      F8  Delete field     F10 Exit
All fields defined                        Pg: 1   Ln: 1   Ps: 1      IO:#
CREATE - Creates a new file or screen
```

When you are happy with the end product press **F10** and the following prompt appears:

Are you through defining this screen (y/n)

Press **Y** for Yes and the screen definition will be saved to disk.

Entering Data into a Customised Screen

You may have just created your own screen and saved the definition to disk but the screen display is still the old standard screen. To use your newly created screen you will have to load

44   *Chapter 3: The Data Manager*

it into memory. To do this move to Command list 4 and follow this sequence of commands:

PROMPT   **ENTER**

                                                              L: Load
Enter filename: **CUSTOMER**

You already have CUSTOMER loaded but this does not matter. When you press **enter** the following screen display appears:

```
┌─ Window 1 ──────────────────────────────────────────────────┐
│ Number  1-----                                              │
│ Name   Dexter J Booth----------------                       │
│ Address1 The Polytechnic----------                          │
│ Address2 Queensgate---------------                          │
│ Address3 HUDDERSFIELD--------                               │
│ Post-Code HD1 3DH------                                     │
│ Telephone 0484 422288---                                    │
│ FAX 0484 51615                                              │
│ Salesperson Angela-----------------                         │
│ LastMonthSales 123.45--                                     │
│ ThisMonthSales 246.90--                                     │
│                                                             │
│  ┌─ Screens for file CUSTOMER ─────────────────             │
│                                                             │
│      -----> standard       CUSTOMER                         │
│                                                             │
└─────────────────────────────────────────────────────────────┘
```
Enter screen name:
load CUSTOMER screen
File: CUSTOMER   Window 1   Page: 1 Rec: EOF (10) Act:Y
LOAD - opens a database file and prepares it for processing

You are being asked to name the screen you wish to use. Move the arrow using the cursor control keys so that it points to **CUSTOMER** and press **enter**. The new screen then appears. Try entering more records into the file using this newly customised screen. If you are not satisfied with it you can always create another screen with another name and use that one instead - one of the advantages with SMART is that any one file can have a number of different input screens associated with it.

As is usual in an imperfect world we all make mistakes and it is entirely possible that one of the records in your CUSTOMER file is incorrect. How do you correct it? You correct records in a file using the **Update** command that is found on Command list 1.

Update

If you are still entering records into the file press **F10** to finish and answer **Y** to the prompt about updating the keys. Move to Command list 1 and select the **Update** command by pressing **U**. The display immediately moves to the first record in the file and by using the function keys listed in the Control Area you will be able to move forwards and backwards through the records in the file. At any time you wish to amend (or update) a record then place the cursor at the particular field and type in the amendment. You may have to make use of the **Ins** (Insert) and **Del** (Delete) keys to do this.

When you have finished updating records press **F10** and the following prompt appears;

> Do you wish to update the keys now (y/n)

Respond with **Y**.

Find

Again on Command list 1 is the command **Find**. This command permits you to locate all those records that contain a particular piece of information. You may wish to try this command for yourself. It will, however, be explained in detail in a later Chapter.

Save, Load and Unload

On Command list 4 you will see there are five commands three of which are **Load**, **Save** and **Unload**. If you select **Save** by pressing **S** then all the records in the file will be saved to disk. If you select **Unload** by pressing **U** the following prompt appears:

> Select option: All File Screen

Select **A** for **All** and the file will first be saved to disk and then unloaded from memory. The Display Window will then be empty. To retrieve the file display you must select **Load** by pressing **L**. The prompt will then ask for the filename and a display of available files will appear at the bottom of the display window. You only have one file, CUSTOMER, and the arrow is pointing at it. Simply press **enter** and this file is automatically selected. Next you are asked which screen you wish to accompany the file. Select your customised screen by placing the arrow next to it and pressing **enter**. You could equally well type in the name of the screen.

So there we are. You can now create your own file, customise a screen for it, enter records into it and amend (or update) them at will. Also, you can save, unload and load a file with an accompanying screen. Before we finish this Chapter there are just three other commands that we need to be familiar with at the moment. The first is the **Browse** command which produces a display of all the records in a file with each record just taking up one screen line. The second is the **Order** command which puts the records in alphabetical or numerical order and the third is the **File-Specs** command which allows you to view the specifications that you laid down when you defined the file.

Browse

Move to Command list 1 and select the following sequence of commands:

PROMPT   **ENTER**

                                                                           B: Browse
Select option: All Fields Off   A: All

Now the entire file is viewed with one record to a line. Using the cursor control keys you can move up and down and across the screen to view those parts of the records not currently displayed. Try it.

Order

Whilst you are in Browse mode we shall put all the records into alphabetical order by customer name. Move to Command list 2 and select the following sequence of commands:

PROMPT   **ENTER**

                                                                           O: Order
Select option: Index   Key   Sequential   K: Key

You are now presented with a display of all the fields in a box at the bottom of the display window. There are three key fields as can be seen by the **k** at the side of **Number**, **Name** and **Salesperson**. The arrow is pointing at **Number** so move the arrow to **Name** with the cursor keys and press **enter** to select this key.

And now you see all the customers listed in alphabetical order. Why not now try to put the records in alphabetical order by **Salesperson**. What do you notice about the groups of records for each Salesperson?

To turn the Browse mode off, select

PROMPT	ENTER
	B: Browse
Select option: All Fields Off	O: Off

and the screen returns to the single record display.

File-Specs

Move to command list 2 and select **File-Specs** by pressing **F**. You are then confronted with the following options:

Select option: Calculated-Fields Data-Ranges Field-Info General Key-Fields
                Running-Totals

There are no **Calculated-Fields** or **Data-Ranges** set. Selecting **Field-Info** produces the following display:

Field No	Field Title	Type	Length	Key	Total	Status
1	Number	N0	6	Y	N	N
2	Name	A	24	Y		N
3	Address1	A	20	N		N
4	Address2	A	20	N		N
5	Address3	A	20	N		N
6	Post-Code	A	10	N		N
7	Telephone	A	12	N		N
8	FAX	A	12	N		N
9	Salesperson	A	17	Y		N
10	LastMonthSales	N2	7	N	N	N
11	ThisMonthSales	N2	7	N	N	N

F4 Next screen   F2 Print screen   F10 Exit
file-specs   field-info
File: CUSTOMER   Key: 1   Window: 1   Page: 1   Rec: EOF (1)   Act: Y
FILE-SPECS - list file specifications of current file

The **Status** of a field refers to whether the field has been further designated as **mandatory entry** or **read only** when customising the screen - the **N** stands for **no-status**. We shall say more about this in a later Section.

Why not repeat the **File-Specs** selection only this time choose the options **General**, **Key-Fields** and **Running-Totals** in turn.

Recap and Review

We have created a file called CUSTOMER complete with a customised screen. We have entered data into the file and later updated it. We have browsed the file and ordered it against a key. Finally we have taken a look at the various parameters that specify the file by using the command File-Specs. You should now have an elementary idea of what a file management system is all about.

What now follows are the Commands that appear within the five command lists displayed in the Control Area.

Command list 1 : Autohelp Browse Create Delete Enter Find Help Print Update

Autohelp : Toggles the Autohelp line on or off. This means that the Autohelp display can be switched on or off.

Browse : Permits the Records in a file to be viewed as a list in the Display Area - now referred to in the Data-Manager as the Data Window.

Create : Allows a file to be created. This is achieved by defining the fields that comprise each record.

Delete : De-activates an active record (signified by **Act: Y**) or Activates a de-activated record (**Act: N**) in a file. Active records within a file can be manipulated whereas de-activated records cannot. This could be used to manipulate a selected number of records in a file whilst ignoring others.

Enter : Permits information to be entered into a file. By this means information is placed into each record in the file.

Find : Finds specific items within a Database file. It allows you to search for specific items contained in the information stored in the file.

Help : Provides assistance with any of the Commands

Print : Prints information from the Database file to either a Printer or to Disk

Update : Allows previously entered information in a Database file to be changed. In many cases information that has been entered manually at the keyboard is incorrect. This command allows you to return to an incorrect record and correct it.

Command list 2 : File-Specs   Key   Order

File-Specs : Displays the specifications of a given file. This command is useful for keeping a track of how a file has been constructed.

Key : Permits manipulation of key fields.

Order : Orders the records in a file in some specific sequence. Typically you may wish to order a collection of sales enquiries in the order of their date or the order of their value.

Command list 3 : Paint

Paint : Allows the screen background and text displays to be colour customised.

Command list 4 : Directory   Index   Load   Save   Unload

Directory : Displays the files that are on the disk. Every file has a name and this command allows you to keep track of the file names you have used.

Index : A list of specific records from a file. If you wished to continually put your records into some predefined order then you could store this predefined order in what is called an index. We shall say more about indexes in a later Chapter.

Load : Loads a file from the disk into memory so that it can be manipulated.

Save : Saves a file to disk for future use.

Unload : Saves a file to disk and then unloads it from memory. This frees the memory space for other uses. There is an upper limit of 40 files that can be resident in memory at any given time.

Command list 5 : Confidence Execute F-Calculator Parameters Text-Editor

Confidence : Sets the Confidence Level for the user. This ranges from 1 to 5.

Execute : Executes a previously written program written in the SMART 4GL programming language. We shall not be considering this aspect of SMART in detail until the penultimate Section.

F-Calculator : Calculates the values of a specified function. This acts much as a programmable hand-calculator would.

Parameters : Permits the configuration of the Data-Manager to differ from the configuration of the SMART System generally. By configuration is meant the various means whereby SMART interacts with such things as the Disk Drive, the Printer, the Screen etc. This is a technical aspect that we shall not deal with here.

Text-Editor : Allows a text file to be created for use within a SMART Application. For example, a pre-written SMART program may require text to be displayed that contains instructions on how to proceed. This text could be constructed using the Text-Editor.

The following is a list of various commands and the subsequent options that appear when those commands are selected.

Create : 1. FILE - <Name> - Fixed length / Variable length - No-password / Password - New / Matching / Similar

2. SCREEN - <Name> - No-password / Password - New / Matching / Similar

Find : [Field] - Equal / Greater than / Less than / Partial - <information> - Backwards / Global / Ignore Case / Whole word

Print : File / Page / Record

File-Specs : Calculated fields / Data-ranges / Field-info / General / Key-fields

Key : Add / Delete / Organise / Update

Order : Index / Key / Sequential

Chapter 4 : The Spreadsheet

Objectives

When you have completed this Chapter you will be able to:

- Understand the concept of the SMART Spreadsheet
- Insert text, numbers and formulas into a Worksheet
- Insert arithmetic symbols as text into a Worksheet
- Insert blank rows and columns into a Worksheet
- Change the format of a cell entry and the column width
- Copy and move block of cells within a Worksheet
- Save, unload and load a Worksheet

Introduction

We have all met spreadsheets at some time or another but we may not have referred to them as a spreadsheet. Let's assume that you are going to buy a house for £70,000 and that the mortgage rate is currently at 10% per annum simple interest. We want to know the cost of buying the house over 10, 20 or 30 years so we draw up a table.

Mortgage Period	10 years	20 years	30 years
Cost of House	70,000	70,000	70,000
Interest at 10%	70,000	140,000	210,000
Total Cost	140,000	210,000	280,000

This table is arranged in regular **rows** and **columns**. It is called a **spreadsheet**.

If, after drawing up this spreadsheet we found out that the interest rate had been changed to 11% then the three **Interest** values would have to be changed along with the corresponding **Total Costs**. We would have to draw up another spreadsheet.

Mortgage Period	10 years	20 years	30 years
Cost of House	70,000	70,000	70,000
Interest at 11%	77,000	154,000	231,000
Total Cost	147,000	224,000	301,000

It does not take a lot of effort to re-draw this spreadsheet but imagine the effort required if there were hundreds of rows and columns all with entries that depended upon each other. It would be a very tedious task indeed. Fortunately, however, we now have the **electronic spreadsheet** which enables us to reproduce the second sheet simply by changing the **10% to 11%** - **the Interest values and Total Costs then being automatically updated.**

The SMART spreadsheet permits numbers, entered in a regular array of rows and columns, to be manipulated at will. The spreadsheet can be constructed so that the value of one number can be made to depend on the value of a second number. So that if the second number is changed the spreadsheet automatically re-calculates the value of the other number. In this way very complicated spreadsheets can be constructed that allow the user to apply the **'What if ...'** principle. **What** happens to all the other numbers **if** we change this number? The possibilities for projecting the consequences of different situations are endless.

To distinguish the word spreadsheet (meaning the program) from the word spreadsheet (meaning the tabulated information) the SMART System refers to the latter as the **Worksheet**.

The Screen Display

Select the **Spreadsheet** from the Introductory Screen by pressing **S** and the following display appears:

```
        1         2         3         4         5         6         7
    ┌─────────────────────────────────────────────────────────────────┐
  1 │ ▓▓▓▓▓▓▓▓▓                                                       │
  2 │                                                                 │
  3 │                                                                 │
  4 │                                                                 │
  5 │                                                                 │
  6 │                                                                 │
  7 │                                                                 │
  8 │                                                                 │
  9 │                                                                 │
 10 │                                                                 │
 11 │                                                                 │
 12 │                                                                 │
 13 │                                                                 │
    └─────────────────────────────────────────────────────────────────┘
```

Enter:

Worksheet: (none)   Loc: r1c1   FN: Font: Standard
ENTER - enter a formula, a value or text into the current cell

This is a **Worksheet**. It contains a number of boxes - called **cells** - arranged in regular rows and columns. The cells are not marked out but they are there nonetheless. Each cell is 10 characters wide and a single character deep. Along the top of the screen are displayed the **column numbers** and down the left hand side of the screen are displayed the **row numbers**. Every cell on the spreadsheet can be identified by giving the numbers of the row and column in which it is located - this is called the **cell address**.

At the moment the **cursor** - the highlight - is in the cell that is in both **row 1** and **column 1**. This cell, then, has address

r1c1

At the bottom of the screen is the usual **Control Area** which contains the single word **Enter**. Below this are the **Status line**, and the **Autohelp line**. As you see it is all very similar to the Time-Manager and the Data-Manager displays.

The status line describes the name of the current **Worksheet** - here it is **(none)** as the Worksheet is as yet unnamed - and the position of the cursor, or highlight, is given as **Loc: r1c1**.

Entry Mode And Command Mode

Unlike the Data-Manager the Spreadsheet has **two modes** of operation. These are the **Entry Mode** and the **Command Mode**. At the moment the Worksheet is in Entry Mode - it is

54   *Chapter 4: The Spreadsheet*

ready to accept information into its cells from the keyboard. The alternative to Entry Mode - Command Mode - can be activated by pressing the **Esc** key. Try it and you will see the screen display change to

```
            1        2        3        4        5        6        7
  1    ▓▓▓▓▓▓▓▓
  2
  3
  4
  5
  6
  7
  8
  9
 10
 11
 12
 13
```
Command list 1: **Autohelp** **Blank Copy Delete Edit Find Goto Help**
                     Insert Name Print Report Scroll Vcopy
Worksheet: (none)   Loc: r1c1   FN: Font: Standard
AUTOHELP - remove/restore help line at bottom of screen (toggle)

Now this is even more like the Data-Manager. Again we have **five** different Command lists. Take a look at them, you already know how to move from one list to another.

To reduce the number of visible commands for this introduction to the spreadsheet, set the Confidence Level to 1 by selecting **Confidence** on Command list 5 just as we did for the Data-Manager.

Now the Command lists will look as follows:

Command list 1:   Autohelp Blank Copy Delete Edit Help Insert Move Print

Command list 2:   Colnumbers Paint Rownumbers Titles

Command list 3:   Fill Justify Newname Reformat Text-Format Value-Format
                  Width

Command list 4:   Directory Index Load Save Unload

Command list 5:   Confidence Execute F-Calculator Parameters Text-Editor

Pressing **Esc** again will move you back to Entry Mode.

Cursor and Sheet Control

The cell containing the cursor is referred to as the **active cell** because it is ready to receive an entry of text, a number or a formula. The active cell can be changed simply by using the cursor control keys to move the cursor around the Worksheet. Try it, press the **up, down, left, right arrows** as well as **PgUp, PgDn, Home** and **End**.

What is seen on the screen is not the entire Worksheet but only a part of it. The complete Worksheet can have as many as 9999 rows and 999 columns. To view other parts of the Worksheet it must be scrolled either left/right or up/down. This is done using the cursor control keys - try it.

Information Entry

Each cell on the Worksheet is capable of containing;

> **Text**
> **Numbers**
> **A Formula**

Text Text is entered in Entry Mode directly from the keyboard. Provided the first character is not a number or an arithmetic symbol, such as + for example, the spreadsheet automatically recognises the entry as text.

Let's try the following. Make sure that you are in Entry Mode - press Esc if you are in Command Mode - and place the cursor in **r1c1**. Now type in the name **Angela** and notice what happens in the Control Area.

As soon as you press the **A** the **Enter:** disappears and on the line below the word **Angela** appears as you type. It also appears in the cell at **r1c1**. When you have finished press enter and the Control Area displays

> **Enter:**
> **Text: Angela**

This is telling you that the highlighted cell at r1c1 contains the text **Angela**.

Numbers Numbers are also entered straight from the keyboard.

Now try this. Move the cursor to cell **r1c2** and type in the number **123.45**. As soon as you press the number 1 the Control Area display changes from **Enter:** to **Enter Value:** - by starting with a number the spreadsheet automatically knows you are entering a number. Again, the number appears in the Control Area as you type it but it does not appear in the cell at r1c2. Only when you press enter does the number appear on the Worksheet. The Control Area then displays

Enter:
Value: 123.45.

Formulas   A formula can be entered into a cell provided the user indicates first that a formula is to be entered. This is done by starting the entry with = followed by the formula.

Try this. Move the cursor to cell **r1c3** and type in the following

=r1c2

As soon as you type in = the Control Area display changes to

Enter formula:

Now type in **r1c2** - the Control Area displays;

Enter formula: r1c2

Notice that nothing appears in the cell at r1c3 until you press enter. When you do press enter the number **123.45** appears.

The formula that you wrote told the spreadsheet that you wanted cell **r1c3** to contain the same contents as cell **r1c2** and that is what is in there. Ok, so let's test the water. What happens if we change the contents of cell **r1c2**; will the contents of **r1c3** also change? Try it. Move the cursor to **r1c2**, type in **246.90** and press **enter**. This automatically changes the contents of **r1c2** but look - the contents of **r1c3** are still the same. Does this mean that the formula is not working? No, it means that the Worksheet is not **re-calculating** the formula.

The spreadsheet can be in either **manual** or **automatic** re-calculation mode and right now it is in manual mode. If you look at the Status Line you will see the word **CALC** has appeared. This is a prompt to let you know that the Worksheet formulas need to be re-calculated. How do we make the spreadsheet re-calculate the formula? Easy, press **F5** and immediately the contents of cell **r1c3** change to **246.90**. To put the spreadsheet into automatic re-calculation mode requires the use of a command in Command list 5 that is not displayed at Confidence level 1. We shall return to this feature in a later Chapter.

We are now sufficiently prepared to construct a complete Worksheet and this we shall now do.

Constructing A Worksheet

When we were looking at the Data-Manager in the last Chapter we constructed a customer file for **ABC Supplies**. ABC Supplies are a fast growing company and have a sales force of six out on the road taking daily orders from their customers. The sales force is very keen as their salaries are directly linked to their commissions but of late the management of ABC Supplies have noticed that sales are starting to level off. They are not sure whether the sales force has reached its selling capacity or whether they are becoming complacent. Rather than hire new sales personnel to increase their sales ABC Supplies have decided to run a competition amongst their six Salespersons.

For reasons known only to ABC Supplies the company year is divided into three-week periods so the competition will be run to coincide with these periods. For each three-week period the value of a Salesperson's sales will be totalled and the Salesperson with the highest total will be awarded a free gift. To organise this competition the management are going to use the spreadsheet and enter the sales values each week.

The first thing that has to be done is to enter the names of the all the Salespersons listed at the end of the last Chapter. Do it and you should end up with something like the following:

Enter text

	1	2	3	4	5	6
1	Angela	0.00	0.00			
2	Brian					
3	Clara					
4	David					
5	Erica					
6	Felix					
7						
8						

Use the names shown here because they are the same names that we used in the Data-Manager. Now let's enter a column of numbers. Try the following:

Enter numbers

	1	2	3	4	5
1	Angela	123.45	0.00		
2	Brian	1003.04			
3	Clara	578.11			
4	David	990.25			
5	Erica	1125.69			
6	Felix	774.65			
7					
8					

These we shall take to be the values of the sales for Week 1 of a period. Columns 3 and 4 will be reserved for the next two weeks and column 5 will contain the totals of all three weeks.

Move to **r1c5** in readiness for entering a formula.

Enter Formulas

In **r1c5** enter the following formula:

$$=r1c2+r1c3+r1c4$$

This formula tells the Worksheet that the contents of cell **r1c5** will contain the sum of the contents of cells **r1c2, r1c3** and **r1c4**. Notice how **123.45** appears in this cell. If you make a mistake press **Esc** until you are able to re-start the entry. Now move to cell **r2c5** - just below - and we shall enter a similar formula. Enter

$$=SUM(r2c2:4)$$

That's a lot shorter and it produces the desired result **1003.04**. The use of the **colon** (:) in c2:4 means **from column 2 to column 4** so the formula reads as

the SUM of the contents of the cells in row 2 from column 2 to 4

The word **SUM** is called a **function** and there are many other functions that can be used in formulas. You might peruse the SMART Spreadsheet Manual just to see how many functions are available - there is a large number of them.

We still have formulas to enter into cells **r3:6c5** but to do this we shall move into Command Mode and use the **Copy** command.

Copy

Press **Esc** to put the sheet into Command Mode. Move to Command list 1 where you will see the command **Copy**. Make sure that the cursor is at cell **r2c5** - the cell to be copied - and then follow this sequence of commands:

PROMPT	ENTER
	C: Copy
Select option: Down From Right	D: Down
Select option: Row Single-Cell	S: Single-Cell
Enter number of copies	4 (enter)

You have made four copies downwards of the single cell where the highlight resides. Instantly, each of the cells **r3:6c5** fill with the same numbers. Press **F5** and the numbers all change. They are now the same numbers as those that appear in cells **r3:6c2**. Put the sheet in Entry Mode and move the cursor from cell **r3c5** down through each cell to **r6c5** and keep your eye on the Control Area. You will notice that the formulas are all different. For example, in cell **r3c5** the formula is

$$SUM(r3c2:4)$$

whereas in the cell below - cell **r4c5** - the formula is

$$SUM(r4c2:4)$$

How amazing, the **Copy** command has not only copied the formula but it has adjusted each copy to make it apply to the correct cells. We shall say more about this in a later Section.

By now your Worksheet should look something like the following:

	1	2	3	4	5
1	Angela	123.45	0.00		123.45
2	Brian	1003.04			1003.04
3	Clara	578.11			578.11
4	David	990.25			990.25
5	Erica	1125.69			1125.69
6	Felix	774.65			774.65
7					
8					

The next entries into the sheet, on row 7, will be the totals of columns 2 tto 5.

Type in the word **TOTAL** into cell **r7c1**. In cell **r7c2** type in the formula:

$$=SUM(r1:6c2)$$

and the number **4,595.19** should appear. Now copy that formula into cells **r7c3:5** and press **F5** to re-calculate to end up with the following display:

	1	2	3	4	5
1	Angela	123.45	0.00		123.45
2	Brian	1003.04			1003.04
3	Clara	578.11			578.11
4	David	990.25			990.25
5	Erica	1125.69			1125.69
6	Felix	774.65			774.65
7	TOTAL	4595.19	0.00	0.00	4595.19
8					

At this stage you might like to put some numbers into columns 3 and 4 just to check that everything is working as expected. Try it but don't forget to use **F5** to re-calculate the formulas when you need to.

As it stands the Worksheet does what it is supposed to do but it is rather boring to look at. Let's liven it up a bit by spacing things out and putting a title on the sheet.

Insert

The first thing we shall do is to separate the totals line from the entries above and to do this we must **Insert** a blank row. Move the cursor to **r7c1** and put the sheet into Command Mode and on Command list 1 you will see the command **Insert**. Follow this sequence of commands:

PROMPT	ENTER
	I: Insert
Select option: Block Columns Rows	R: Rows
Enter number of rows	1 (enter)

and immediately the contents of row 7 move to row 8 and row 7 is left blank - you have inserted a blank row between the row the cursor was on and the row **above**. Notice that the formulas have adjusted to accommodate this change.

To emphasise the separation we have achieved we shall now put in some **underlines**. Place the cursor in cell **r7c2**, press **Esc** for Entry Mode and use the **minus sign** (-) to form the underline. How strange, you enter ------- and the cell contains the number **0.00**. The reason for this is because the minus sign is an **arithmetic symbol** and so the sheet was expecting a number. To use **arithmetic symbols** as **text** you must first precede your entry with ". Try it again. You will notice that as you press " the message **Enter text above:** appears and as you enter the minus signs they also appear in the cell. Just use 9 minus signs.

When you have done this, place a row of equal signs (=) in r9c2, under the total. When this is complete, Copy the underlines to produce a display similar to the following:

	1	2	3	4	5
1	Angela	123.45	0.00		123.45
2	Brian	1003.04			1003.04
3	Clara	578.11			578.11
4	David	990.25			990.25
5	Erica	1125.69			1125.69
6	Felix	774.65			774.65
7		-------------	-------------	-------------	-------------
8	TOTAL	4595.19	0.00	0.00	4595.19
9		=======	=======	=======	=======

So that we shall know what the columns refer to we shall put headings above each column. Insert three rows at the top of the sheet and put in the headings as shown.

	1	2	3	4	5
1	SALESPERS	WEEK 1	WEEK 2	WEEK 3	TOTAL
2					
3	Angela	123.45	0.00		123.45
4	Brian	1003.04			1003.04
5	Clara	578.11			578.11
6	David	990.25			990.25
7	Erica	1125.69			1125.69
8	Felix	774.65			774.65
9		-------------	-------------	-------------	-------------
10	TOTAL	4595.19	0.00	0.00	4595.19
11		=======	=======	=======	=======

Width

Notice that there is not enough room to enter **SALESPERSON** as the cell is only 10 characters wide. We can solve this problem. Put the sheet in Command Mode, place the highlight in r1c1 and move to Command list 3 where you will find the **Width** command. Follow this sequence of commands:

PROMPT	ENTER
	W: Width
Enter width:	1 2
Select option: Columns All	C: Columns
Enter number of columns:	1

Now the entire column is 12 characters wide and you can enter **SALESPERSON** in the heading.

Justify

Notice also the **screen format** of the entries. All the text entries are **left-justified** and all the number entries are **right-justified**. It would be nice if the headings could be centred and this we can do by selecting the **Justify** command in Command list 3. Place the highlight in **r1c1** and follow this sequence of commands in Command Mode:

PROMPT	ENTER
	J: Justify
Select option: Left Center Right	C: Center
Select option: Block Columns Rows All	R: Rows
Enter number of rows:	1

and immediately all the entries in row 1 are centred.

Spillover

Finally we should give the entire spreadsheet a heading. Insert 2 rows at the top of the sheet and enter into **r1c1** the following;

Sales Summary By Week And By Period

This is certainly longer than 10 characters, but look what happened. The cell expanded to allow the text to fit in - this is called **spillover**. Finish off the Worksheet so that it looks as follows:

	1	2	3	4	5
1	Sales Summary By Week And By Month				ABC Supplies
2					
3	SALESPERSON	WEEK 1	WEEK 2	WEEK 3	TOTAL
4					
5	Angela	123.45	0.00		123.45
6	Brian	1003.04			1003.04
7	Clara	578.11			578.11
8	David	990.25			990.25
9	Erica	1125.69			1125.69
10	Felix	774.65			774.65
11		-------------	-------------	-------------	-------------
12	TOTAL	4595.19	0.00	0.00	4595.19
13		=======	=======	=======	=======

Save, Unload and Load

We shall now save this Worksheet on the Disk under the name **SALES**. Move to command list 4 and select **Save**. Enter the following:

PROMPT	ENTER
	S: Save
Enter Worksheet name:	SALES

The Worksheet can be unloaded by using the **Unload** command and loaded using the **Load** command.

Recap and Review

We have constructed a Worksheet called SALES. We have entered text, numbers, arithmetic symbols and formulas into the sheet. We have changed the width of a cell, justified and reformatted its contents. We have inserted rows and copied blocks of information. Finally we saved the entire Worksheet to disk.

What now follows is a list of the Commands displayed in the five Command lists in the

Control Area. You might try each command in turn to familiarise yourself with them.

Command list 1 : Autohelp Blank Copy Delete Edit Help Insert Move Print

Blank : Removes information from the Worksheet. This command could be used to remove an entire block of information to permit new information to be entered.

Copy : Copies information from one area of the Worksheet to another area.

Delete : Removes Rows and Columns from the Worksheet. This command can be used to tidy up a Worksheet by deleting rows or columns of empty cells.

Edit : Permits entries to the Worksheet to be amended when it would be too tedious to simply overwrite the information contained in a cell. This situation can occur if a cell contains a long formula. We shall say more about this later.

Insert : Inserts Rows and Columns into the Worksheet. Just as Delete removes rows and columns, this command can put rows and columns of empty cells into the Worksheet. This is often used to assist in making the appearance of the sheet more attractive.

Move : Moves information from one area of the Worksheet to another. Unlike Copy which leaves the original information where it is and merely copies it elsewhere, this command literally moves the information.

Command list 2 : Colnumbers Paint Rownumbers Titles

Colnumbers : Toggles the display of Column numbers on or off. Often, a display looks better if these numbers are omitted.

Paint : Permits the screen background and text display to be colour customised.

Rownumbers : Toggles the display of Row numbers on or off.

Titles : Fixes Rows and Columns to make them independent of other row and column manipulations. Typical of this is when a Worksheet is scrolled across the screen. Ordinarily the left hand columns disappear as new columns appear from the right. It may be that you would like certain cells containing descriptive text to remain where they are whilst other cells scrolled on and off the screen. This feature is controlled using this command.

Command list 3 : Fill Justify Newname Reformat Text-Editor Value-Format Width

Fill : Fills an area of the Worksheet with incremental or decremental values. For instance you may want a list of numbers from 1 to 1000 in the cells of the first column. This command can be used to avoid having to enter each number individually.

Justify : Specifies the location of information within a cell. Text is usually started from the left hand side of a cell and numbers usually end at the right-hand side of a cell. This justification can be changed.

Newname : Allows the current Worksheet to be renamed.

Reformat : Sets the format of numerical information. Numbers can take various forms, for example the thousands can be separated from the hundreds by a comma, a blank space or neither. This command sees to that.

Value-Format : Selects a default Format for new numerical entries. It may be that earlier entries have the numbers in one format and later numbers in another. This command permits this facility.

Width : Sets the width of a cell in numbers of characters. This command is often used to tidy up the appearance of a Worksheet. For example, a column of single digit numbers could be located in a cell of width 1 rather than a cell of default width 10.

Command list 4 : Directory Index Load Save Unload

Index : Lists all Worksheets that are currently active.

The other commands in this and the following list are similar to the same commands in the Data-Manager.

Command list 5 : Confidence Execute F-Calculator Parameters Text-Editor

The following is a list of some commands available in the Spreadsheet and the subsequent options when the commands are selected.

Blank : Block / Column / Rows / All

Copy : Down / From / Right

Delete : Block / Columns / Rows

Paint : Border / Cursor / Formulas / Text / Values / Locked-cells / Window

Titles : Drop / Fix

Justify : Left / Center / Right

Reformat : Block / Columns / Rows / All / Formula-display

Text-Format : Left / Center / Right

Value-Format : Bar / Date / E-Notation / Normal

Chapter 5 : The Wordprocessor

Objectives

When you have completed this Section you will be able to :

- Create a document by entering text at the keyboard
- Insert text into the Document
- Delete text from the Document
- Undelete text in the Document
- Copy and move text within the Document
- Set the indentation, margin and tabs of the Document
- Toggle the ruler display on and off
- Password protect your Document
- Save, unload and load your Document to and from Disk.

Introduction

The **SMART Wordprocessor** enables the complete management and handling of documents. Again, like the Spreadsheet, the Wordprocessor operates in two modes - **Entry Mode** and **Command Mode**. You enter the **Wordprocessor Module** from Command list 1 of the SMART Introductory Screen by pressing **W**. The display shows us that we are automatically in **Entry Mode**.

```
┌─ Window 1 ─────────────────────────────────────────────────────┐
│                                                                │
│                                                                │
│                                                                │
│                                                                │
│                                                                │
│ 0|||||||| L|||||||| 2|||||||| 3|||||||| 4|||||||| 5|||||||| 6|||||||| R|||||| │
└────────────────────────────────────────────────────────────────┘
F1 Help        F3 Find   F5 Replace     F7 Zoom      F9 Repeat
F2 Next menu   F4 Goto   F6 Font Select F8 Execute   F10 Quit
Document (none) Pg: 1 Ln: 1 Ps: 10 FN: 0 Font: Standard Insert: ON
TEXT-ENTRY - normal Text Entry Mode
```

The top of the screen is the display area - the Document Window - where the document will appear as it is typed. Notice the cursor - a flashing line under a diamond shape; the flashing line indicates where the next typed character will appear and the diamond shows the end of the text. As you type in characters this cursor moves across the screen. Try it, type in

Once upon a time there were three bears, Father bear, Mother bear and little Baby bear. They all lived together in a small thatched cottage in the middle of the wood. One day a young girl called Goldilocks . . .

When you type in this passage do not press the **enter** or **return** key until you have typed in the third full stop after Goldilocks, then press enter twice. The display should then look something like the following:

```
┌─ Window 1 ─────────────────────────────────────┐
│                                                │
│      Once upon a time there were three bears, Father bear, Mother
│      bear  and  little  Baby bear.  They  all  lived  together  in  a
│      small  thatched  cottage in the middle of the wood.  One day  a
│      young girl called Goldilocks . . .
│
│
│
│   0|||||||||L|||||||||2|||||||||3|||||||||4|||||||||5|||||||||6|||||||||R||||||
└────────────────────────────────────────────────┘
```

Notice how the text automatically **wraps round** as you type and adjusts itself on the screen to align with the right hand edge. This is known as **wraparound** or **right-justification**. Notice also the reverse **P** which signifies the end of a paragraph - put there when you pressed the **enter** key.

At the bottom of the screen is a ruler on which is marked an **L** and an **R**. The **L** signifies the position of the left-hand edge and the **R** the right-hand edge of the text as it appears on the screen.

Also on the ruler the numbers **2**, **3**, **4** and **5** are highlighted which indicates that a **Tab** is set at these places. Try pressing the tab and typing a character to see the effect.

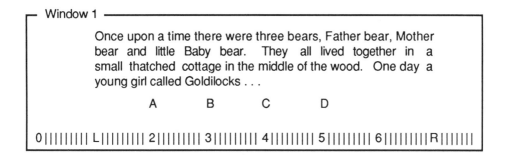

In the Command Area you will see a list of what are called **Quick Keys**. There are **nine** such lists and they can be accessed in sequence by pressing the **F2 - Next menu** function key. Try it to see what is displayed. Any quick key that begins with an **Alt** such as **Alt-F1** means the combination of **F1** with the **Alt** key. A combination of a key with the **Ctrl** key is prefixed with a ^.

The Status line displays, amongst other things, the name of the current document and where the cursor is located in the document - the page number, the line number and the column number (Ps for position).

For now leave the Entry Mode and change to Command Mode by pressing the **Esc** key.

As expected the Control Area now displays the familiar command lists. Move to Command list 5 and set the confidence level at 1. The commands that remain visible are then:

Command list 1: Autohelp Copy Delete Help Insert Move Print Undelete

Command list 2: Indent Margin Tabs

Command list 3: Newname Paint Ruler

Command list 4: Directory Index Load Password Save Unload

Command list 5: Confidence Execute F-Calculator Parameters Text-Editop

We wish to create a document but before we do this we must lay out the page on which it is to be typed. First, clear the screen. Move to Command list 4, select **U** for **Unload** and at the prompt:

Save modified document first (y/n):

enter **N** for **No**. We are now ready to lay out the page for the next document.

Laying out the Page

Laying out the page means that we must set the left- and right-hand margins, set the indent and any tabs that we shall wish to use.

Margins We shall now readjust the **default** size of the page width by re-setting the margins. To do this we must be in Command Mode so make sure that this is the case. Move to Command list 2, select **Margin** and enter the following:

PROMPT	ENTER
	M: Margin
Select option: Left Right Temp-Release	L: Left
Enter new left margin, or use Tab or cursor control keys to move to column:	5

As you move the cursor you will notice the flashing block - alternatively you can just type in the number 5.

Now set the **right margin** at column **75**.

Indent The indent is the left-hand space that lies between the margin and the first character of a new paragraph. Currently the Indent is set at zero - there is no indent. We shall set one - select **Indent** from Command list 2.

PROMPT	ENTER
	I: Indent
Enter new indent, or use Tab or cursor keys to move to column:	9

The 9 will appear when you move the cursor to the correct place - notice that the indent position is measured from the margin and not from the edge of the screen.

Tabs To set a tab select Tabs on Command list 2:

PROMPT	ENTER
	T: Tabs
Select option: Normal Decimal	N: Normal

You are now presented with a list of functions for setting tabs.

F3 Set F4 Unset F5 Left 10 F6 Right 10 F9 Clear all F10 Finished

Try them all to see how they work. In our document we shall only require one tab set at column **25**. A **decimal Tab** aligns numbers on their decimal point.

The Document

The document that we shall create here is a Company Memo that announces the winner of the ABC Supplies sales competition and exhorts the sales force to continued good efforts. We are now ready to type the document into the Document Window but first we must be in Entry Mode - press the **Esc** key.

Copy the following **Departmental Memo** taking note of just two instructions:

1. Do not press the enter key at the end of a line. Just continue typing a paragraph one character after another. The only time you will press enter is when you wish to start a new paragraph.

2. Do not worry about making mistakes. If you should make a few, all the better. Just leave them and continue typing. We shall correct all mistakes later. In fact the letter as written contains a number of errors that we shall have to correct.

ABC Supplies   Sales Memo

SUBJECT : Sales Figures And Competition Result

Now that the Company has settled down into its new selling proceedures I fel that it time to start making that extra effort that will make all the diffrence between continuing as we are and becoming a leading supplier in the region we serve. I shuld like to congratulat all the members of our Sales Team who have maintained theri sles record consistently over the past two or three months. To spurr you all on to higher sales levels the managment has decided to run a Sales Competition. This competitin will be based on the yuor sales performance figures accumulated evry week for each of our three wek Compny Periods. At the end of each period the top saelsperson will be awarded a free gift of substantial value. If this competition proves to be successfull - by which i mean our sales figures increese - then the competition will be reviewed to make it even more atractive

Thankyou all once again for your continuiuing effort and I wish you all success in the future.

> **Sincerly**
>
> **Jane Doe**
>
> **Slaes Mnager**

In your document you may see hyphens that you did not put there. This is done automatically by the Wordprocessor to attain the right-justification.

Editing

This Memo is far from perfect so we shall have to do some editing. There are a number of keys that you will have to be aware of :

> **The Cursor Keys** : Using these keys you will be able to range over the document without affecting it in any way.
>
> **The Back-Arrow Key** : This key can be used to delete characters. As the cursor moves backwards it deletes a character.
>
> **The Insert Key** : The insert key is either **ON** or **OFF**. Its Status is displayed on the status line. If it is **ON** then you can type with impunity and it will insert each character as it is typed. If it is **OFF** the typing will **overtype** what is already on the screen. The state of the Insert can be toggled on and off by simply pressing the **Ins** key - try it. You will notice that in Entry Mode the cursor is a flashing line when **Ins** is **ON** and a flashing square when **Ins** is **OFF**.
>
> **The Delete Key** : Pressing the delete key will delete that character under the cursor. Notice how the text moves back to fill the gap and so maintains the left- and right-justification.
>
> **The Enter Key** : Pressing the **enter** key will insert a new paragraph. If the **insert** key is **OFF** it will also delete the character under the cursor at the time.

Using these keys you are now in a position to edit the document. The obvious mistakes of your own doing you can correct yourselves.

Spelling mistakes can be identified using the SMART Spell-Checker but in this Chapter we shall not use it. For now just look through the document and try to locate all those words that are misspelt and correct them. Only by doing this will you gain a familiarity of moving around the screen and inserting and deleting at will.

As an example of this let us break the document up into paragraphs. Make sure that you are in Entry Mode so that we can insert.

Insert

To improve the appearance of the document and its readability we are now going to break the document into paragraphs. Go to Entry Mode and make sure that **Insert** is **ON** - you will see this indicated on the right-hand side of the status line. If **Insert** is **OFF** then press the Ins key once.

Now place the cursor on the word I on the sixth line of the letter and press **enter** twice. Immediately a new paragraph is created. Do the same with **Now that this ....** and **If this competition ....** to form a total of four paragraphs.

Another feature of a well-presented letter is to remember that after a full stop there should be **two** blank spaces, not one. Insert blank spaces where appropriate.

Next, we shall improve the document from within Command Mode.

Delete

Press **Esc** to enter Command Mode and move to Command list 1. Place the cursor on the S of **Sincerely**, select **Delete** and enter the following sequence of commands:

PROMPT	NTER
	D: Delete
Select option: Block Line Paragraph Remaining Sentence Word:	W: Word

The word **Sincerely** disappears. Now move into Entry Mode (Press **Esc**) and type in

Yours

We have changed **Sincerely** for **Yours**. Now we relent and change our mind. We wish to put **Sincerely** back.

Undelete

Press **Esc** to change to Command Mode, place the cursor on the **Y** of the word **Yours** and select the following commands:

PROMPT	ENTER
	U: Undelete

74   Chapter 5: The Wordprocessor

Immediately **Sincerely** reappears tacked onto the beginning of **Yours**. Undelete is a useful facility for retrieving accidentally deleted text. But beware, it will only undelete the **last** deletion. Now we must get rid of the **Yours** and to do this we shall use the **Delete Block** option. Place the cursor on the **Y** of **Yours**, move to Command list 1 and select the following:

PROMPT   **ENTER**

                                                                     D: Delete

Select option: Block Line Paragraph Remainder
                 Sentence Word: B: Block

We now wish to **mark the block**. To do this make a note of the message in the Control Area:

Use cursor to mark block
F2 Drop new anchor   F10 or ENTER end block

With the cursor on the **Y** of **Yours** we press **F2**. This **drops the anchor** at the beginning of the block of characters. Now move the cursor to the paragraph marker after the **s** of **Yours** (notice the highlight as you move the cursor) and press either **F10** or **enter**. The **Yours** disappears.

The next improvement is to interchange the first two sentences and this we do with the **Move** command.

Move

Place the cursor over the **N** of **Now** in the first sentence of the letter, move to Command list 1 and select the following:

PROMPT   **ENTER**

                                                                     M: Move

Select option: Block Line Paragraph Remainder
                 Sentence Word :   S: Sentence

Immediately the entire sentence disappears. Do not worry it hasn't been lost it is being stored in the computer's memory ready for being **Inserted** where we wish it to be.

Now move the cursor to the end of what is now the first sentence and press **I** for **Insert** on

Command list 1. The first and second sentences have now been interchanged.

The same procedure is followed for the **Copy** command, also on Command list 1 - try it.

Fonts

You will see on the status line that the **Font** is the **Standard** font. This refers to the typeface that will appear on the document when it is printed. There are a number of different fonts available but for now we shall demonstrate just one of them - we shall **underline** the title of the memo. Make sure that you are in Entry Mode and place the cursor on the S of **SUBJECT** at the head of the letter.

Enter **Ctrl-U** (press **U** whilst holding down the **Ctrl** key) and you will see that in the status line the **Font** has changed from **Standard** to **Standard-U**. This means the same font as before but **underlined**. Now retype the heading:

> **SUBJECT : Sales Figures And Competition Results**

Was **Insert ON** or **OFF**? If it was **OFF** then fine, but if it was **ON** you will have to do some more editing.

Now press **Ctrl-U** again and the font returns to **Standard**.

In this manner a number of different fonts can be made use of.

There are a number of other changes that can be effected to further improve the style and these are left to you.

By the time you have finished editing and amending the document it should look something like the following;

> ABC Supplies   Sales Memo To All Sales Personnel
>
> <u>**SUBJECT: Sales Figures And Competition Result**</u>
>
> I should like to congratulate all the members of our Sales Team who have maintained their sales record consistently over the past two or three months.
>
> Now that the Company has settled down into its new selling procedures I feel that it is time to start making that extra effort that will make all the difference between continuing as we are and becoming a leading supplier in the region we serve. To spur you all on to higher sales levels the management has decided to run a Sales Competition. This competition will be based on your sales performance figures accumulated every week for

each of our three-week Company Periods. At the end of each period the top salesperson will be awarded a free gift of substantial value.

If this competition proves to be successful - by which I mean our sales figures increase - then the competition will be reviewed to make it even more attractive

Thank you all once again for your continuing effort and I wish you all success in the future.

Sincerely

Jane Doe

Sales Manager

Save, Unload and Load

By now you will be familiar with these commands on Command list 4. **Save** the document under the name **SALEMEM1**. Then **Unload** the document. Now **Load** the document and you will see the prompt

Enter document or text filename:

Enter **SALEMEM1** or just press **enter** as the pop-up window is displaying the file name with the arrow pointing at it. We shall explain the reason for the word **text** in the prompt in a later Section.

The document written using the Wordprocessor will have to be printed for circulation amongst the members of the Sales Team.

Printing The Document

In Command Mode move to Command list 1, select **Print** and enter the following:

PROMPT	ENTER
	P: Print
Select option: Normal Enhanced Options Preset Template	N: Normal
Enter document or text filename:	SALEMEM1
Select option: Printer Disk	P: Printer
Enter number of copies:	1

Enter start page number: 1
Enter end page number: 1

and the document is then sent to the printer.

Recap and Review

We have laid out a page and constructed a document called SALEMEM1. We have edited by deleting, undeleting, moving, inserting and changing the font. We have also edited in Entry Mode using the cursor keys in combination with a selection of other keys. Finally we have saved the document and then printed it.

What now follows is a list of the Commands that are displayed in the five Command Lists in the Control Area.

Command list 1 : Autohelp Copy Delete Help Insert Move Print Undelete

Undelete : This command retrieves text that has been previously deleted. It sometimes happens that you will delete text from a document only to find that it should not have been. This command allows the situation to be remedied.

Command list 2 : Indent Margin Tabs

Indent : Sets the indentation of the first word of the first line of a new paragraph.

Margin : Sets the Left and Right MARGINS.

Tabs : Permits the setting of text and decimal TABS.

Command list 3 : Newname Paint Ruler

Ruler : Toggles the display of the ruler on or off. The ruler displays the page width and the TAB settings.

Command list 4 : Directory Index Load Password SaveUnload

Password : Allows a Document to be protected by attaching a password to it. This prevents anyone not knowing the password from viewing the document.

Command list 5 : Confidence Execute F-Calculator Parameters Text-Editor

What now follows is a list of some commands available in the Wordprocessor and the various options that occur when those commands are selected:

Delete : Block / Line / Paragraph / Remainder / Sentence / Word

Move : Block / Line / Paragraph / Remainder / Sentence / Word

Margin : Left / Right / Temp-release

Tabs : Normal / Decimal

Paint : Border / Window / Text-block

Password : Attach / Remove

Section 2 The Data-Manager

This Section consists of a description of the SMART Data-Manager. The intention of this Section is to develop further the introductory ideas of the Data-Manager discussed in the Overview Section.

When you have completed this Section you will be able to **Create, View, Query** and **Organise** a file. You will also be able to Create a file with a **Customised** screen and to create the links that will make it interact with other files. You will be able to define **Table** and **Form Reports**. Finally you will have been exposed to the programming facility of the Data-Manager in preparation for a further Section dealing specifically with **Project Processing**.

This Section is divided into nine Chapters :

- **An Amplified Review**
- **Ordering Records**
- **Creating Files**
- **Lookups**
- **Relations**
- **Transactions**
- **Reports**
- **The Remember Mode**
- **Additional Commands**

Chapter 1 : An Amplified Review

Objectives

When you have completed this Chapter you will be able to:

- Appreciate the various interactive, database features of the Data-Manager
- Recognise the complete set of commands available at Confidence level 3
- Select commands and appreciate the use of Quick Keys
- Distinguish between active and inactive records
- Distinguish between Loading a file and Activating a file

Introduction

The purpose of this Chapter is to review and amplify the points discussed in Chapter 3 of Section 1. We shall require access to all available commands and to ensure this the Confidence level must be set at **3**. If you are in doubt about the default Confidence level enter the Data-Manager Module, move to Command level 5 and set the Confidence level at 3.

Data Management and the Components of a Database

All organizations collect and store information to enable them to function. Much of this information is collected and collated manually and much of it is handled electronically. The advantages of electronic handling are clear - it is efficient and it is accurate. Repetitive tasks are performed perfectly every time and storage and retrieval are performed in a fraction of the time it takes to perform the equivalent operations manually. Whether the system that manipulates information be manual or electronic we refer to it as an **information system**.

A typical manual information system consists of a filing cabinet inside of which are a collection of files. Each individual file contains a collection of records in which information is recorded. This information will have been entered into each record in specific formats - for example, name, address, telephone number and record number. These pre-set formats are called fields.

The electronic system replaces the filing cabinet with a **Database**. The Database is a collection of files that are stored typically on a disk. Just as with the manual system, each file consists of a number of records on which information is stored in fields.

Database Features

Any manipulation of information that can be performed with a manual Information System can also be done with an electronic system. There are, however, facilities within an electronic system that have no equivalent in a manual system.

Calculated Fields

The SMART System has the ability to perform calculations between fields and insert the result of that calculation into the record. For example given two fields, one for **Unit Price** and one for **Quantity** it is quite a simple matter to define a third field that automatically takes as its value the product of Unit Price and Quantity to produce a **Total Cost**.

Password Protection

The SMART Data-Manager allows you to protect a particular file with a **password**. Such a password can be used to control access to confidential information. This is equivalent to having access to the filing cabinet key except the password can operate at the file level.

Data Entry Status

It is possible to specify the **entry status** of any field. Ordinarily this status is such that entry of information into a field is optional - you can enter information or not as you wish. The status can be changed to **mandatory**, where information must be entered or it can be changed to **read-only** where information can only be **read** and not **written** - in the latter case the original information will have be put there by the Data-Manager system. This status is imposed when the **screen** associated with a file is created.

Data Range

A **data range** can be specified for a field. This means that data entered that lies outside the range will not be accepted. This is a further assurance of accuracy.

Printing Reports

The **report** facility for the SMART Data-Manager permits information to be gleaned from the Database with speed and accuracy and complied into a predefined report format.

General Manipulation

The ability to **query** the Database and thereby locate specific information quickly is one of the more important functions of a Database. There are a number of different ways to do this and we shall consider them all extensively later on.

An Interactive Database

An **interactive** Database is one where a record field in one file can be **linked** to a record field in another file to facilitate an interaction between records in the two files. A typical use of this facility could occur where a customer's name and address were required to be entered onto an invoice. If all the customer details are contained in one file and the invoices in another then SMART provides the facility to link those two files together. In this way, just entering a customer's code number onto an invoice will cause the name and address to appear automatically, being taken from the appropriate record in the Customer file. There are a number of different ways of interactively activating the SMART Data-Manager and we shall consider each one in a later part of this Section.

The Data Manager Display

Having entered the Data-Manager module you are confronted by a screen that is divided into four distinct areas.

>**The Data Window** The uppermost area is called the **Data Window**. It is here that all information that is entered into the system is displayed.
>
>**The Control Area** This consists of two lines available for text display just beneath the Data Window. It is here that the user receives prompts for information entry and it is here that error messages are displayed should an error occur. Also listed here are the five Command Lists that allow the user to manipulate the Data-Manager
>
>**The Status Line** This line contains information relating to the file or record currently visible in the Data Window. This information consists of:
>
>>**File: XXXXX** This is the name of the file currently being viewed. It is possible to have a number of different files **activated** at the same time but only one can be viewed at a time in any one window.
>>
>>**Window: 1** This is the window number currently being viewed. It is possible to have up to 50 windows.
>>
>>**Page: 5** This is the page number of the particular record being viewed. It is possible for an individual record to have up to 15 screen pages.
>>
>>**Rec: 10** The number of the record being viewed. Sometimes the letters EOF appear here. This indicates the End Of File - the last record in the file. It is possible to have up to 999,999 records in any one file with up to 255 fields per record. The individual record is limited to 1,000 characters up to a maximum of 4096 characters per record..
>>
>>**Act:** This is followed by **Y** or **N** and indicates whether or not a particular record is **active**. Any temporarily inactive records cannot be manipulated.

The Autohelp Line This line of text at the bottom of the screen displays a short description of the Command currently highlighted in the Control Area or the Command just selected from the Control Area. There is a further HELP facility that is accessible via the **F1** Key.

HELP

A comprehensive description of any one of the available Commands can be displayed on the screen and, if desired, printed out. First select the command that you require help on by highlighting it. Then press the **F1** function key. Immediately a brief description of this command appears in a pop-up box at the bottom of the Data Window. Press **F1** again and a more detailed description of the command's operation appears. If this description covers more than a single screen of text the remaining text can be viewed via the **PgDn** key.

During this process the following appears in the Command Area :

        F2 Print Help   **F3 Help Index**   **F10 Finish**   **Cursor Keys**

Press **F3** and all the commands are listed alphabetically. Any command can then be selected by using the cursor keys to move the arrow to the desired command. Again, press **F1** and the HELP for that command appears.

Pressing **F10** causes the HELP display to disappear, returning the user to the Command Mode.

Selecting Commands and Quick-Keys

There are five Command lists. Each list can be viewed in the Control Area by entering the list number. Alternatively, pressing / displays the **next** Command list and pressing \ displays the **previous** Command list.

To select a command one can either use the highlight and **enter** or simply press the first letter of the displayed command. It is also possible to select a command that is not in the currently displayed list. This is done using what are called the **quick-keys**. For example, no matter which Command list is being displayed **Alt-L** will automatically activate the **Load** command. The ability to use these quick-keys comes as familiarity with the System grows; we shall describe them as and when we use them.

Viewing Files

In Chapter 3 of Section 1 we created a file in the Data-Manager called CUSTOMER. We shall now load this file into memory and take a close look at it.

Command list 4 : Load   **Quick-Key : Alt-L**

Selecting **L** for **Load** on Command list 4 or using the quick-key **Alt-L** causes a pop-up screen to appear at the bottom of the Data Window containing a list of file names. You can now enter the word **CUSTOMER** into the Control Area followed by enter or alternatively you can use the cursor keys to place the arrow next to CUSTOMER and then press **enter**. Next appears a second pop-up window:

```
┌─── Screens for file CUSTOMER ──────────────────┐
│    ----> standard    CUSTOMER                  │
└────────────────────────────────────────────────┘
```

Enter screen name:

There are two different ways to display this particular file. You can use the **standard screen** where the fields are just listed one beneath the other down the screen or you can use the **CUSTOMER screen** which has been custom designed. Select the **CUSTOMER** screen and a display similar to the following appears in the Data Window:

```
┌──────────────────────────────────────────────────────────────────┐
│                              Number -----------                  │
│   Name -----------------------------                             │
│                                                                  │
│   Address1 -----------------------------                         │
│   Address2 -----------------------------                         │
│   Address3 -----------------------------   Salesperson --------- │
│                                                                  │
│   Post-Code --------------------           LastMonthSales ------ │
│                                                                  │
│   Telephone ----------------------         ThisMonthSales ------ │
│                                                                  │
│       FAX ----------------------                                 │
│                                                                  │
└──────────────────────────────────────────────────────────────────┘
```

Command list 1: Activate Directory File Index Load Read Save Unload Write
File: CUSTOMER   Window: 1   Page: 1 Rec: 1 (xxx)   Act: Y
LOAD - opens a database file and prepares it for processing

The status line tells you that you are looking at a File called CUSTOMER in Window 1 (we have only got one window at present) What you see is Page 1 of the first Record (there is only one page to each record in this file). Also the record is **active** (**Y** for **Yes**). The value of xxx will depend upon the number of records that you entered into the file when you created it in Chapter 3 of Section 1.

Active and Inactive Records

The current record is active as indicated by the status line

Act: Y

To inactivate this record move to Command list 1 and select the **Delete** command:

Command list 1: Delete   **Quick Key: Alt-D**

The status display now reads **Act: N** - the record is now inactive and cannot be manipulated. Press **D** for **Delete** again and the record becomes active again - **Delete** is a toggle that alternately activates and de-activates the currently displayed record.

Entering Information

With the CUSTOMER file loaded, move to Command list 1 and select **E** for **Enter** and the file is now prepared for information to be entered into the records. So that we shall have some common records to discuss in the rest of the book enter the following five records:

AlphArtcraft   Davenports
131 Berry Lane   12 High Street
Chumley   Upley
CH2 3OH   UU12 0VW

Personal Enterprises Reliable Supplies
Zenith House   Lord Manor
Park Road   Lord Lane
Humworth   Thripton
HZ6 PR1   TN5 7ML

Jones Craftware
74 Middle Way
Quayside
QS8 1CD

F5 and F6

When you have completed your entry you will press **F10** to leave Entry Mode. Having done this you will be able to view all the records in the file by pressing **F5** and **F6**. Think of the file as a card index and each record is a particular card. As you flip from one record to another you will notice that the entries on each record change. What you are looking at is a file containing a list of names and addresses of the customers of the company ABC Supplies. Each record is numbered sequentially and this number can be used as a code for the customer - we shall say more about this later. Also included in each record is the name of the salesperson who deals with that customer, and the latest two months sales figures.

To take a look at the field specifications move to Command list 2 and enter the following:

PROMPT   **ENTER**

                                                                  F: File-Specs

Select option: Calculated-Fields Data-Ranges
                Field-Info General Key-Fields
                Running-Totals   F: Field-Info

The display of the field specifications now appears.

Field No	Field Title	Type	Length	Key	Total	Status
1	Number	N0	6	Y	N	N
2	Name	A	24	Y		N
3	Address1	A	20	N		N
4	Address2	A	20	N		N
5	Address3	A	20	N		N
6	Post-Code	A	10	N		N
7	Telephone	A	12	N		N
8	FAX	A	12	N		N
9	Salesperson	A	17	Y		N
10	LastMonthSales	N2	7	N	N	N
11	ThisMonthSales	N2	7	N	N	N

F4 Next screen   F2 Print screen   F10 Exit
field-specs field-info
File: CUSTOMER   Window: 1   Page: 1   Rec: 1 (xxx)   Act: Y
FILE-SPECS - list file specifications of current file

The fields are numbered in the first column and named in the second. The third column headed Type has just two different entries. A stands for alphanumeric so these fields will hold their information as characters. Any numbers written in alphanumeric format cannot be arithmetically manipulated. N2 stands for a numeric field with 2 places of decimals. The last two fields store their information as numbers and will not permit letters to be entered. The fourth column stipulates the maximum number of characters that can be entered into each field. The last two fields permit a number up to 7 digits long including the decimal point. So the largest number that these fields can store is 9999.99. The column headed Key we shall discuss in a moment. The column headed Total concerns only the numeric fields. It is possible to generate a running total of all the record values of a particular field. The column headed Status shows the entry status of that particular field. The possible options are:

    n: No Entry Status (it is not obligatory to enter information)
    m: Mandatory Entry Status (information MUST be entered into this field)
    r: Read Only Status (information cannot be entered at the keyboard it can only be read)

Blank: The field is not displayed on the screen.

NOTICE that it is possible for a field to exist and hold a value yet not be displayed on the screen.

Key Fields

Any field can be designated to have a **special key field status**. A **key field** is a specified field whose information can be used to assign an order to the records in a file. For example, you will see that the Number field is a key field (it has a **Y** in the Key column). This means that the records in this file could be arranged in ascending or descending order of Number. Similarly Name is also a Key Field so the records could be arranged into ascending or descending order of Names. Whether it is ascending or descending is determined when the key is created during the creation of the file. Both of these keys have been designated as ascending Keys. A file can have up to **15** keys assigned to it.

Also listed under the **File-Specs** options are :

Calculated-Fields : This gives information relating to any calculated fields in the record. There are none here.

Data-Ranges : There are no ranges specified on any of the fields.

General : Select this option and have a look at what it tells you.

Key-Fields : This list the two key fields in this file.

Running-Totals : There are no running totals specified in this file.

Range through all the possible options to see the sort of information that each one holds.

Browsing a File

A further Command that displays the entire File is the **Browse** command. Move to Command list 2 and select the following sequence of commands:

PROMPT	ENTER
	B: Browse
Select option: All Fields Off	A: All

Choosing the **All** option permits all the fields to be displayed on the screen with each record taking just one line of text. With large files the records can be scrolled by using the Cursor Keys. Try it.

Choosing the **Fields** option permits you to select just those fields that you wish to see displayed for each record. Choosing the **Off** option returns the Data Window to the state that it was at prior to making the Browse selection.

NOTE : Quick Key Alt B selects Browse All.

We shall look at the Browse Mode in more detail in the next Section when we look at Organizing Files.

Unload, Save and Activate

To complete the discussion of commands in this Chapter there are three further Commands that require mention, all of them on Command list 4.

Command list 4 : Unload   **Quick Key : Alt-U**

This command is used to **Unload** a file or a screen from memory. The options are:

All File Screen

The process of Unloading a file also **Saves** the files to disk.

Command list 4 : Save   **Quick Key : Alt-S**

This command **Saves** a file to disk without Unloading it.

Command list 4 : Activate   **Quick Key : NONE**

This **Loads** a file but does not display it unless the current screen is empty unlike the Load command which will cause the current display to be displaced.

Exiting the Data-Manager

To leave the Data-Manager press **F10**. You are then faced with a list of options in the Control Area. Among these options are the other SMART Modules and the word **Quit**. Selecting any of the Modules causes you to **exit** the Data-Manager and **enter** the chosen module. Selecting **Quit** causes you to exit not only the Data-Manager but also the SMART System.

Chapter 2 : Ordering Records

Objectives

When you have read this Chapter you will be able to:

- Order a file sequentially, by key or by index
- Understand how a key field works
- Add, Delete, Organize and Update Keys
- Create a Sort Definition
- Create a Sort Index
- Create a Query Definition
- Create a Query Index
- Understand the effect of the various Query Options
- Use the Query Clauses

Introduction

In this Chapter we shall be concerned with various manipulations that can be performed on a file. These manipulations usually concern the obtaining of information contained in the various records. To this end we shall be concerned with Ordering and Sorting records and with Querying their contents. Make sure that the Confidence level is set at 3 and that the CUSTOMER file is Loaded.

Browse and Order

We begin by Browsing the CUSTOMER file and displaying all the fields in each record.

Command list 1 : Browse All   **Quick Key : Alt-B**

The order in which the records appear is their **natural** or **sequential** order - this is the order in which they were **entered into the file**. You will notice that the numbers are in ascending order but the customer names are in no order at all. We shall now see the use of a **key**.

We are going to arrange this display so that the customer names are in alphabetical order - ascending order. We do this using the fact that this field is a key field that has been pre-defined to be an **ascending key**. Move to Command list 2 and select the following commands:

PROMPT	ENTER
	O: Order
Select option: Index Key Sequential	K: Key

The Sequential option is the natural order - the order in which they were entered into the file and the order in which they are currently displayed. The option Index we shall cover later; for now select the option Key by pressing **K**.

A list of all the available fields appears in a pop-up screen with the letter **k** alongside those fields that are key fields. Move the arrow using the cursor keys until it is against **Name** and press **enter**. Immediately, the list of records appears in the Browse mode in alphabetical order of Name. This demonstrates the purpose of a key field.

How a Key Field Works

When a field is assigned to be a key field a separate file is created called a **key file** - and there is a key file for each key field. This key file keeps a track of the values of that field in all the records of the original file. These files can be maintained by using the Key command on Command list 2.

Command list 2 : Key   Quick Key : Alt G

Selecting this command produces the following list of further options :

Add   Delete   Organize   Update

You can now make any field into a key field by using the **Add** option, or remove the key attribute from a field by using the **Delete** option.

> **Update:** When new records are added to the file each new value of a key field is added to the end of the appropriate key file. However, the important aspect of the key file is that these values be arranged in ascending or descending order. This is what the Update option does. It rearranges the values in the key file to put them into the required order. This file can then be used as a reference file to put the display of the original file records into the required order.
>
> **Organize:** Sometimes a key file is damaged or in some way made inoperable. The option Organize is used to remedy this. By looking at all the records in the original file the key files are reconstructed

Sort

Any file can have up to 15 fields in a record designated as key fields. It is, however, possible to have all 15 keys used up yet still require the file records to be listed in ascending or descending order of a further non-key field. To order records with respect to a field that is not a key field we must use the **Sort** command.

The action of the Sort command is in two parts:

A Sort Definition is constructed.

The Sort Definition is then used to create a file called an Index that holds the values of the field in question in ascending or descending order. The Index is equivalent to the key file for a key field.

Having created the Index the records can be ordered against that Index. Let's try it.

Command list 2 : Sort   **Quick Key : Alt-J**

Selecting the Sort command produces the following further options:

Define   Now   Predefined   Undefine

Define: This option permits the construction of the Sort Definition that can be used to create an Index File that holds the appropriate field values from all the records. We shall use this to create an Index to allow us to Sort the CUSTOMER file into descending order of ThisMonthSales, which is not a key field.

Move to Command list 2 and select the following sequence of commands:

PROMPT	ENTER
	S: Sort
Select option: Define Now Predefined Undefine	D: Define
Enter name of sort definition:	CSORT
Select field:	[11]: (ThisMonthSales)

Choose D for Descending and press F10 to Finish

This will now create the Sort Definition CSORT. Nothing happens on the screen. To actually put the display into the required order we must first create the **Sort Index** using the **Sort Predefined** option.

To create the Sort Index select the following commands from Command list 2:

PROMPT	ENTER
	S: Sort
Select option: Define Now Predefined Undefine	P: Predefined
Enter sort definition:	CSORT
Enter sort index:	CSORT

We use the same name as the Sort Definition for convenience only - it is not necessary to use the same name.

We can now Order the file against this Index.

94   *Chapter 2: Ordering Records*

        Command list 2 : Order   **Quick Key : NONE**

Move to Command list 2 and enter the following sequence of commands:

PROMPT	ENTER
	O: Order
Select option: Index Key Sequential	I: Index
Enter index filename:	CSORT

The records on the screen will now be displayed in descending order of **ThisMonthSales**.

    Now: The Now option following the selection of the Sort command allows you to both create a Sort Definition and a Sort Index in one operation.

    Undefine: The Undefine option following the selection of the Sort command will delete a Sort Definition from the disk.

Query

The **Key**, **Sort** and **Order** commands deal with the entire collection of records within a file. Sometimes, however, it may be desired to deal with just a few of the records. For example, you may wish to deal only with those Customers whose spent less than £100 last month.

To achieve this we shall **Query** the CUSTOMER file. As with the Sort command we must first create a **Query Definition**, followed by a **Query Index** before we can **Query** the file.

Command list 2 : Query   **Quick Key : Alt-Q**

To achieve our object enter the following :

PROMPT	ENTER
	Q: Query
Select option: Count Define High-Low Manua Now Predefined Undefine	D: Define
Enter query definition name:	CQUERY

The **Query Definition Screen** now appears and the criterion is entered into it:

```
┌─ Query Editor ─────────────────────────────────────┐
│ [10] < 100                                         │
│                                                    │
│                                                    │
│                                                    │
│                                                    │
│                                                    │
└────────────────────────────────────────────────────┘
F1 Help      F3 Find     F5 Replace      F7 Insert line     F9 Repeat
F2 Calc      F4 Goto     F6 List fields  F8 Delete line     F10 Finished
                                         Line: 1 Column: 9    Insert: ON
QUERY - select records meeting specified criteria
```

The formula on the screen is the criterion against which records will later be selected - [10] denotes field number 10, LastMonthSales. It is the **Query Definition**.

Having defined the Query we now create the **Query Index** file that will contain references to those records that satisfy the criterion in the definition - that is, all records where last month's sales were less than £100.

From Command list 2 enter the following :

PROMPT	ENTER
	Q: Query
Select option: Count Define High-Low Manual Now Predefined Undefine	P: Predefined
Enter query definition filename:	CQUERY
Select option: Index Neither Screen	I: Index
Enter name of index:	CQUERY

We give the Index the same name as the Definition - again for convenience only. The appropriate records are then selected for the Index file. To display only those records that satisfy our criterion we use the Order command on Command List 2.

PROMPT	ENTER
	O: Order
Select option: Sequential Index Key	I: Index
Enter name of index:	CQUERY

Now if you Browse through the CUSTOMER file you will see that there are fewer records - these are the only records where the criterion was satisfied.

96 *Chapter 2: Ordering Records*

In summary, for both Sort and Query we follow these steps:

1. **Create a Sort or Query Definition by using option Define**
2. **Create a Sort or Query Index by using option Predefined**
3. **Order the file by using Order Index.**

Query Options

When querying the file we came across a large number of possible options. We shall now consider these individually.

Selecting the Query command from Command list 2 produces the following list of options :

Count Define High-Low Manual Now Predefined Undefine

Count: Select the fields you wish to count and a report is printed counting the number of records with each unique data item in the key field. The file must be in key order to use this option. For example, putting the CUSTOMER file in key order Name and then counting on field [11] - ThisMonthSales, the following printout is obtained:

QUERY:	Count duplicates
File:	CUSTOMER
Key:	Name
Field:	ThisMonthSales
Date:	DD/MM/YY
54.50	Count : 1
125.00	Count : 1
0.50	Count : 1
1.35	Count : 1
95.00	Count : 1

(This count list is just an illustration and not necessarily what you would obtain)

High-Low: This option selects records containing the highest, lowest or both highest and lowest values. Following this option is

Select option: High Low Both

followed by

Select option: All Category

> **All:** selects records containing the highest and/or lowest data items in the entire CUSTOMER file.

Category: selects the records containing the highest and/or lowest data for each unique item in a key field. This option requires the file to be in key order. Choosing the option results in the following prompts:

How many members to keep (1-10)

It allows up to 10 highest and/or lowest items to be retained.

Select field:
Enter index file:

After the records have been scanned the total number retained is noted in the Control Area.

N Record(s) selected. Enter any key

Manual: This option allows you to select the records without specifying a criterion. Each record is viewed in turn and is selected or not by entering **Y** or **N** according to the prompt:

Select record (y/n):

The complete selection in then saved in an Index.

Now: This option permits you to both select and query the current file in one step. It does not save the query definition. Following this selection the following options are available:

Index Neither Screen

Index: creates an Index for future use.

Screen: allows the selected records to be viewed on the screen.

Neither: This option can be used if only a count of the records selected is required. The count appears in the control area. It can also used when the criterion contains a **Replace** clause - see below.

Predefined: This option is followed by **Index Screen Neither** in the same manner as the **Now** option.

Undefine: This option deletes a previously created Query Definition.

Special Query Clauses

There are two special clauses that can be used within a query definition. These are **Where** and **Replace**.

Where:

Where [field] = [expression]. To use this clause the file must be ordered by the field referenced in the clause. See Order Key or Order Index. The advantage of using this clause is that it speeds up the selection process. If the WHERE were not used then every record in the file would be tested whereas, since the records are ordered, the likely candidates for selection are grouped together and the Where clause takes advantage of this. Only one Where clause can be used in a criterion, for example **where [Name] = "Jones"**.

Replace:

A replace clause can be added to the end of a Query Definition and takes the form:

>**Replace [field] = [expression] ... [field] = [expression]**

or

>**Replace [field] = [field] ... [field] = [field]**

Each named field in the selected records is given the value of the [expression] or [field].

Replace Delete and Replace Activate:

Each selected record is made either **inactive** by **delete** or **active** by **activate**.

NOTE : Query cannot replace the contents of Calculated fields.

Chapter 3 : Creating Files

Objectives

When you have read this Chapter you will be able to:

- Understand fully the field options that are available when creating a file
- Create a file
- Create a Screen to accompany a file
- Understand the meaning of field Entry Status

Introduction

In Chapter 3 of Section 1 we created a file called CUSTOMER and an associated screen, also called CUSTOMER. In this Chapter we wish to extend the ABC Supplies system to include a SUPPLIER file, a STOCK file and an ORDERS file.

The SUPPLIER File

In Chapter 3 of Section 1 we created a file called CUSTOMER and below we display the File-Specs of that file.

Field No	Field Title	Type	Length	Key	Total	Status
1	Number	N0	6	Y	N	N
2	Name	A	24	Y		N
3	Address1	A	20	N		N
4	Address2	A	20	N		N
5	Address3	A	20	N		N
6	Post-Code	A	10	N		N
7	Telephone	A	12	N		N
8	FAX	A	12	N		N
9	Salesperson	A	17	Y		N
10	LastMonthSales	N2	7	N	N	N
11	ThisMonthSales	N2	7	N	N	N

F4 Next screen   F2 Print screen   F10 Exit
field-specs field-info
File: CUSTOMER   Window: 1   Page: 1 Rec: 1 (xxx) Act: Y
FILE-SPECS - list file specifications of current file

ABC Supplies have been using their CUSTOMER file satisfactorily for some time now and they wish to expand their system to include a SUPPLIER file. Their SUPPLIER file will be similar to the customer file with the exception that the Salesperson field will be omitted. To create the SUPPLIER file we must first load the CUSTOMER file and then Create SUPPLIER Similar to CUSTOMER.

Load the CUSTOMER file and CUSTOMER screen using Load from Command list 4 or Quick Key Alt L. When this file is resident in memory move to Command list 1 and enter the following:

PROMPT	ENTER
	C: Create
Select option: File Screen	F: File
Enter the new filename:	SUPPLIER
Select option: Fixed-Length Variable-Length	F: Fixed-Length

A file with a Fixed-Length format stores the total number of characters for each record regardless of the number actually entered. This can make for faster access to particular records but does use up more disk space than is needed to fully store the information held in a file. A file with a Variable-Length format only stores those characters entered. This uses less disk space but does make access to particular records slower.

Select option: No-Password Password	N: No-Password
Select option: New Matching Similar	S: Similar
Select database filename:	CUSTOMER

The screen now displays the File Definition screen.

```
┌─ Creating file ─────────────────────────────────────────────────┐
│   Fld No    Title           Type    Length    Running Total    │
│                                                                 │
│     1       Number          N0      6              N           │
│     2       Name            A       24                         │
│     3       Address1        A       20                         │
│     4       Address2        A       20                         │
│     5       Address3        A       20                         │
│     6       Post-Code       A       10                         │
│     7       Telephone       A       12                         │
│     8       FAX             A       12                         │
│     9       Salesperson     A       17                         │
│    10       LastMonthSales  N2      7              N           │
│    11       ThisMonthSales  N2      7              N           │
│                                                                 │
└─────────────────────────────────────────────────────────────────┘
```

F3 Calc fld F7 Insert field F10 Exit   PgUp Prev page Home First Entry
F4 Del calc F8 Delete field Esc Abandon PgUp Next page End Last entry
Title can be up to 16 characters long

CREATE - creates a new file or screen

Notice the available function keys in the Command Area. Because we are now on Confidence level 3 there are more than were available when we were on Confidence level 1 in Section 1.

To define the fields for SUPPLIER delete the Salesperson field using F8. Next change the Number field to Supplier Code. When you are asked to specify the type of field you will see a greater number of options to choose from:

   A Alpha **I** Inv name **N** Num **C** Counter **D** Date **T** Time **S** SSN **P** Phone

Alpha is still alphanumeric

Inv name will sort on the last word of the field rather than the first

Num is still numeric

Date, Time, SSN - Social Security Number and **Phone** are all predefined formats for their entries. **SSN** and **Phone** are in USA format.

Counter A Counter field is a whole number field that is automatically entered. Each record will have a number one greater than its predecessor - we shall designate the Supplier Code to be a Counter field of length 6. Finally, designate fields [1] - Supplier Code and [2] - Name to be ascending key fields.

When you have completed this process you can Create a screen, also called SUPPLIER,

Similar to the CUSTOMER screen. When you do this you will find that, again, you have a greater number of function keys to use than hitherto. Also you will be able to enter text into the record straight from the keyboard. Perhaps the most striking facility that we gain at this Confidence level is the ability to draw lines and boxes using the F4 key. How? - as follows:

Lines Place the cursor where you wish the line to start and press F4. Move the cursor horizontally to where you wish the line to end and press enter. Hey presto - a line appears.

Boxes Place the cursor where you wish a corner of the box to be and press F4. Move the cursor to where you want the diametrically opposite corner to be and press enter - and there is the box.

Entry Status

The Entry Status of a field can be optional entry, mandatory entry or read only entry. The Entry Status is assigned using the Alt F7 keys. The default status is one of optional entry. Make the Name field a mandatory entry field by using the Alt F7 key. Place the cursor on the Name field and press Alt F7 and the field status changes to read-only signified by an r. Press Alt F7 again and the status changes to mandatory signified by an m. Press Alt F7 a third time and the status reverts to the default status of optional entry. Press Alt F7 twice more to ensure that the supplier's name has a mandatory entry status. Go ahead and create a screen for the SUPPLIER file. The following is a suggestion for the design of the SUPPLIER screen:

```
+----------------------------------+----------------------------------+
| ABC Supplies  SUPPLIER FILE      | Supplier Code: --------------    |
+----------------------------------+----------------------------------+
|   Name:       m---------------------|                               |
|                                     |    Purchase Details           |
|   Address:    ---------------------|                                |
|               ---------------------|                                |
|               ---------------------|    Last Month: ----------      |
|   Post Code:  ----------           |                                |
|                                    |    This Month: ----------      |
|   Telephone:  ----------           |                                |
|        FAX:   ----------           |                                |
+----------------------------------+----------------------------------+
```

F1 Help F3 Ins w/o title F5 Prior fld F7 Ins fld AF7 E-status F9 Clr Page
F2 Next Menu G4 Box/Line F6 Next Fld F8 Del fld AF8 Range F10 Exit
All fields defined   Pg: 1   Ln: 1   Ps: 1
CREATE - creates a new field or screen

Notice that in this screen all the field names have been entered from the keyboard and the field itself entered using the F3 key - insert without title.

When you are satisfied that the screen has been completely designed press **F10** to terminate the process.

Next you will want to see the screen attached to the file. At the moment the screen that is attached to the file is the standard screen so we must Load the screen called SUPPLIER.

Command list 4 : Load   **Quick Key : Alt-L**

Load the file SUPPLIER again, this time with screen SUPPLIER. Immediately the new screen appears. If you now enter data into it you will see the effect of both the counter field Supplier Code and the mandatory status of the Name field. The Supplier Code is entered automatically and you are forced to enter data into field [2] - Supplier Name - try getting past it just by pressing enter.

To ensure that there is some commonality between your SUPPLIER file and the descriptions in this book enter the following suppliers:

Top Equipment	Harcastle Hardware
18 New Road	51 Smith Street
Stedley	Amborough
ST1 1TS	AM2 1BQ
Betty's	Lamps 'N Lanterns
2 Beauville Ave	Old Smithy
Enerfield	Crumble Lane
London	Wickley
EN2 2OR	W13 5OP
Gadgets Galore	
Gismo House	
Western Way	
Fumboro	
FBO 2PN	

When you have entered a number of suppliers into the SUPPLIER file move to Command list 4 and Unload All to clear both the CUSTOMER and the SUPPLIER files out of memory.

The STOCK File

Having created the SUPPLIER file Similar to the CUSTOMER file we shall now create the STOCK file that contains information concerning the stock obtained from the suppliers and sold to the customers. The fields for this file will be:

Chapter 3: Creating Files

Field Number	Field Name	Field Type	Length	Key	Status
1	Stock Code	C	6	Y	N
2	Stock Name	A	20	N	M
3	Supplier Code	N0	6	Y	N
4	Quantity In Stock	N0	4	N	N
5	Cost Per Unit	N2	7	N	N
6	Total Value	N2C	8	N	N

Notice field [6]. This is a Calculated field.

Calculated Fields A Calculated Field is a field whose contents are obtained from applying a formula calculation. The Total Value field is obtained by multiplying the number of a particular item in stock by the cost of that item.

Designate field [6] to be a Calculated Field when the field parameter values have been defined. Place the cursor in the Field Type column on the Total Value line and press F3 - you will notice in the control area that F3 is annotated as Calc Field. When you press F3 the Display Window displays the Formula Editor screen:

```
┌─ Formula Editor ─────────────────────────────────┐
│                                                  │
│                                                  │
│                                                  │
│                                                  │
│                                                  │
│                                                  │
└──────────────────────────────────────────────────┘
F1 Help     F3 Find    F5 Replace     F7 Insert line    F9  Repeat
F2 Calc     F4 Goto    F6 List fields F8 Delete line    F10 Finish
                                      Line: 1  Column: 1  Insert: ON
```
CREATE - creates a new file or screen

It is into this Formula Editor screen that the formula to be used in the calculation is entered. The cursor is at the top left hand corner of the screen and the formula can be entered either as:

[Quantity In Stock] * [Cost Per Unit]

or simply as

$$[4] * [5]$$

The square brackets are mandatory. If, during the entry of the formula, you are unsure of either the exact name or number of the fields then pressing F6 will display a list of the available fields from which selections can be made.

When you have completed the definition of the STOCK file you may wish to design a screen to accompany it. The following is a suggestion:

ABC Supplies STOCK FILE	Stock Code Number: --------
Stock Item : ---------------------------- Description : --------------------------------- Quantity In Stock : --------------------	Supplier Code: ----------
Cost Per Unit: ----------------	Total Value: £ --------------

Now enter the following into the STOCK file (and anything else you may wish to include).

Item	Cost
Artist Easels	20.00
Outdoor Lights	60.00
Indoor Lanterns	183.75
Electric Mobiles	16.00
Looms	275.50

The Customer Order File

When one of the ABC Supplies sales personnel receives an order they enter the details of the order onto a Sales Order form. At the end of the day these paper forms are forwarded to the Main Office where they are entered into the computer. This enables the administration to generate invoices and keep a watch over their stock levels. The file that contains the Sales Orders is called ORDERS and the field specification is as follows:

Field No	Field Title	Type	Length	Key	Total	Status
1	Order Number	C	6	Y		M
2	Date	D	8	N		N
3	Customer Code	N0	6	Y		M
4	Customer Name	A	24	Y		N
5	Address1	A	20	N		N
6	Address2	A	20	N		N
7	Address3	A	20	N		N
8	Post-Code	A	10	N		N
9	Item1Code	N0	6	N		N
10	Item1Name	A	20	N		N
11	Item1Price	N0	7	N		N
12	Item1Number	N0	2	N		N
..	....	..	..	..		..
21	Item4Code	N0	6	N		N
22	Item4Name	A	20	N		N
23	Item4Price	N0	7	N		N
24	Item4Number	N0	2	N		N
25	Total Price	N2C	8	N		N
26	VAT	N2C	3	N		N
27	Total Value	N2C	8	N		N

Fields [25], [26] and [27] are all Calculated Fields. Field [25] is the sum of all the item prices multiplied by the number ordered. Field [27] is this sum increased by the current VAT rate (15%). Create this file and a screen to accompany it. The following is a suggestion for the screen named ORDERS:

```
+---------------------------------+-----------------------------+------------------+
| ABC Supplies  ORDER FORM        | Order Number: -----------   | Date: --- --- ---|
+---------------------------------+-----------------------------+------------------+
| Customer Details                | Item     Description      Price     No         |
|                                 |  1  --------  --------------  --------  ----   |
| Customer Code: -------------    |  2  --------  --------------  --------  ----   |
|                                 |  3  --------  --------------  --------  ----   |
| Name:     ------------------    |  4  --------  --------------  --------  ----   |
|                                 +------------------------------------------------+
| Address:  ------------------    |                                                |
|           ------------------    |   Total Price:  ------------------             |
|           ------------------    |   VAT: ( ----- )                               |
| Post Code: --------------       |                                                |
|                                 |   Total Value:  ------------------             |
+---------------------------------+------------------------------------------------+
```

Notice that the Customer Code has a mandatory entry status. To illustrate how this record will be entered enter the following information:

Date:	Press F5 for automatic date entry
Customer Code:	1
Customer Name:	Dexter J Booth
Address:	The Polytechnic
	Queensgate
	Huddersfield
Post Code:	HD1 3DH
Item 1:	1
Description 1:	Artist Easel
Price 1:	20
No 1:	2

The calculated fields will fill in automatically.

When you entered this record you will probably have had the feeling that you had been here before. So you had, it contains details that you have already entered into other files - the CUSTOMER file and the STOCK file. It would be rather nice if we could call up that information without having to enter it all over again, and so we can. This is the subject of the next Chapter.

Chapter 4 : Lookups

Objectives

When you have read this Chapter you will be able to:

- Define a Lookup between two files
- Use multiple Lookups for data entry and updating

Introduction

There are many times when information entered into a file is already contained in another file. In such a situation it is much more efficient and convenient for that information to be directly copied from one file to the other without it having to be entered in detail at the keyboard. For example, if a customer places an order with ABC Supplies then the customer details are going to be required on the order form. To avoid typing these details into the order form they can be copied directly from the CUSTOMER file using what is called a Lookup. There are many advantages in this method of entering information into a file; it avoids spelling errors, it is fast and it avoids tedium.

Lookups

We shall now define a Lookup between the ORDERS file and the CUSTOMER file that will automatically enter the customer's details onto an order record when the customer's code is entered. The process of defining a Lookup involves a number of stages:

1. The screen must be Split into two Windows.

2. Both files must be loaded, one into each Window. The CUSTOMER file is the source file - the information is going to come from this file, and the ORDERS file is the destination file - this is where the information is going to.

3. A link is established between the two files by linking a field n the destination file to a field in the source file. These link fields must be of the same type and contain information common to both files.

4. The source file link field must be a key field and the file must be in key order by the link field.

5. The destination file must be in the current window.

6. The lookup can then be defined.

Defining a Lookup

To make sure that we start with an empty memory move to Command List 4 and **Unload All**. We are now ready to define the Lookup.

Stage 1: Split the screen into two windows

Move to Command list 3 and enter the following sequence of commands:

PROMPT	ENTER
	S: Split
Select option: Horizontal Vertical	V: Vertical
Move cursor to new window border and press	Enter

Move the cursor to the center of the screen and press enter. The screen now looks as follows:

```
┌─ Window 1 ──────────────┐  ┌─ Window 2 ──────────────┐
│                         │  │                         │
│                         │  │                         │
│                         │  │                         │
│                         │  │                         │
│                         │  │                         │
└─────────────────────────┘  └─────────────────────────┘
```

Command list: 3 Border Close Link Paint Split Unlink Zoom
File: (none)   Window: 1
SPLIT - split the current window into two windows

Stages 2 and 3: Load the source and destination files into each window and order them by key.

Move to Command list 1 and enter the following sequence of commands:

PROMPT	ENTER
	G: Goto
Select option: File Record Window	W: Window
Enter window number:	1

And now on Command list 4:

	L: Load
Enter filename:	ORDERS

Enter screen name:	ORDERS

On Command list 2:

	O: Order
Select option: Index Key Sequential	K: Key

and select key field [3] - **Customer Code**.

So far we have loaded the ORDERS file into window 1 and have ordered the file against key field [3] - Customer Code. Make sure that you have followed this procedure and that you fully understand what you have done. When you are completely clear repeat the process by loading the CUSTOMER file into window 2 and ordering against key field [1] - Number.

Stages 4 and 5: Linking the files together and defining the Lookup

Go to window 1 - the destination file ORDERS, move to Command list 2 and enter the following sequence of commands:

PROMPT	ENTER
	L: Lookup
Select option: Define Index Load Remove Undefine	D: Define
Enter lookup definition filename:	ORDCUST

The following display appears:

112   Chapter 4: Lookups

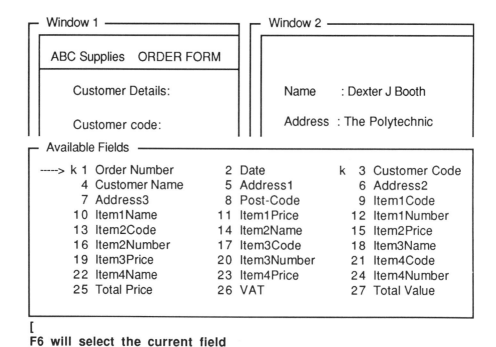

Move the arrow to field [3] - Customer Code and press enter. The following prompt appears in the command area:

Select source filename: **CUSTOMER**

and the screen now displays:

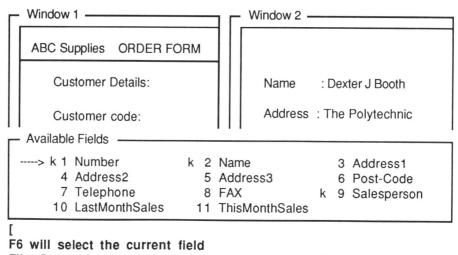

The arrow is pointing at field [1] - Number, press **enter**.

You have now established the link between Customer Code in the destination file and the customer Number in the source file. **NOTE: all these operations must be performed whilst you are in the window containing the destination file.**

We are now ready to continue the Lookup definition using the Lookup Definition screen that has now appeared.

```
┌─ Lookup Definition ─────────────────────────────────────────────┐
│     Field           Source field              Dest. field       │
│  ──> 1         ----------------------         Order Number      │
│      2         ----------------------         Date              │
│      3         ----------------------         Customer Code     │
│      4         ----------------------         Customer Name     │
│      5         ----------------------         Address1          │
│      6         ----------------------         Address2          │
│      7         ----------------------         Address3          │
│      8         ----------------------         Post-Code         │
└─────────────────────────────────────────────────────────────────┘
```
F1 Help   F7 Insert a field   PgUp Prev group   Up arrow   Prev line
F10 Finished F8 Delete field   PgDn Next group Down arrow Next line
Source: CUSTOMER   Destination ORDERS

The first entry that we wish to transfer is the Customer Name so move the arrow down to line 4 and press **F7** to insert a field. The available fields are then displayed from which we select field **[2] - Name**. This field then appears on line 4 of the Lookup Definition screen in the Source column.

This means that the contents of field [2] - Name - of the source file CUSTOMER will be copied into field [4] - Customer Name - of the destination file ORDERS.

Repeat this process to ensure that all the relevant customer details will be copied. Your final Lookup Definition screen should look as follows:

```
┌─ Lookup Definition ─────────────────────────────────────────────┐
│    Field          Source field              Dest. field         │
│      1        ----------------------       Order Number         │
│      2        ----------------------       Date                 │
│      3        ----------------------       Customer Code        │
│      4        Name                         Customer Name        │
│      5        Address1                     Address1             │
│      6        Address2                     Address2             │
│      7        Address3                     Address3             │
│      8        Post-Code                    Post-Code            │
│      9        ----------------------       Item1Code            │
│     10        ----------------------       Item1Name            │
└─────────────────────────────────────────────────────────────────┘
```

F1 Help   F7 Insert a field   PgUp Prev group   Up arrow   Prev line
F10 Finished F8 Delete field   PgDn Next group Down arrow   Next line
Source: CUSTOMER   Destination ORDERS

Press **F10** when the definition is complete.

Using A Lookup

To use a Lookup both the source and destination files must be loaded into separate windows, ordered against their respective keys and the Lookup itself must also be loaded.

We already have both files loaded and ordered against their respective link fields. We shall now load the Lookup. Move to Command list 2 and enter the following sequence of commands:

PROMPT	ENTER
	L: Lookup
Select option: Define Index Load Remove Undefine	L: Load
Enter lookup definition filename:	ORDCUST

Before we enter information into the ORDER file we should like to see the entire record on our screen - at the moment the screen is still split. Ensure that you are in Window 1, move to Command list 3 and enter the following:

PROMPT	ENTER
	Z: Zoom

and immediately the screen fills with the ORDERS record. Move to Command list 1 and select **Enter** to commence entering information.

The cursor is flashing on the order number, press **enter**. To enter the Date press **F2** - or today's date if your computer does not remember today's date. You are now ready to enter the customer details. In Customer Code enter the number **1** and immediately all the customer details appear - magic! That is the effect of the Lookup.

Closing Down

When you have finished entering records press **F10** and at the prompt

> Do you wish to update keys now? (y/n)

respond with **Y** and then **Unload All** to unload the two files. Select the **Zoom** command on Command list 3 and retrieve the Split screen display. On the same command list 3 select **Close** to close window 2. **NOTE: you cannot Close an Un-Zoomed window.** Now move to Command list 2 and enter the following:

PROMPT	ENTER
	L: Lookup
Select option: Define Index Load Remove Undefine	R: Remove

It is important to remember that Lookups are not automatically removed when you unload the files that they were connected to.

Stock Items

We can now define lookups that will bring in the stock details whenever we enter a stock code onto the order. We shall require four such Lookups, one for each possible stock item on the order. Define these Lookups for yourself and call them ORDSTOC1 to ORDSTOC4. Load the two files just as we did for the last Lookup - the ORDERS file in window 1 and the STOCK file in window 2 - and use the respective Item Code Number in the ORDERS file as the link with the Stock Number in the STOCK file for each Lookup. When an Item Code is entered into the record the respective Lookup should bring into the record both the Item Name and the Item Price.

When you have tested your Lookups ORDSTOC1 to ORDSTOC4 why not Load the Lookup ORDCUST as well and enter a few more records. See how much easier it is to enter records - fast and accurate.

Chapter 5 : Relations

Objectives

When you have read this Chapter you will be able to:

- Understand that a relationship can be established between files
- Create a Relate Definition
- Use a Relate Definition
- Understand the various Relate options

Introduction

ABC Supplies have found a need for a new file. They have a STOCK file where each record gives the details of a stock item and the code number of the supplier from whom they obtain the item. Unfortunately, when the stock file was created it did not include the supplier's name and address and so the management has decided to create a file that does include these details.

We have already seen how to create a new file and how to create a file similar to an old one. We are now going to see how a new file can be created by joining two files together - we do this using the Relate command to be found on Command list 2.

Loading the Two Files

The two files we are going to join together are the SUPPLIER file and the STOCK file. We need both of these files to be loaded into separate windows and ordered by the field that is going to link them together - the Supplier Code.

By now you should be able to do this but if you are unsure the necessary sequence of commands follows:

PROMPT	ENTER
	U: Unload
Select option : All File Screen	A: All
	S: Split
Select option: Horizontal Vertical	V: Vertical
Move cursor to desired location and press enter	
	L: Load
Enter filename:	STOCK
Screen: Standard STOCK	STOCK

Chapter 5: Relations

	O: Order
Select option:	K: Key
Enter key field number:	3
	G: Goto
Select option: Record File Window	W: Window
Enter number of window:	2
	L: Load
Enter filename:	SUPPLIER
Screen: Standard SUPPLIER	SUPPLIER
	O: Order
Select option:	K: Key
Enter key field number:	1

By now you should have STOCK in Window 1 ordered against the key field [3] - Supplier Code, and SUPPLIER in Window 2 ordered against the key field [1] - the Supplier Code. These are the two fields that will be used to link the files together.

Ensure that you are in Window 1 and move to Command list 2:

Relating The Two Files

The Relate command is found on Command list 2

Command list 2 : Relate   Quick key : Alt-N

PROMPT   **ENTER**

                                                                 R: Relate
Select option: Define Predefined Undefine   D: Define

To produce a new File we must first use **Define** to create the Relate Definition. Having done this we use the Predefined option to create the new file. **Undefine** deletes the Relate Definition from the disk.

> **Define** To begin the Relate Definition we must recognise that we have two files both in key order where the keys are going to link the files together. Consequently, the linking key fields must be identical in Type and Size - which they are. Having connected the two files together in this way we can continue to specify the Relationship that will join them together into a new file called STOCSUPP.

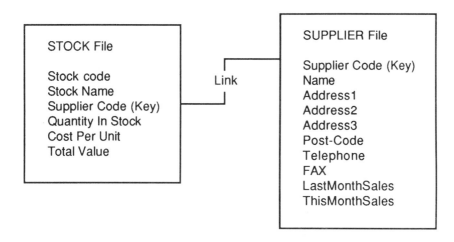

PROMPT	ENTER
Enter relate definition filename:	**STOCSUPP**
Select database filename:	**SUPPLIER**

Because you are resident in Window 1 you are going to link the other file to the current file - SUPPLIER is linked to STOCK and not the other way round.

Immediately the following screen is displayed:

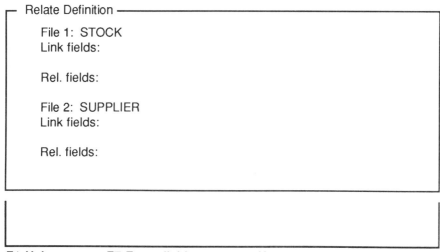

RELATE - create a file based on a relationship between two files

120   *Chapter 5: Relations*

You are now being asked to define the actual relationship by

        1 Defining the link fields
        2 Defining the fields that form the relationship.

The Relationship

The relationship consists of all those fields from the two files that will be used to create the new file.

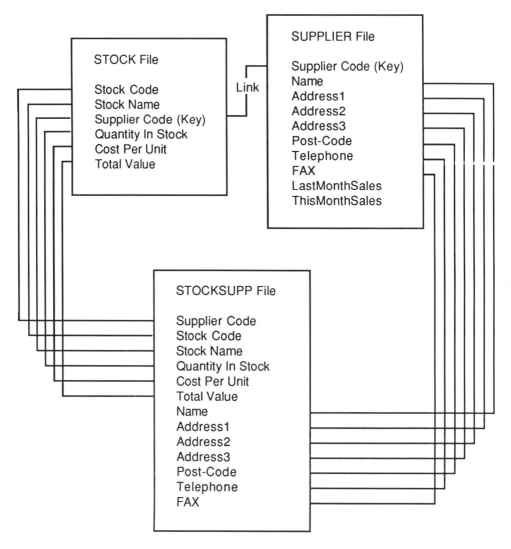

To complete the Relate Definition the Link and Rel. fields are entered onto the screen. This is done by placing the arrow against the line you wish to enter and pressing F7. The list of

available fields then appears in a pop-up display area at the bottom of the screen. By placing the arrow against those fields desired and pressing F6 for each one the final definition will appear as shown:

```
┌─ Relate Definition ─────────────────────────────────────────┐
│     File 1: STOCK                                            │
│     Link fields:   [3]                                       │
│                                                              │
│     Rel. fields:   [1;2;4;5;6]                               │
│                                                              │
│     File 2: SUPPLIER                                         │
│     Link fields:   [1]                                       │
│                                                              │
│ --> Rel. fields:   [2;3;4;5;6;7;8]                           │
├─ Available fields ──────────────────────────────────────────┤
│    k  1   Number         k  2  Name         3  Address1      │
│       4   Address1          5  Address3     6  Post-Code     │
│       7   Telephone         8  FAX          9  LastMonthSales│
│       10  ThisMonthSales                                     │
└──────────────────────────────────────────────────────────────┘
F1 Help         F7 Enter fields           Up arrow     Previous line
F10 Finished    F8 Delete current line    Down arrow   Next line
```

RELATE - create a file based on a relationship between two files

Pressing F10 terminates this definition. The next stage in the creation of the file is to select the Predefined option after the Relate command. Before we do this it will be instructive to consider exactly how the new file is to be created.

There are a number of different ways that the new file can be created and we shall consider the detail of just one - the Intersect method.

Intersect

With the two original files loaded into their respective windows and ordered against their linking key fields the computer will move from record to record in the STOCK file, looking at the value of the Supplier Code each time. Having read the value of the Supplier code the computer will then look at each record of the SUPPLIER file in turn until a match is found in the value of the Number field. When a match is found then a record of the new file will be created, writing into it the contents of the relevant fields from the two original files. In this way the new file will eventually contain records each of which were obtained by matching the values of the two linking key fields. We can represent this diagrammatically as follows:

Intersect

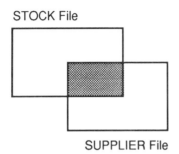

STOCK File

SUPPLIER File

The intersect operation places a record in the new file for every match in the values of the two linking fields.

The other possibilities are:

Not-Intersect

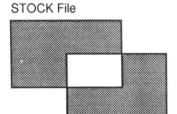

STOCK File

SUPPLIER File

The not-intersect puts a record in the new file when no match occurs between the link fields.

Subtract

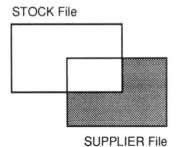

STOCK File

SUPPLIER File

The subtract operation creates a new record for each item of the link field in file 2 for which there is no match in file 1.

Union

STOCK File

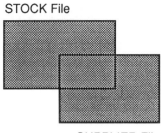

SUPPLIER File

The union operation puts a record in the new file when;

    a) there is a match
    b) there is no match.

To continue with the creation of the new STOCSUPP file (we shall give it the same name as the file definition though this is not necessary) enter the following sequence of commands:

PROMPT	ENTER
	R: Relate
Select option: Define Predefined Undefine	P: Predefine
Enter relate definition filename:	STOCSUPP
Select option: Intersect Not-Intersect Subtract Union	I: Intersect
Enter name of new file:	STOCSUPP

This is followed by the prompt:

Saving new file definition

The new file STOCSUPP is now created and resident on the disk. To view the new file it will have to be Loaded. A close inspection of the File Specifications will reveal the fact that there are no key fields. If you want to have key fields you will have to Add them using the Key command on Command list 2. Similarly, the screen automatically provided is the Standard screen. If you wish a customised screen then you will have to create one in the usual manner.

Chapter 6 : Transactions

Objectives

When you have read this Chapter you will be able to:

- Perform a Transaction on a file

Introduction

At the end of a month ABC Supplies wish to find out how much each customer has purchased. During the course of any particular month a customer will make more than one purchase from ABC Supplies. Each purchase will be recorded on a record in the ORDERS file so at the month's end a transaction will have to be performed that accumulates each customer's purchases.

Transactions

We shall assume that the ORDERS File has a large number of completed records, each one relating to a particular order. What we now wish to do is to find the total value of each customer's purchases by adding together the Total Value of all the records pertaining to individual customers. This is where the Transaction Command comes in.

First of all we must create a new file called TOTALORD that contains the following :

Field No	Field Title	Type	Length	Key	Total	Status
1	Number	C	6	Y		N
2	Customer Code	N0	6	Y	N	N
3	Customer Name	A	24	Y		N
4	Order Value	N2	10	N	N	N

Just as we did with the Relate command we must link this file with the ORDERS file, and we shall do this using the Customer Code field [2] of the TOTALORD file and the Customer Code field [3] of the ORDERS file. Naturally, both files must be in key order by the linking field which indicates that the TOTALORD file must already contain some records. Indeed it does - it should contain one record for each customer. These must be created beforehand. This can be accomplished by entering data into each record in turn but leaving the Order Value field empty. The Customer Name could be entered using a Lookup and this task will be left to you. There is no need to enter anything in the Order Value field.

Defining the Transaction

We shall now assume that we are at the month's end and that the ORDERS file contains this month's orders. We shall also assume that the TOTALORD file exists and contains one record for each customer. The TOTALORD file is in Window 2, the ORDERS file is in Window 1, and both files are ordered against their linking key fields:

[2] - Customer Code - for TOTALORD
[3] - Customer Code - for ORDERS

Go to Window 2 and move to Command list 2. Enter the following sequence of commands:

PROMPT	ENTER
	T: Transaction
Select option: Define Predefined Undefine	D: Define
Enter transaction definition filename:	TOTALORD

(we use the same name as the file though this is not essential)

Select source filename:	ORDERS

The source of the data is obviously in the ORDERS file and the next question to be asked is whether the destination file or the source file is to be the driver. This should be explained.

The driver file is the file that is searched first. The link field in the driver file is located and the transaction then causes the driven file to be searched until the link field contents match. This may occur in more than one record within the driven file. When a match is achieved the driver file record is searched for the appropriate fields whose data is to be sent to the driven file and the data is transacted. The transaction can be in one of three forms:

> 1. ADD the data in the source field to the destination field
> 2. SUBTRACT the data in the source file from the destination field
> 3. MOVE the data in the source field to the destination field

We are ready to continue;

PROMPT	ENTER
Select option: D-Driver S-Driver	S: S-Driver

Link with [3] Customer Code in the ORDERS file and [2] Customer Code in the TOTALORD file.

The following screen is then displayed:

SmartWare: A Beginner's Guide: Section 2 127

```
┌─ Transaction Definition ──────────────── driven link: Customer Code ─┐
│                                                                      │
│    SOURCE FIELD      DESTINATION FIELD    ACTION   LINK   DRIVER LINKS│
│                                                                      │
│   ---> ----------    Number                 -       ---   3 Customer C│
│        ----------    Customer Code          -       ---              │
│        ----------    Customer Name          -       ---              │
│        ----------    Order Value            -       ---              │
│                                                                      │
└──────────────────────────────────────────────────────────────────────┘
F7 add action    F8 remove action    F3 copy destination    F10 Finished

File: CUSTOMER   Key: 2   Window: 2       Page: 1  Rec: 1 (xxx)  Act: Y
TRANSACTIONS - transfer data between files based on matching fields
```

Place the arrow against the Order Value and press **F7**. You are then presented with the list of available fields in the ORDERS file. Select Total Value and enter **A** for add in the ACTION column. By now the display should look as follows:

```
┌─ Transaction Definition ──────────────── driven link: Customer Code ─┐
│                                                                      │
│    SOURCE FIELD      DESTINATION FIELD    ACTION   LINK   DRIVER LINKS│
│                                                                      │
│        ----------    Number                 -       ---   3 Customer C│
│        ----------    Customer Code          -       ---              │
│        ----------    Customer Name          -       ---              │
│   ---> Total Value-- Order Value            A        3               │
│                                                                      │
└──────────────────────────────────────────────────────────────────────┘
F7 add action    F8 remove action    F3 copy destination    F10 Finished

File: CUSTOMER   Key: 2   Window: 2       Page: 1  Rec: 1 (xxx)  Act: Y
TRANSACTIONS - transfer data between files based on matching fields
```

Press **F10** to finish.

You are then asked whether the entire file is to be used each time -answer **Y** for yes to this question. If you were to answer **N** for No to this question then the transaction would only act on those records that had been entered since the last time the transaction had been run.

The final question is

Delete records in driver (y/n)

Answer **N** and the transaction definition is saved.

Executing the Transaction

To execute the transaction we must use the Transaction Predefined option.

PROMPT	ENTER
	T: Transaction
Select option: Define Predefined Delete	**P: Predefined**
Enter transaction definition filename:	**TOTALORD**
Select option: Audit No-Audit	**N: No-Audit**

The Transaction now begins immediately. If the Audit option had been selected then an audit report would have been created and sent either to the disk or the printer. This report produces one line for every driver link that gives the Driver record number, the link field data and the driven record number.

When the Transaction is complete **Zoom** into Window 2 and look at each record of the TOTALORD file. You will see that every order placed by a particular customer has had its value added into the Order Value field of the appropriate record of the TOTALORD file.

Chapter 7 : Reports

Objectives

When you have read this Chapter you will be able to:

- Understand the difference between a Table and a Form Report
- Define a Page layout for either a Table or a Form Report
- Create a Table Report
- Produce a printed copy of a Table Report
- Create a Form Report
- Produce a printed copy of a Form Report

Introduction

The SMART Data-Manager is capable of generating two kinds of report, A Table Report and a Form Report. We shall consider each one in turn. Information from the records in a database file can be compiled into a table consisting of rows and columns. This is the Table report. Such a table can possess headings, footings, page numbers, sub-totals of numeric information as well as grand totals.

An alternative to the Table Report is the Form Report. A Form Report consists of information entered into a sequence of forms, each of which has a layout similar to a file record.

To produce either report we must first define how the report is to fit onto the sheet of paper that we are using in the printer. Having done that we must define how the information from the database file is to be presented on the report itself. We shall now consider these aspects of report generation.

Table Reports

The Table Report that we shall produce will contain a tabulation of all the Orders made to date. For every Order we shall record:

   Order Record Number
   Customer Code
   Customer Name
   Total Value

We shall also provide a Grand Total of the value of all the Orders. Before we begin to define the report we must load the ORDERS file accompanied by the ORDERS screen and order the file against key field [1] - the Order Number. When it is loaded and ordered, move to Command

130   *Chapter 7: Reports*

list 1 and enter the following sequence of commands:

PROMPT	ENTER
	R: Report
Select option: Define Print Undefine	D: Define
Enter report definition filename:	TABLEREP
Select option: Form Table Page:	P: Page

Before the decision is made to use a Table or a Form report the Page must be defined, so here we select the Page option. The screen now fills with the various parameters that define the Page upon which the Table will be printed. The default parameters will not be described here, instead we shall just describe those parameters that have to be changed to ensure that the Page is correctly defined for the Table.

Page Length   6 6

The default is 66 but if your paper is A4 the Page Length should be 70.

Page Width   8 0

The standard width of A4 is capable of taking 80 characters.

Page Numbers: Left Right Center Left-right Right-left No-numbers

Each page of the report can be numbered or not as wished. The options Left-right and Right-left refer to switching the page number from left to right or vice versa. This is particularly useful if the report is to form part of a book with its pages back-to-back.

Lines per inch : 6   8

We choose 6.

Characters per inch: 10   12   17

We chose 10.

The next prompt is asking if there is a Form on this page. This must be answered as No. Press **PgDn** to move to the Table parameters.

IS THERE A TABLE ON THIS PAGE   Yes

We are setting up the page parameters to permit it to contain a Table.

Location of upper left corner of table
      Line   3
      Column   3

Location of lower right corner of table
        Line 60
        Column 78

Which File-screen will be processed for this table
        File: ORDERS
        Screen: ORDERS
Is this file a driver or driven file: Driver

Always use the Driver option unless the table is linked to a form on the same page.

Double space body of table: No

Press **F10** to complete this definition. You are then faced with the prompt:

              Select option: Form Table Page

Press **T** for **Table**.

Immediately the **Table Definition** screen appears.

```
┌─ Table Definition ──────────────────────────────────────────┐
│                                                             │
│   + ------------------------------------------------------- │
│                                                             │
│                                                             │
│                                                             │
└─────────────────────────────────────────────────────────────┘
┌─ Options ───────────────────────────────────────────────────┐
│                                                             │
│                                                             │
│                                                             │
│                                                             │
│                                                             │
└─────────────────────────────────────────────────────────────┘
```

Select option: Columns   Breakpoints   Grand-total   Report-title
Report: TABLEREP   Line: 1   Col: 1   F10 Finished   Esc Cancel
REPORT - Print or define a table or form

Every report will consist of a **Title** that describes the nature of the report, a **body** which contains the report itself and, possibly, **footnotes** that augment the information in the body of the report. Typically, the outline of a report is as follows:

```
┌─────────────────────────────────────────────┐
│   PAGE as set up in the Page Definition     │
│   ┌─────────────────────────────────────┐   │
│   │ REPORT Title                        │   │
│   ├─────────────────────────────────────┤   │
│   │                                     │   │
│   │        BODY Of The Report           │   │
│   │                                     │   │
│   ├─────────────────────────────────────┤   │
│   │ REPORT Footnote                     │   │
│   └─────────────────────────────────────┘   │
└─────────────────────────────────────────────┘
```

Every table report is in the form of columns of data. Sometimes these columns will consist of numbers that end with a Grand Total of all the numbers in the column. Sometimes there may be category breaks with or without **sub-totals** within a column. These are located using the **Breakpoints** option

So far we have set up the Page size and the Table size that is to fit on the Page. We shall now set up the **Title** and **Footnotes** using the **Report-title** option.

PROMPT		ENTER
Heading		
Title Justification:	Left Center	Center
	Line: 1	Customer Orders
	Line: 2	-------------------
	Line: 3	
Blank Lines After Heading 0 1 2 3		2
Footing		
	Line: 1	----------------
	Line: 2	4 Week Period
	Line: 3	----------------
Blank Lines After Footing 0 1 2 3		2

Date in heading: Alpha-date Numeric-date No-date   Alpha-date
Lines to enclose report: Yes No   Yes

Pressing **F10** to complete this process returns you to the previous set of options:

PROMPT		ENTER
Select option:	Columns Breakpoints Grand-total Report-title	C: Columns

We are now going to enter information into the body of the report.

Select option:	Calculated Field Text Edit Move Remove	F: Field

We must first enter those fields contained in the ORDERS file that we wish to include in the report. Selecting Field causes the available fields to be displayed. Move the cursor to the first space on the top line (it will probably be there already) and select the field **Order Number**.

The Field Options screen now appears in the bottom half of the Data Window.

```
┌─ Field Options ──────────────────────────────────────┐
│     Column width: 5                                   │
│     Heading Lines                                     │
│        Line 1:                                        │
│        Line 2: Order                                  │
│     Heading Justification: Left  Right  Center  None  │
│                                                       │
│     Precision: 0                                      │
│     Field Justification: Left  Right  Center          │
│     Commas: Yes  No                                   │
└───────────────────────────────────────────────────────┘
```

Re-set the parameters to match those given here.

Press **F10** to complete this field and the field heading will be displayed in the top half of the Display Window.

We have defined the location of the field whose contents are to be listed and we have given the list a heading.

Now move the cursor to the 9th space on the Table Definition screen and select Field again. Choose Customer Number, change the heading to Customer and re-set the width to 8 with a Center justification. Set the Field Justification to Center and press **F10** to complete this field location.

Continue in this manner so that the following are entered:

Space	Field	Width	New Name
33	Customer Name	20	Customer Name
59	Total Value	11	Total Value

Press **F10** to complete this part of the definition. Press **F10** once again and we return to the first set of options:

Select option: Columns Breakpoints Grand-total Report-title

So far we have defined and located on the Table the field headings and contents to be entered from the ORDERS file. All that remains to be defined are the Breakpoints and Grand Total

Breakpoints

Breakpoints are used to break a report into separate sections. This could be a very useful feature if, for example, a report was required that summarised information according to Sales Territory. In this case a break would be imposed between each Sales Territory with the next Territory starting on a new page. ABC Supplies do not have Sales Territories or any categories into which the report is to be broken. Accordingly, we shall not impose any Breakpoints into our Report.

Grand Total

Select Grand Total by pressing **G** and the following options appear:

Select option: Add Remove Edit

Press **A** to Add the Grand Total and the following screen appears:

```
┌─ Table Definition ─────────────────────────────────────────────────┐
│   Order      Customer    Customer Name                Total Value  │
│ + ---------  --------    ------------------------     -----------  │
│   *****      ********    ************************    **********   │
│                                                                    │
│ G-totals: Key                                                      │
└────────────────────────────────────────────────────────────────────┘
┌─ Options ──────────────────────────────────────────────────────────┐
│   Output Lines                                                     │
│           Line 1: Blank  Underscore  Double  Results  Omit         │
│           Line 2: Blank  Underscore  Double  Results  Omit         │
│           Line 3: Blank  Underscore  Double  Results  Omit         │
│           Line 4: Blank  Underscore  Double  Results  Omit         │
│           Line 5: Blank  Underscore  Double  Results  Omit         │
│                                                                    │
│           Results line label:   Total                              │
│           Lines to skip after breaks:  0  1  2  3  4  5  new-page  │
│                                                                    │
└────────────────────────────────────────────────────────────────────┘
```

Select option: Columns   Breakpoints   Grand-total   Report-title
Report: TABLEREP   Line: 1   Col: 59   F10 Finished   Esc Cancel
REPORT - Print or define a table or form

Every Grand Total can use up to five lines on the report. Here the first line is an underline, the second line is the actual total and the third line is a double underscore for emphasis. The last two lines are omitted.

The last question to answer on this screen is:

> **Position of the first printed character (optional):**
> **Line: 0**
> **Column: 0**

Setting these at 0 and 0 ensures that the total will be printed on the next available line.

Press **F10** to complete this specification and the screen changes to:

136 *Chapter 7: Reports*

```
┌─ Table Definition ─────────────────────────────────────────────────────────┐
│    Order        Customer       Customer Name                    Total Value │
│ + ------------------------------------------------------------------------- │
│    *****        **********     *************************        *********** │
│                                                                              │
│  G-totals: Key                                                               │
└──────────────────────────────────────────────────────────────────────────────┘
┌─ Options ────────────────────────────────────────────────────────────────────┐
│                                                                              │
│                                                                              │
│                                                                              │
│                                                                              │
└──────────────────────────────────────────────────────────────────────────────┘
```

Use cursor and press Enter to select grand-total columns or F7 to clear
Break key-field Grand-totals
Report: TABLEREP   Line: 1   Col: 59   F10 Finished   Esc Cancel
REPORT - Print or define a table or form

Move the highlight to the Total Value column and press enter and the word **tot** appears in the Total value column.

We have now set the location of the Grand Total. Now press **F10 four times** in succession. Twice to complete the Grand Total specification, once to complete the Table Definition and once to complete the Report definition.

All that is now required is to print the Report. From Command list 2 enter the following sequence of commands:

PROMPT	**ENTER**
	R: Report
Select option: Define Print Undefine	P: Print
Enter report definition filename:	TABLEREP
Select option: Disk Printer Screen	P: Printer

and the following report is issued at the printer:

                    Customer Orders
                    ----

                                                1 January 1980

Order   Customer   Customer Name   Total Value
----
1   1   AlphArtcraft   100.00
2   1   AlphArtcraft   250.00
3   2   Davenports   150.00
4   3   Personal Enterprises   200.00

                                         Total 700.00
                                                =====

----
4 Week period

                              Page 1

A Breakpoint could have been added to the Table Definition with a sub-total that would cause a break and sub-total after the two entries of customer AlphArtcraft.

Form Report

Whereas a Table Report is printed in the form of rows and columns of text and numbers, a Form Report is printed in a form similar to a database file record. As with the Table Report we must first define the page on which the Form is to be placed. Having done this we must then define the layout of the Form. The Form can contain database file fields, text, calculated items, page numbers and labels. All of these can be placed in the body of the Form to suit the user.

A useful document to have around the Company would be a list of Suppliers and the Parts that they supplied. We already have a file called STOCSUPP that contains all this information so we shall now generate a Form Report based on this file.

Load STOCSUPP screen standard. When it is loaded move to Command list 1 and enter the following sequence of commands:

138 *Chapter 7: Reports*

PROMPT	ENTER
	R: Report
Select option: Define Print Undefine	D: Define
Enter report definition filename:	FORMREP
Select option: Form Table Page:	P: Page

Before we can define the Form report the Page must be defined.

The screen now fills with the various parameters that define the Page upon which the Table will be printed. The default parameters will not be described here, instead we shall just describe those parameters that have to be changed to ensure that the Page is correctly defined for the Form.

    Page Length   66

The default is 66 but if your paper is A4 the Page Length should be 70

    Page Width   80

The standard width of A4 is capable of taking 80 characters

    Page Numbers: Left Right Center Left-right Right-left No-numbers

Each page of the report can be numbered or not as wished. The options **Left-right** and **Right-left** refer to switching the page number from left to right or vice versa. This is particularly useful if the report is to form part of a book.

    Lines per inch : 6   8
    Characters per inch: 10   12   17

    IS THERE A FORM ON THIS PAGE   Yes

We are setting up the page parameters to permit it to contain a FORM.

    Location of upper left corner of form
            Line 1
            Column 1

    Location of lower right corner of form
            Line 60
            Column 78

    Which File-screen will be processed for this form
            File: STOCSUPP
            Screen: Standard

Is this file a driver or driven file: Driver

Press **F10** to complete this definition. You are then faced with the three options :

Form Table Page

Select Form and immediately the Form Definition screen appears. A form report consists of pages on which information is placed in specific locations. The entire report will then consist of a collection of pages in much the same way as a file consists of a number of records. We must now lay out the various areas that will constitute a page of the report.

The Control Area for the Form Definition screen contains the following options:

Calculated-Field Label Page-Number Text Duplicate Edit Move Remove

Ensure that the cursor is at the top left hand corner of the screen and select **Text**.

You are then asked to define the area that the text is to occupy. Move the cursor until the line/column reading on the Status Line reads

Line 4 Column 22

and press **enter**. The area is then highlighted. This is the principle of the form definition - make sure you know where you are, where you want to go, make your selection and then define the area.

Now enter the required text in this area as follows:

Report FORM 1.

Suppliers and Parts

Next move the cursor to Line 6 Column 1 and select Text again. Move the cursor to Line 12 Column 14 and press enter. Now type in the text as follows:

Stock Number

        Item
      Quantity
       Price

      Value

Move the cursor to Line 6 Column 17 and select Field. Move the cursor to Line 6 Column 24 and press enter. You are now prompted to select a field. Select field [2] - the Stock Code.

140 *Chapter 7: Reports*

Repeat this process so that between Line 8 Column 17 and Line 12 Column 17 you have inserted fields [3],[4],[5] and [6] and between Line 8 Column 46 and Line 10 Column 74 you have inserted fields [7], [8] and [9].

Finally we shall insert the page number in the area between Line 1 Column 61 and Line 1 Column 74 - this is done by selecting Page-Number.

When you have finished, the form should look something like the following:

```
┌─ Form Definition ────────────────────────────────────────┐
│   Report FORM 1                                   page # │
│                                                          │
│   Suppliers and Parts                                    │
│                                                          │
│         Stock Number   [2]              [7]              │
│                                         [8]              │
│                 Item   [3]              [9]              │
│             Quantity   [4]                               │
│                Price   [5]                               │
│                                                          │
│                Value   [6]                               │
└──────────────────────────────────────────────────────────┘
┌─ Options ────────────────────────────────────────────────┐
│                                                          │
│                                                          │
└──────────────────────────────────────────────────────────┘
```

Select option: Calculated fields   Label   Page-Number   Text
                     Duplicate   Edit   Move   Remove
Report: FORMREP   Line: 1   Col: 6   F10 Finished   ESC Cancel
REPORT - print or define a table or form

Having now defined the form press F10 to complete. Press **F10** twice more and the Report Definition is saved to disk. Now we can see the end result. Move to Command list 1 and enter the following:

PROMPT   **ENTER**

                                                  R: Report
                                                  P: Print
                                                  FORMREP
                                                  P: Printer

The following is a typical page from the FORMREP Report:

Report FORM 1 page 1

Suppliers and Parts

        Stock Number   1
                                   Top Equipment
              Item Artist Easel   18 New Road
         Quantity 12   Stedley
            Price 20.00
            Value 240.00

Chapter 8 : The Remember Mode

Objectives

When you have completed this Section you will be able to :

- Appreciate the existence of the programmability of the Data-Manager
- Generate a simple program using the Remember Mode

Introduction

All of the SMART Data-Manager Commands are capable of being written into two files - a Program-File and a Text-File. At any later time this Text-File can be read by us. The Program-File can be read by SMART and the commands executed in sequence. The content of these Program-files is called a program and the language that the program is written in is the SMART language - the ordinary commands that you have been using throughout this Chapter.

This method of generating an executable program can be done in two different ways:

>Directly Written Programs
>The Remember Mode

Directly Written Programs

The commands for an executable program within the SMART Data-Manager can be written in much the same way as writing a program in any other high-level language. Because this method of generating programs is a topic in its own right we shall leave its consideration to a later Section of the book.

The Remember Mode

The SMART System can be put into Remember Mode so that any Commands that are activated at the keyboard are remembered by SMART and automatically listed in sequence in a text file. This will then constitute an executable program that can be executed at any time so duplicating all the Command selections made previously.

Order Entry

After we had created the five Lookups we demonstrated how to use them when entering data into the ORDER File. This was a long procedure and one that was to be repeated every time the ORDER file was used for entering orders. Instead of having to remember the procedure

144   *Chapter 8: The Remember Mode*

every time we use it we shall perform it in **Remember Mode** and generate a simple program. This program can then be executed every time we wish to enter information into the ORDERS file.

Move to Command list 5 and enter the following sequence of commands:

PROMPT	ENTER
	R: Remember
Select option: Compile Delete Edit Finish Help Print Start	S: Start

Now execute the entry of data into the ORDER File.

COMMANDS		EXPLANATION
4	Unload All	Clear the memory of any loaded or active files
3	Split Vertical	Split the screen about one third the way across from the left
1	Goto Window 2	Move the cursor to window 2
3	Split Vertical	Split window 2 into two in the middle
1	Goto Window 1	Move into window 1
4	Load ORDERS screen ORDERS	Load ORDERS file into window 1
2	Order key [1]	Order against the Order Number key field
1	Goto Window 2	Move into window 2
4	Load CUSTOMER screen CUSTOMER	Load CUSTOMER file into window 2
2	Order key [2]	Order against key field Customer Code
1	Goto Window 3	Move into window 3

4	Load STOCK screen STOCK	Load the Stock file into window 3
2	Order key [1]	Order against key field Stock Code
2	Load lookup ORDCUST Load lookup ORDSTOC1 Load lookup ORDSTOC2 Load lookup ORDSTOC3 Load lookup ORDSTOC4	Load five lookups
1	Goto Window 1	Move into window 1
3	Zoom	Zoom into the ORDERS screen
1	Enter	Enter information into the ORDERSfile a record at a time. It is not actually necessary to enter any records at this stage. Press F10 when finished.
4	Key Update	Update the ORDERS key files
3	Zoom	Un-zoom window 1 to display the three split windows
3	Close Close	Close windows 2 and 3
4	Unload All	Unload all files
2	lookup Remove ORDCUST lookup Remove ORDSTOC1 lookup Remove ORDSTOC2 lookup Remove ORDSTOC3 lookup Remove ORDSTOC4	Remove the five lookups

This completes the Order Entry sequence. Now move to Command list 5 and enter the following

146 *Chapter 8: The Remember Mode*

PROMPT	ENTER
	R :Remember
Select option: Compile Delete Edit Finish Help Print Start	F:Finish
Enter project filename:	ORDERS

This completes the Remember Mode process. Now let us look at the program we have written. Again, on Command list 5 enter the following sequence of commands:

PROMPT	ENTER
	R: Remember
Select option: Compile Delete Edit Finish Help Print Start	E: Edit
Enter project filename:	ORDERS

Just look at the listing - it duplicates exactly everything that you did to perform data entry into the ORDERS File.

```
unload all
split vertical 2 25
goto window 2
split vertical 2 50
goto window 1
load ORDERS screen ORDERS
order key [1]
goto window 2
load CUSTOMER screen CUSTOMER
order key [1]
goto window 3
load STOCK screen STOCK
order key [1]
lookup load ORDCUST
lookup load ORDSTOC1
lookup load ORDSTOC2
lookup load ORDSTOC3
lookup load ORDSTOC4
goto window 1
zoom
enter
key update
zoom
close
close
unload all
lookup remove ORDCUST
```

lookup   remove   ORDSTOC1
lookup   remove   ORDSTOC2
lookup   remove   ORDSTOC3
lookup   remove   ORDSTOC4

Press **Esc** to quit this display and we shall now **Execute** this program - again from Command list 5.

PROMPT	ENTER
	E: Execute
Enter project filename:	**ORDERS**

Now everything that you performed manually is performed automatically. All that need concern the user now is how to actually enter information into an ORDERS record. Isn't that a useful facility? We shall be saying more about Project Processing in the penultimate Section.

If you wish to have a hard copy of this program then select **Remember Print** on Command list 5

Chapter 9 : Additional Commands

Objectives

When you have completed this Chapter you will have been introduced to the following Commands not explicitly covered in the previous text :

- Find
- Scroll
- Link
- Unlink
- Border
- Display
- File
- Utilities
- Macro
- Parameters
- Read, Write and Send

Introduction

When we re-set the Confidence level to 3 we found a number of commands displayed that were not displayed at Confidence level 1. A few of these additional commands have not been used in this Chapter and we shall briefly review those here.

Command list 1   **Quick-Key**

Find   F3

Find searches a field or set of fields in the current file for specified data and displays the record in which the data is found. It will Find Equal, Find Greater-Than or Find Less-Than. It will also Find Partial or Find Whole word only. It also searches Backwards from the current record, Globally starting from the first record and will do so Ignoring Case.

Scroll   NONE

Scroll displays records in a file one record after another automatically. It is possible to Scroll both forwards (Next) or backwards (Previous) at speeds ranging from 1 (slowest) to 10.

Command list 2   Quick Key

Utilities   NONE

Utilities perform additional file maintenance operations. These are:

Alter-Count: Changes the next value in counter fields.

Concatenate: Appends data from another file to end of the current file.

Duplicates: Delete records with duplicate Key Field values.

Erase: Erases a File or a custom Screen from disk.

File-Fix: Reconstructs lost or damaged Physical Index (PIX) files or screen files. However, when recovering screen files only the standard screen is recovered. All custom screens are lost.

New-Password: Changes the password.

Purge: Erases inactive records - those that have been Deleted - from a file.

Restructure: Permits data transfer into the current file from a file with a different structure.

Totals-Recalc: Re-calculates all running totals.

Command list 3   Quick-Key

Link, Unlink   NONE

Link ties together two windows for the purpose of displaying corresponding records. Data is matched in linked fields which should contain data common to both files. Unlink severs the link. Two linked files can be made to Scroll together.

Border   NONE

Toggles the Border of the Data Window ON or OFF.

Display   NONE

Toggles between the Colour display and the Monochrome display.

Command list 4	Quick-Key

File NONE

File permits various disk-file management operations: Copy, Erase, Rename and New-Directory. The latter changes the current data path. The file location should be explicitly defined stating Drive, Path and Filename. If no extension is given to the filename all such files will be affected.

Command list 5	Quick-Key

Macro Alt-M

Macro permits the redefinition of almost any key on the keyboard to output a series of alternative characters. A Macro key definition can consist of up to two full lines of characters and can be used to define your own personal Quick-Keys.

Parameters NONE

Parameters permits the setting of default items that control the operation of the SMART Data-Manager.

Read, Write and Send

These commands are the subject of Section 5.

There are three commands that have not been mentioned. These are **Text-Editor, Input-Screen** and **F-Calculator**. They are common to all the SMART Modules and will be covered later in the book.

Section 3 : The Spreadsheet

This Section consists of a description of the SMART Spreadsheet. The intention is to develop further the introductory ideas of the Spreadsheet discussed in the Overview Section.

When you have completed this Section you will be able to Create, Edit and Print a Worksheet. You will understand the differences between absolute and relative cell references. You will be able to use multiple Worksheets connected to each other via windows. You will also be able to generate Graphs and Reports from a Worksheet. Finally you will have been exposed to the programming facility of the Spreadsheet in preparation for the penultimate Section of the book dealing with Project Processing specifically.

This Section is divided into twelve Chapters:

- **An Amplified Review**
- **Creating a Worksheet**
- **The Matrix Command**
- **The Appearance of the Worksheet**
- **Printing the Worksheet**
- **Worksheet Maintenance**
- **Windows and Multiple Worksheets**
- **Graphs**
- **The Graphics Edit Mode**
- **Reports**
- **The Remember Mode**
- **Additional Commands**

Chapter 1 : An Amplified Review

Objectives

When you have completed this Chapter you will be able to:

- Appreciate the role of the electronic spreadsheet
- Recognise the various features of the SMART Spreadsheet
- Appreciate the two modes of operation within the spreadsheet

Introduction

The purpose of this Chapter is to review and amplify the points discussed in Chapter 4 of Section 1. Though the topics discussed are the same they are considered in more detail.

Data Management and the Role of the Spreadsheet

There are many occasions within an organization when data is required to be both displayed and manipulated in a tabulated format. Many times this data is collected and manipulated manually and much of it is handled electronically. The advantages of electronic handling are clear - it is efficient and it is accurate. Repetitive tasks are performed perfectly every time and storage and retrieval are achieved in a fraction of the time it takes to perform the equivalent manual operations.

For example, a company may require a list of the sales made by each of its component Departments each month. This list may be required to be accompanied by a tabulation showing each Department's sales performance in relation to its previous month's figures and its percentage contribution to the entire Company's sales. This is typical of a **tabular** approach to data manipulation and is an ideal application for a **spreadsheet**.

Spreadsheet Features

The **SMART Spreadsheet** is the module within the SMART System that permits information to be stored and easily manipulated within a tabular format. Such tabular formats are traditionally referred to as Spreadsheets but to distinguish the **spreadsheet module** from individually created sheets within the system, SMART refers to the latter as **Worksheets**. Every Worksheet in SMART starts out as a large grid of 9999 rows and 999 columns of **cells**. Each cell is located at the intersection of a row and a column. Since each cell can be thought of as a particular row/column combination each cell can be addressed as such. For example, The cell that is at the intersection of the **10th row and the 15th column** is called the **r10c15 cell** - here the **r** stands for **row** and the **c** for **column**.

Each cell is capable of containing **text, numbers** or **a formula**. The numbers can be manipulated by using all the usual arithmetic operations. The formulae are very comprehensive and can contain references to the contents of other cells - one cell can contain the results of complicated manipulations that have been achieved by referring to the contents of other cells. Because of this the Worksheet is said to be completely **interactive**. A further feature of the SMART Worksheet is that a cell can contain a reference to another cell in another Worksheet. This feature permits a three dimensional approach to Worksheet interaction.

The SMART Spreadsheet allows you to protect a particular Worksheet with a **password** and this can be used to control access to confidential information.

The Spreadsheet Display

Having entered the Spreadsheet Module from the **Introductory Screen** by selecting S on the **Main Menu** you are confronted by a screen that is divided into four distinct areas.

The Worksheet Window The uppermost area is called the Worksheet window. It is here that the current Worksheet and all the data entered at the keyboard are displayed.

The Control Area This consists of two lines available for text display just beneath the Worksheet window. It is here that the user receives prompts for data entry and it is here that error messages are displayed should errors occur. Also displayed here are the five Command Lists that allow the user to manipulate the Spreadsheet. We shall say more about this area later when we discuss the two modes of operation of the Spreadsheet.

The Status Line This line contains information relating to the Worksheet currently visible in the Worksheet window. This information consists of :

Worksheet: NAME This is the name of the Worksheet currently being viewed.

Loc: r2c3 This is the location of the highlight in the Worksheet window. It is the address of the cell that is currently available for data entry.

FN: This refers to the **font** in the current cell. It is a number ranging between 0 and 12 as there are 13 fonts available in the SMART Spreadsheet.

FONT: Standard This is the font to be used for new entries into the Worksheet. **Standard** is the default font that is used whenever a new Worksheet is created.

CALC This word appears on the right hand side of the Status Line whenever you change the structure or contents of a Worksheet while the Spreadsheet Module is in the **manual re-calculation** mode. We shall say more about this later.

CIRC This word appears on the Status Line when your Worksheet has formulae that result in a **circular reference** - we shall say more about this later.

The Autohelp Line

This line of text at the bottom of the screen displays a short description of the command currently highlighted in the Control Area or the Command just selected from the Control Area. There is a further HELP facility that is accessible via the **F1** Key.

HELP

A comprehensive description of any one of the available Commands can be displayed on the screen and, if desired, printed out. First select the Command that you require help on by moving the highlight to it. Then press the **F1** function key. Immediately a brief description of this command appears in a pop-up box at the bottom of the Data Window. Press **F1** again and a more detailed description of the Command's operation appears. If this description covers more than a single screen of text the remaining text can be viewed via the **PgDn** key. During this process the following appears in the Command Area :

F2 Print Help   F3 Help Index   F10 Finish   Cursor Keys

Press **F3** and all the Commands are listed alphabetically. Any Command can then be selected by using the Cursor Keys to move the arrow to the desired Command. Again, press F1 and the HELP for that Command appears. Pressing **F10** causes the HELP display to disappear, returning the user to the Command Mode.

Selecting Commands and Quick Keys

There are **five** Command lists. Each list can be viewed in the Command area by entering the list number. Alternatively, pressing / displays the next Command List and pressing \ displays the previous Command List.

To select a command one can either use the highlight or simply press the first letter of the displayed Command. It is also possible to select a Command that is not in the currently displayed list. This is done using what are called the **Quick-Keys**. For example, no matter which Command list is being displayed, **Alt-L** will automatically activate the **Load** command that is displayed on Command list 4. We shall describe these quick keys as and when we use them. The complete list can also be viewed in the Control Area by pressing **F2**.

The Two Modes of Operation

When you first enter the Spreadsheet you will see the word **Enter:** followed by a flashing cursor. The Spreadsheet is now in the **entry mode**. This means that anything that you enter

158   *Chapter 1: An Amplified Review*

at the keyboard will be entered into the highlighted cell. Try it. As you type alphabetic characters they appear in the cell. If you start by typing numbers they will only appear in the cell after you have pressed **enter**. We shall say more about the Enter Mode later on in the book. There are two Modes of operation within the Spreadsheet. To move from one mode to another you must press the **Esc** key.

The second mode of operation is the **Command mode**. In this mode the Control Area contains the various Command Lists. It is from within this mode that you will learn to manipulate the Worksheet and its contents.

Moving Around the Worksheet

Because of the very large size of the entire Worksheet, the window area only shows a part of the Worksheet. It is possible to move around the Worksheet using various keys - the cursor keys.

The current position is denoted by a highlight. It displays the cell into which data can be immediately entered via the keyboard. By pressing the arrow keys you can move this cursor up, down, left and right. Try it. You will notice that when you try to move the highlight off the screen it stays where it is and the column or row numbers change. The best way to visualise what is happening is to imagine a large numbered sheet with the screen lying on top of it.

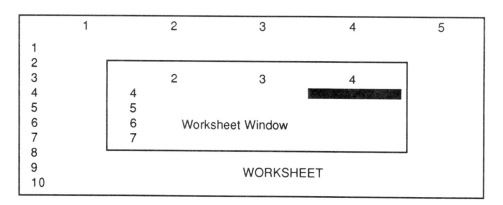

As the cursor keys are pressed the highlight moves around the Window. When the highlight comes up to the boundary of the Window, pressing the cursor keys causes the window to move across the Worksheet. We shall now look at the cursor control keys in more detail as they depend upon the mode in which the Worksheet is being operated.

Special Commands in Entry Mode

In **entry mode** most of the keys on the keyboard will contribute to the intended contents of a cell. However, occasions will arise when you wish to move around the Worksheet without wishing to move to Command Mode. This can be done using the cursor control keys.

PgUp and PgDn These cause the Window to **scroll** one window height up or down.

Ctrl-Arrow These cause the Window to **scroll** one window width in the direction of the arrow.

Ctrl-Home The highlight moves to the first entry in the Worksheet.

Ctrl-End The highlight moves to column 1 of the row that contains the last entry in the Worksheet.

Special Commands in Command Mode

Command list 1: Goto   Quick Key: F4

Ordinarily the **Goto** command is used to move to a particular cell or block of cells on the current Worksheet or to move to another **Active** Worksheet that is not the currently displayed Worksheet. Other times you will wish to move around the sheet without wishing to name cells or blocks of cells. In Command Mode this can be done by combining the **Goto** command with the cursor control keys.

After selecting the Goto Command from Command list 1 the following take effect :

Home	Goto upper-edge. The highlight moves up the current column to the first row of the Worksheet that contains data.
End	Goto lower-edge. The highlight moves down the current column to the last row of the Worksheet that contains data.
Ctrl-Arrow	Goto left (or right)-edge. The highlight moves in the direction of the arrow along the current row to the first or the last column of the Worksheet that contains data.

Exiting the Spreadsheet

To leave the Spreadsheet press **F10**. You are then faced with a list of options in the Command Area. Among these options are the other SMART Modules and the word Quit. Selecting any of the Modules causes you to **exit** the Spreadsheet and **enter** the chosen Module. Selecting Quit causes you to exit not only the Spreadsheet but also the SMART System.

Chapter 2 : Creating A Worksheet

Objectives

When you have completed this Section you will be able to:

- Appreciate the concept of a Block of cells
- Point to a cell and a Block of cells
- Copy a cell and a Block of cells
- Understand the difference between absolute and relative cell references.

Introduction

Because we shall require the full command power of the Spreadsheet in this Section we must set the Confidence level at 3. Do this - the **Confidence** command is found on Command list 5.

You will recall from Chapter 4 of Section 1 that we created a Worksheet that listed the weekly sales of each Salesperson employed by ABC Supplies. The Worksheet also listed a period total of sales based on a three-week period. The reason for the three-week period was due to the fact that the salesforce were paid weekly and the sales commission was paid two weeks in arrears. By using a three-week accounting period, wages paid at the end of the last week of a period also included commission for the first week of the same period. Last week the Board of ABC Supplies decided that as the salesforce was due to grow quite significantly in the next few months they would have a better cash flow if they paid their salesforce monthly (every fourth week) rather than weekly and included commission from the last month's sales.

Loading a Worksheet

ABC Supplies were still intent on running their sales competition so the Worksheet that had been created to tabulate their weekly sales figures will have to be amended. This we shall now do.

Command list 4: Load   **Quick Key: Alt-L**

PROMPT   **ENTER**

                                           L: Load
Enter worksheet name: **SALES**

SALES is the name we gave to the Worksheet and now this should be displayed in the

Worksheet Window.

	1	2	3	4	5
1	Sales Summary By Week And By Period			AB	C Supplies
2					
3	SALESPERSON	WEEK 1	WEEK 2	WEEK 3	TOTAL(£)
4					
5	Angela	123.45			123.45
6	Brian	1003.04			1003.04
7	Clara	578.11			578.11
8	David	990.25			990.25
9	Erica	1125.89			1125.89
10	Felix	774.65			774.65
11		------------	------------	------------	------------
12	TOTAL	4595.19			4595.19
13		======	======	======	======

Inserting a Column

We are going to need an extra column between the **WEEK 3** and the **TOTAL** columns to permit **WEEK 4**'s sales to be listed. Before we do this make a note of the formula in cell **r5c5** - move the highlight to that cell and move to **enter mode** and the formula appears in the Control Area. It reads:

r5c2 + r5c3 + r5c4

We shall be referring to this in a little while. Now we are ready to insert a column. Make sure that you are in Command Mode and displaying Command list 1.

Place the highlight at the top of the **WEEK 1** column in **r1c2** and enter the following:

PROMPT   **ENTER**

                                                           I: Insert
Select option: Block   Columns   Rows   C: Columns
Enter number of columns: 1

Immediately the four columns headed **WEEK 1** to **TOTAL** all move one column to the right leaving a blank column to the left of the **WEEK 1** column. You may think this is rather silly because we are now going to have to amend all the entries in the Worksheet, and so we are. The blank column will now have to be the **WEEK 1** column and all the other columns will have to changed accordingly. We could have simply inserted a column between **WEEK 3** and **TOTAL** and saved a lot of effort. However, it was done for a good reason. Take another look at the formulas in the **TOTAL** column.

Cell References

Move the highlight to cell **r5c6** which is the new location of Angela's total sales. Put the Worksheet into **Entry Mode** and in the control area you will see the following formula displayed:

r5c3 + r5c4 + r5c5

The formula **still refers to the original weekly sales** despite the fact that the addresses of the cells have changed. The formula has been adjusted to cater for the amendment made to the Worksheet. This ability of the Spreadsheet to adjust formulas is an essential feature for efficient Worksheet construction. Care, however, must be taken when a formula is **Copied** from one cell to another.

Copying Formulas

To illustrate the problems associated with copying formulas we shall start with an empty Worksheet so **Unload** the current Worksheet SALES.

When the Display window has been cleared move the highlight to cell **r1c1**, put the Worksheet into Entry Mode and enter the number **10**. Now move the highlight to the adjacent cell at **r1c2** and enter the formula:

r1c1

Press F5 to re-calculate the sheet and the number **10** appears in cell **r1c2**. We now wish to Copy the formula in **r1c2** into **r2c2**. Place the highlight in **r1c2**, put the Worksheet in **Command Mode**, move to Command list 1 and enter the following sequence of commands:

PROMPT	ENTER
	C: Copy
Select option: Down From Right	F: From
Enter name or block reference:	press enter
Enter name or block reference:	r2c2

Press F5 to re-calculate the Worksheet and the number **0** appears in cell **r2c2**. We were wanting to see the number 10 so what has gone wrong?

Move to Entry Mode, place the highlight in cell **r2c2** and in the Command Area you will see the formula **r2c1**. A formula has been **Copied** but it has been incorrectly adjusted - or has it?

Still in Entry mode, move the highlight back to the original formula cell at **r1c2** and overwrite the existing formula by entering a new formula. Enter

r[1]c[1]

Press **F5** to recalculate the Worksheet and the number **10** is still there. Now put the

Worksheet in Command Mode, move to Command list 1 and **Copy** the formula cell **r1c2** to **r3c2**. When the Worksheet is recalculated the number **10** appears. Great - success, but why? The difference lies in the cell references **r1c1** and **r[1]c[1]** in the original formula.

Absolute Cell References When we used the cell reference

$$r[1]c[1]$$

in cell r1c2 we actually referred to the cell located **on row 1 column 1**. When we copied the formula into cell **r3c2** the cell reference did not change - it still referred to the cell at row 1, column 1. This form of cell reference is referred to as an **absolute cell reference** - it refers to a **specific cell by using that cell's address**.

Relative Cell References When we used the cell reference

$$r1c1$$

in the first formula in cell **r1c2** we actually referred to the cell located **on the same row and one cell to the left** - we referred to the cell **r1c1** in a **relative** manner. When the cell was copied it still referred to **the cell on the same row and one cell to the left** - cell **r2c1**. A relative cell reference refers to a cell's position **relative** to the formula cell.

Both absolute and relative cell references will adjust themselves when rows and columns are inserted and when cells are moved. Only when cells containing formulas are copied does the difference between the two forms of cell address become apparent.

To return to the amendments required to be made to the SALES Worksheet we must re-**Load** SALES. As far as this Worksheet is concerned it is left to you to complete. You will have to enter **text** to re-label the headings, you will have to enter **formulas** as the ones there are now incorrect and you will have to enter **numbers** to check that the formulas work. Your efforts should be rewarded with a Worksheet that looks as follows:

	1	2	3	4	5	6
1	Sales Summary By Week And By Period					ABC Supplies
2						
3	SALESPERSON	WEEK 1	WEEK 2	WEEK 3	WEEK 4	TOTAL(£)
4						
5	Angela	123.45				123.45
6	Brian	1003.04				1003.04
7	Clara	578.11				578.11
8	David	990.25				990.25
9	Erica	1125.89				1125.89
10	Felix	774.65				774.65
11		------------	------------	------------		------------
12	TOTAL	4595.19				4595.19
13		======	======	======		======

You may find that after changing the numbers in those cells that are the subject of formulas the formulas are not automatically recalculated. This will be because the Worksheet is in **manual recalculation** mode - you will be able to tell by the word **CALC** that appears in the status line. To put the Worksheet into automatic recalculation mode so that any changes are immediately reflected in the formula cells move to Command list 5 and enter the following:

PROMPT   **ENTER**

                                                              A: Auto-Recalc
Select option: Automatic   Display   Iterate
                Manual   A: Automatic

Now go back to Entry Mode and change one of the numbers in a cell that is referenced in a formula. You will see the word **CALC** flash on and off on the Status Line and the formula will be automatically recalculated.

The Prize Worksheet

ABC Supplies, realising the value of the SALES Worksheet as a source of information for the salesforce, have decided that they would like it to remain just as it is with the sales personnel listed in alphabetical order. Copies of this can then be sent each week to every member of the sales force to allow them each to see how well everybody is selling.

This raises the problem of deciding who has won the monthly prize for the best sales. Obviously, with just six salespersons it is an easy matter to run down the list to find the highest monthly sales figure. With an increased sales force this becomes more laborious so it has been decided to create a separate Worksheet that does the job automatically. To do this we first unload the Worksheet SALES. Move to Command list 4 and enter the following:

PROMPT	ENTER
	U: Unload

The screen is now cleared. To create the PRIZE Worksheet we shall want to copy information from the SALES Worksheet. We can do this in one of two ways. We can split the screen into two windows, load SALES into one window and copy information into the Worksheet in the second window. Alternatively, we can merely **Activate** the SALES Worksheet and work with a single window. We shall do the latter. Move to Command list 4 and enter the following;

PROMPT	ENTER
	A: Activate
Enter worksheet name:	SALES

If we wish to view this Worksheet at any time we must first use the **Goto** command.

The first items we wish to copy from the SALES Worksheet are the list of salespersons. Move to Command list 1 and enter the following:

PROMPT	ENTER
	C: Copy
Select option: Down From Right	F: From
Enter name or block reference:	SALES.r1:10c1
Enter name or block reference:	Enter

The Block of cells on the Worksheet SALES are referenced by using the name of the Worksheet followed by a **dot** and then the Block reference. The second prompt asking for name or block reference refers to the location the cells are to be copied **to**. By pressing **enter** the are copied into a column starting from where the cursor is located.

We now wish to copy the final monthly totals into an adjacent column to the list of names. However, the totals column on the SALES Worksheet contain formulas and if we copied these they would not bring with them the sales figures. To overcome this problem we shall use the **Vcopy** command that only copies the **values** displayed in a cell when those values are obtained by using formulas.

Repeat the above process using Vcopy on Command list 1 and the final result should look as follows:

	1	2	3	4	5
1	Angela	123.45			
2	Brian	1003.04			
3	Clara	578.11			
4	David	990.25			
5	Erica	1125.69			
6	Felix	774.65			
7					
8					

Moving a Block of Cells

At the moment the Worksheet is without any labelling at all. We shall want to put a heading on the Worksheet for future identification purposes, but first of all we shall move this block of information to a more central position on the screen. We do this by using the **Move** command on Command list 1.

PROMPT   **ENTER**

                                                                    M: Move
Select option: Block   Column   Rows: B: Block
Enter name or block reference:

Here, instead of entering the block reference we shall use a method called pointing.

> **Pointing** Pointing is a general method of identifying a cell or a block of cells without having to be concerned about knowing the cell references. The principle is as follows:
>
> 1 Place the highlight on the topmost left hand cell of the block. This can be done using the cursor keys.
>
> 2 Press **F2** to **drop the anchor**. You will see what this means next.
>
> 3 Move the highlight to the bottom-most right-hand cell of the block. As you do so the cells of the block are all highlighted - hence the use of the phrase 'drop the anchor'.
>
> 4 When all the cells of the block are highlighted press **Enter** and this completes the pointing process.

At the prompt requesting the block to be identified **point to the block** - you will see the cell references appear in the Control Area. Following this procedure you are then requested to state where you wish the block to move to;

168   *Chapter 2: Creating a Worksheet*

PROMPT	ENTER
Enter name or block reference:	r5c1

Immediately the information is moved to the new location.

Now we are ready to label the Worksheet to make it look as follows:

	1	2	3	
1	ABC Supplies			
2				
3	Monthly PRIZE Selection			
4				
5	Angela	123.45		
6	Brian	1003.04		
7	Clara	578.11		
8	David	990.25		
9	Erica	1125.69		
10	Felix	774.65		
11				

Sorting

To select the prizewinner we shall **Sort** those rows containing names and monthly figures so that the figures are in descending numerical order. Move to Command list 2 and enter the following:

PROMPT	ENTER
	S: Sort
Enter name or block reference:	Point to r5:10c1:2
Select option: Ascending Descending	D: Descending
Select option: Row Column	C: Column
Enter column number(s) of sort key:	2

Immediately the information in the Worksheet is rearranged to appear as follows:

	1	2	3	
1	ABC Supplies			
2				
3	Monthly PRIZE Selection			
4				
5	Erica	1125.69		
6	Brian	1003.04		
7	David	990.25		
8	Felix	774.65		
9	Clara	578.11		
10	Angela	123.45		
11				

Chapter 3 : The Matrix Command

Objectives

When you have completed this Section you will be able to :

- Appreciate the power of the Matrix Command
- Use the Matrix command to perform addition, division, multiplication or subtraction on a block of numbers in a Worksheet

Introduction

The **Matrix** command is a most remarkable facility within SMART that has many varied applications. Indeed, almost a whole Section could be devoted to this command alone.

The word **Matrix** is a mathematical term but before you immediately turn to the next Chapter let me assure you that we shall not be doing any mathematics here - at least if we do, it will be painless. In mathematics, a **Matrix** is a rectangular array of numbers and there is a large and comprehensive section of mathematics that deals with the manipulation of such matrices. Here we shall be concerned with just one problem. How do you change an entire block of numbers by a fixed amount?

The PRICE Worksheet

Every company that sells, needs a price list and ABC Supplies is no exception to the rule. We want to construct a price list that lists the names of the items to be sold and their prices. The prices will be listed in units, tens and hundreds. Multiple purchases will be discounted according to the following:

> ten units of a single item - 15% discount
> a hundred units of a single item - 30% discount

Set up the PRICES Worksheet to look as follows:

172 Chapter 3: The Matrix Command

	1	2	3	4
1	PRICE List			ABC Supplies
2				
3	ITEM	Price Per	Price Per	Price Per
4		Unit	10	100
5				
6	O/door Lite	87.50	743.75	6125.00
7	Indoor Lant	226.50	1925.25	15855.00
8	Elec Mobile	24.00	204.00	1680.00
9	Loom	345.00	2932.50	24150.00
10	Art Easels	35.00	297.50	2450.00
11				
12				

The prices in the third and fourth columns are obtained using formulas. For example, the formula in cell **r6c3** is

$$(r6c2)*10*0.85$$

So now we have the price list. What happens when the prices are to be changed?

Changing the Prices

Every three months ABC Supplies reviews its price structure. This year inflation has been fairly steady at around 5% per annum and at the last prices review the management of ABC Supplies decided that a 5% increase in prices across the board was called for. This meant that all the unit prices in the price list had to be increased by 5%.

With just five items shown on the price list this should be a simple matter but what if the company has 5000 items - not so funny! Fortunately the Matrix command is ideally suited for this problem. Move to Command list 4 and enter the following sequence of commands:

PROMPT	ENTER
	M: Matrix
Select option: Aux Diagonal Eigen Invert Multiply N-Solve Parallel Regression Sweep Transpose Upper	P: Parallel
Enter matrix block:	Point to r6:10c2
Select option: Add Div Mult SubM:	Mult
Enter matrix block, value or single cell:	1.05
Enter matrix block:	Point to r6:10c2

This latter command locates where the new prices are to be located - in place of the old prices. You will then see the prices change - they have all increased by 5%. Press **F5** to re-calculate the Worksheet and the job is complete.

	1	2	3	4
1	PRICE List			ABC Supplies
2				
3	ITEM	Price Per	Price Per	Price Per
4		Unit	10	100
5				
6	O/door Lite	91.88	780.94	6431.25
7	Indoor Lant	273.83	2021.51	16647.75
8	Elec Mobile	25.20	214.20	1764.00
9	Loom	362.25	3079.13	25357.50
10	Art Easels	36.75	312.38	2572.50
11				
12				

This deserves a little explanation.

Select option: Aux Diagonal Eigen Invert Multiply
              N-Solve Parallel Regression Sweep
        Transpose Upper   **P: Parallel**

This large collection of possibilities represents an amazingly powerful range of command options. The option **Parallel** permits the block of cells to be manipulated on a cell by cell basis.

Select option: Add Div Mult SubM: Mult

This set of options shows that the individual cells of the block - the matrix - can be added to, divided, multiplied or have subtracted from them another matrix of numbers. We chose to multiply each cell of the block by the same number - **1.05** - which represents an increase of 5%.

If you are at all mathematically inclined you may wish to play around with this command - it really is fascinating. If you are not mathematically inclined don't worry - we have now finished with it in this book.

Chapter 4 : The Appearance Of The Worksheet

Objectives

This Chapter presents a review of all the available commands that assist in creating a pleasing and easy to read presentation.

Introduction

The appearance of a Worksheet can be just as important as its contents. If the sheet cannot be read with ease then the contents could be almost worthless. For this reason we shall now spend some time considering the various commands that are available for rearranging the information on the Worksheet to both make it pleasant to look at and easy to read.

Insert, Move, Width, Colnumbers, Rownumbers, Border

We have already met these commands before so we shall only briefly mention their uses here.

Insert Blank rows and columns can be inserted into the Worksheet. This feature can be used to make space for row labels and column headings or simply to space out the entries on the sheet. Any relative cell addresses contained in formulas are automatically adjusted.

Move Whole blocks of information or just one single cell can be moved to another location on the Worksheet. Again, relative cell addresses are automatically adjusted.

Width Despite the fact that text entries can **spillover** into adjacent cells on the same row there are times when text may be required to be confined to a single cell. The width of a cell can range from 0 to 80 characters wide. Width may also be crucial for numerical entries. For example, a twelve-figure number will not fit into a ten-character-wide cell. What happens is that the cell just fills with a row of stars (*). To have the number displayed will require the cell width to be increased.

Colnumbers, Rownumbers, Border These three commands act as toggle switches. They can turn on and off the display of the column and row numbers and the border that surrounds the Worksheet. This is especially useful when the row and column numbers cause interference with the information in the body of the Worksheet.

Formatting a Worksheet

Formatting refers to the location within each cell of the information displayed. For example, in all the Worksheets that have been displayed in this book the text is justified to the left and the numbers are justified to the right. This is not a hard and fast rule. Text and numbers can be justified left, right or centre and numbers can be displayed in a variety of ways.

> **Justify** Justify allows the justification of a block of cells already on the Worksheet to be changed.
>
> **Text-Format** Text-Format sets the default format for all new text entries onto the Worksheet.
>
> **Value-Format** Value-Format sets the default format for all new numeric entries onto the Worksheet. This command not only sets the justification it also sets the style. Numbers can be represented as ordinary decimals - **Normal** - and can include currency symbols, percentage symbols and commas to separate thousands as well as being displayed with up to 9 decimal places. Alternatively, numbers can be represented in scientific notation - **E-Notation** - with a mantissa and exponent. If a cell entry is a date there is a variety of **Date** formats possible.

Reformat

Reformat literally reformats the entire Worksheet according to a number of possible options. The options include all those we have just mentioned. In addition there is an option to display formulas instead of the values those formulas have produced. This latter option permits a Worksheet to be checked against the formulas that have been used.

Titles

The Titles command permits one or more rows or columns to be fixed in a window. Imagine a Worksheet that displays the values of the items purchased by all the company's customers during the last month. Along the top row are the names of all 500 stock items and down the left hand side is the list of 200 customers. You **Goto** cell **r100c350** and there you see the number

100,523.00

Now here is a valued customer who last month bought a significant amount of a particular item. But which item? And which customer? That information is way back on column 1 and row 1. How do you find out? You move **up** the sheet 100 rows to find the stock item, back down to row 100 and then you move **left** 350 columns to find the customer. By the time you reach the customer you have forgotten not only the item name but also the quantity they bought! This is where the **Titles** facility comes in.

Titles is to be found on Command list 2 and using this command it is possible to fix both the **item names** in the first row and the **customer names** in the first column. Then when you **Goto** cell **r100c350** the item names and customer names are still displayed on the first row and first column.

Display and Paint

If you have a colour monitor the **Display** command toggles between colour and monochrome display. The **Paint** command permits a colour customised screen to be designed.

Chapter 5 : Printing A Worksheet

Objectives

When you have completed this Section you will be able to :

- Print the textual contents of a Worksheet
- Print out the formulas contained in the cells of a Worksheet
- Change the fonts and font attributes of any text on the Worksheet

Introduction

As expected any Worksheet can be sent to the printer and a paper copy of either a portion or the complete Worksheet is produced. In addition to this the printout can display the Worksheet with the formulas as formulas or as the results of formulas. This latter is very useful if a large Worksheet containing a large number of formulas contains an error that is proving difficult to locate. By printing out the formulas they can be perused at leisure.

Printing Text

Load the **SALES** Worksheet into memory, move to the Command mode and Command list 1.

PROMPT	ENTER
	P: Print
Select option: Formulas Text	T: Text
Select option: Block Worksheet	B: Block
Enter name or block reference:	Point to r5:10c1:2
Select option: Disk Printer	P: Printer
Select option: Normal Compressed	N: Normal
Enter number of copies:	1

At the printer the appropriate block of text and numbers are printed. The **Compressed** option is useful if the paper is too narrow for the printout to fit. By using compressed print more cells per row can be printed across the page. If the block to be printed does not fit onto the sheet of paper being used then as much of the rows as will fit will be printed and the remainder of the rows will be printed below the first block of printout. Notice also the option of sending the Worksheet to the **Disk**. This permits an ASCII file to be produced that can be accessed at a later time. We shall say more about ASCII files in a later Section.

Printing Formulas

If you select the **Formulas** option then this information is automatically sent to the printer. The block or entire Worksheet must be specified as must the print format - normal or compressed.

Fonts

In the last Chapter we considered the appearance of the Worksheet on the screen. It is of equal importance that we also consider the appearance of the Worksheet as printed out. A lot of this will, of course, be taken care of by our considerations of how the Worksheet looks on the screen, as the formats and justifications are transmitted to the printer as well as to the screen. There is, however, a further option that affects only the printout and this concerns the Fonts of the typeface produced by the printer.

There are eleven possible fonts provided with SMART, each one coded with a number ranging from **0** for **Standard Font** to **9** for **Small Capitals**. In addition each font is capable of having attributes. These are **bold face** and **underlining**. Make sure that you still have the Worksheet **SALES** loaded and place the highlight in **r1c1** - the Worksheet heading. Move to Command Mode and Command list 2 and enter the following;

PROMPT	ENTER
	F: Font
Select option: Change Select	

Change changes the type styles of previously entered information and **Select** changes the type styles of all newly entered information.

	C: Change
Enter new font number:	1 (Italics)

The Worksheet heading now changes colour (or shade in monochrome) to indicate the different type face. On the status line the new font is notified after the label **FN:**. If we had also wanted Bold and Underline we would have entered

1 B U

instead of just **1** at the last prompt. Now print the Worksheet in **Normal** print and you will see the heading of the Worksheet is in bold italics with an underline.

Font-Design

On the SMART Main Menu there is a command **Font-Design** that permits any of the fonts offered by SMART to be edited and so to create your own customised font. This is not a topic to be considered in this book.

Chapter 6 : Worksheet Maintenance

Objectives

The purpose of this Chapter is to review the various commands that can be used to maintain a Worksheet once it has been created.

Introduction

Having created a Worksheet it must always be borne in mind that at some later stage someone other than the person who created the Worksheet will be accessing the information and possibly altering it. This raises the issue of protection both from unauthorised access and from deletion of vital formulas embedded within the sheet.

Unauthorised Access

To prevent an unauthorised person viewing confidential information contained in a SMART Worksheet the Worksheet can be protected with a **Password**. The command for this is found on Command list 4. When this command is selected the following options are displayed:

Attach Remove

Attach Selecting **Attach** permits a **four character** password to be entered. The characters can be any printed character but cannot include a **space**. Once the password is attached the Worksheet must be **Unloaded** after which the only way to successfully **Load** or **Activate** the Worksheet from then on is to type in the password when requested. For added security up to three passwords can be attached to any Worksheet.

There are two **levels** of password protection - save permission and read-only permission. Save permission permits a Worksheet to be accessed and read, edited, printed and then saved to disk in its edited form. Read-only permission permits access to read and also to edit and print the edited sheet but it does not permit the edited sheet to be saved to disk. The first password automatically receives save permission but for the second and third passwords access level has to be specified.

Remove To remove a password the password must be known.

To protect a Worksheet from accidental damage due to careless editing it is possible to protect cells and blocks of cells by **Locking** them.

Lock and Unlock

The **Lock** and **Unlock** commands are found on Command list 2. Using **Lock** the contents of a cell, a block of cells or the entire Worksheet can be protected from editing. Once locked, cells cannot be edited, deleted, blanked or overwritten by Copying or Moving. It is also possible to lock blank cells. Should it be desired to edit a locked cell then it can be done in one of two ways:

Lock Disable This command option temporarily disables the lock thereby permitting editing. The locks can then be reinstated by using **Lock Enable**.

Unlock Unlock destroys the lock status of a cell, block of cells or the entire Worksheet. The distinction between Unlock and Lock Disable is that with Unlock the System does not remember where the locks were. Consequently it is not possible to automatically re-lock that which was unlocked as one can with **Lock Enable**.

Newname and Name

Any current Worksheet can be renamed by using the **Newname** on Command list 3. The **Name** command on Command list 1 is used to name blocks of cells. If a block of cells is assigned a name then any future reference to that block can be done by name rather than by pointing or by using the block address.

File

The **File** command on Command list 4 permits various disk file operations without having to leave the SMART Spreadsheet. Selecting File produces the following options:

Copy Erase New-Directory Rename

The action of all these are self-explanatory except perhaps for **New-Directory**. New-Directory permits the current data path to be changed. With all these options the file must be specified with its extension and no wild cards are permitted.

There are two other commands that assist in maintenance.

Directory and Index

Directory on Command list 4 lists the files on a specific drive and specific directory. Filename extensions must be used though wild cards are permitted. Using this command, information regarding the names of files, the dates they were created and their sizes can be ascertained. The Index command, also on Command list 4, lists all currently active Worksheets. A Worksheet is made active by using the **Load** or the **Activate** command. Index displays the name, the number of entries, the number of formulas and the password status of the Worksheets.

Chapter 7 : Windows and Multiple Worksheets

Objectives

When you have completed this Section you will be able to :

- Split the screen into Windows
- Move from Window to Window
- Zoom and Close a window
- Use external sheet references to connect multiple Worksheets

Introduction

The purpose of this Chapter is to introduce the means whereby different Worksheets can be linked together. This enables new Worksheets to be created using information on existing Worksheets and also enables many different Worksheets to be viewed simultaneously using the **Window** command.

The COST List

Some time back ABC Supplies created a price list for use by their sales personnel when out in the field. Management also need to keep a track of costs and to this end they decided to create a cost list. Because of the similarity of the Cost list with the Price list they decided to use the PRICES Worksheet as the basis from which to start.

Ensure that you are in Command Mode with no Worksheet **Loaded** or **Activated**, move to Command list 3 place the highlight in cell **r2c1** and enter the following;

PROMPT	ENTER
	S: Split
Select option: Horizontal Vertical	V: Vertical

Now the screen is split into two windows and the highlight is in **Window #1**.

```
#1            #2     2           3           4
1  ▓▓▓▓▓      1
2             2
3             3
4             4
5             5
6             6
7             7
8             8
9             9
```

Command list 3:   Close   Fill   Justify   Newname   Reformat   Split
**   Text-Format   Unlink   Value-Format   Width   Zoom**
Worksheet: (none)   Loc: r1c1   FN: Font: Standard
SPLIT - split the current window into two windows

Now Load the Worksheet PRICES into window #1. Press **Alt-L** and select the Worksheet from the pop-up window. This now loads PRICES into window 1 and the list of items are listed down the first column. Next we must **Goto** window #2 and to do this we use the **Goto** command on Command list 1.

PROMPT   **ENTER**

                                                        G: Goto
Enter worksheet, name, cell reference or window: 2

The highlight is now in window #2 and located at **r1c2**. Scroll the Worksheet in window #2 using the cursor left key until the highlight is in cell r1c1 - just press the **left-arrow** once.

We are now ready to Copy the PRICES Worksheet into this second window.

PROMPT   **ENTER**

                                                        C: Copy
Select option: Down   From   Right   F: From
Enter name or block reference: PRICES.r1:10c1:4
Enter name or block reference: enter

The external cell block reference PRICES.r6:10c1 is now addressed and the PRICES Worksheet is copied into window #2. To fill the screen with the Worksheet in window #2 we use the **Zoom** command on Command list 3. This command is a toggle so repeating it returns the screen to the split appearance. **Zoom** into window #2.

Making note that ABC Supplies receive a 5% discount on batch orders of 10 and 20% discount on batch orders of 100 we amend the appearance, edit the formulas and enter the costs of this Worksheet to end up with a display similar to the following:

	1	2	3	4
1	COSTS List			ABC Supplies
2				
3	ITEM	Cost Per	Cost Per	Cost Per
4		Unit	10	100
5				
6	O/door Lite	60.00	570.00	4800.00
7	Indoor Lant	183.75	1745.63	14700.00
8	Elec Mobile	16.00	152.00	1280.00
9	Loom	275.50	2617.25	22040.00
10	Art Easels	20.00	190.50	1600.00
11				
12				

Here we see that ABC Supplied receives a discount for bulk purchases of **5% on batches of 10** and **20% on batches of 100** - you should have edited the formulas to cater for this. This is why ABC Supplies could afford to pass on discounts to their own customers.

When your COSTS Worksheet is complete move to Command list 4 in Command Mode and Save the Worksheet as COSTS.

The PROFIT Worksheet

To assist the management of ABC Supplies in devising an efficient and cost-effective pricing policy they need to know how their profit margins are being maintained. Their profits are, of course, measured by the differences between their selling prices and their buying costs. To help them in their pricing policy the management have decided to create a PROFITS Worksheet which will not only allow them to see what profit is being made on each item, but will also allow them to gauge how low they can charge for an item to remain competitive yet still make a profit.

Just as the COSTS Worksheet is similar to the PRICES Worksheet so is the PROFITS Worksheet. It is now tempting to **Split** window 2 to create Window 3 and copy COSTS or PRICES into Window 3 and repeat the previous procedure to create the PROFITS Worksheet. But this procedure will not succeed because any amendment in Window 3 will also be reflected in window 2 and you will not be able to **Save** the contents of window 3 independently of window 2.

Instead, we shall start over again. Assuming that you have saved the COSTS Worksheet move to Command list 3 in Command Mode to **Zoom** in the split screen display then move to Command list 4 and issue the command

Unload All

You are now left with a split screen with no Worksheet in either one.

Move to Command list 1 and **Goto** window 1 and scroll the window until the highlight is in r1c1. Now **Load** in the PRICES Worksheet. Goto window 2 and **Copy** the Worksheet PRICES. Just as before, we can now amend the appearance of the Worksheet in window 2 to look like a PROFITS Worksheet. For the moment we shall only be concerned with amending appearance, so change the contents of **r1c1** to read **PROFITS** and the contents of **r3c2:4** to read **Profit Per**. We are going to have to amend the formulas in this Worksheet but we cannot do it at the moment. Move to Command list 4 in Command Mode and **Save** the Worksheet in window 2 as PROFITS.

Now issue the Command:

Unload All

and at the prompt:

Are you sure (y/n)

respond with **Y** for Yes. This clears both windows again. Now, on Command list 3, **Close** window 2 to leave just the single window. Since the PROFIT formulas depend upon the contents of both the PRICES and the COSTS Worksheets, we are going to need both of these Worksheets as well as the PROFITS Worksheet loaded or active. We shall choose the **Active** option.

Move to Command list 4 and Load the PROFITS Worksheet. Having done this Activate (Command list 4 again) both the PRICES and the COSTS Worksheets in succession - they will not appear in the Display Window because PROFITS is already there but they are now ready for use. To prove this why not **Goto** PRICES and then you will see the Display change to the PRICES Worksheet. **Goto** PROFITS to enable us to enter some formulas.

In the PROFIT Worksheet move the highlight to the first profit cell r6c2, move to Enter Mode and you will see either

Value 87.50 or 60.00

depending on which Worksheet was copied to form the PROFITS Worksheet. We wish to change this to a **formula**. Press = and enter the following formula

(PRICES.r6c2)-(COST.r6c2)

and the contents of cell **r6c2** changes to **27.50** - the profit. We can now copy this formula into the rest of the appropriate cells knowing that the cell references will be adjusted accordingly. Move the highlight to **r6c2** if it is not there already and select the **Copy** command on Command list 1. We shall now **Copy** this cell into **r7:10c2** and then into **r6:10c3:4**

PROMPT	ENTER
	C: Copy
Select option: Down From Right	D: Down
Enter number of copies:	4

and the column fills with **27.50**. Now we shall Copy into **r6:10c2:4**.

PROMPT	ENTER
	C: Copy
Select option: Down From Right	F: From
Enter name or block reference	enter

We are going to copy from the single cell at **r6c2**.

Enter name or block reference	Point to r6:10c2:4

This now copies the formula into all the appropriate cells which now all display **27.50**. Press F5 to recalculate the Worksheet and the correct profits are displayed in every cell.

		1	2	3	4
1	PROFITS				ABC Supplies
2					
3	ITEM		Profit Per	Profit Per	Profit Per
4			Unit	10	100
5					
6	O/door Lite		27.50	173.75	1325.00
7	Indoor Lant		42.75	179.63	1155.00
8	Elec Mobile		8.00	52.00	400.00
9	Loom		69.50	315.25	2110.00
10	Art Easels		15.00	107.50	850.00
11					
12					

Do not forget to **Save** the PROFITS Worksheet as it has been amended.

Having created the PROFIT Worksheet we are now in a position to evaluate the profits made when items are sold. These profits relate only the the fixed costs and prices on the PRICES and COSTS Worksheets, however, one of the more useful features of Spreadsheets is that they allow **What ... if ... projections**.

What ... if ... Projections

Because the contents of a cell are very easily changed it is possible to review the effects of a single cell change on the rest of the Worksheet very quickly. Using this feature we shall now devise a system whereby we can immediately see the effects on the profits made by ABC Supplies by changes in both the costs incurred and the prices charged. This is the principle behind the **What ... if ...** projections. We ask ourselves **What** is the effect on the profits **if** we change the prices and costs.

The Profit Projection System

We shall want to start the next exercise with a clear slate so if you still have three Worksheets loaded or activated they must all be unloaded. Move to Command list 4 and select the following commands:

PROMPT	ENTER
	U: Unload
Enter worksheet name:	All
Are you sure (y/n):	Y: Yes

The three files are now unloaded and deactivated respectively.

To start the **Profit Projection** sequence load COSTS place the highlight in **r1c1** and **Titles Fix** column 1. **Titles** are on Command list 2.

PROMPT	ENTER
	T: Titles
Select option: Drop Fix	F: Fix
Select option: Columns Rows	C: Columns
Enter number of columns:	1

Now place the highlight in the second column, **Split Vertical** the window and then **Goto** window #2. **Load** PRICES into window #2 and **Scroll** the Worksheet using the cursor keys until the **Prices Per Unit** column is adjacent to the left-hand window border. **Goto** column 2 and **Split Vertical** window #2 and then **Goto** window #3. **Load** PROFITS into window #3 and **Scroll** the Worksheet until the **Profit Per Unit** column is adjacent to the left-hand window border. By now you should have a screen that looks as follows:

	#1	1	2	#2	2	#3	2		3
1	COSTS List								
2									
3	ITEM		Cost Per		Price Per		Profit Per		Profit Per
4			Unit		Unit		Unit		10
5									
6	O/door Lite		60.00		87.50		27.50		173.75
7	Indoor Lant		183.75		226.50		42.75		179.63
8	Elec Mobile		16.00		24.00		8.00		52.00
9	Loom		275.50		345.00		69.50		315.25
10	Art Easels		20.00		35.00		15.00		107.50
11									
12									

Now move to Command list 3 and select the **Link** option.

PROMPT	ENTER
	L: Link
Enter windows to be linked:	1 2 3

Notice the spaces between 1, 2 and 3 - that is necessary. Now that all three windows are **Linked** together they will scroll together. **Goto** window #1 and move to **r2c6** and change the cost of a single **Outdoor Light**. You will see the immediate effect on the profit. If this has not changed then your Worksheet may well be in manual **Recalculation** mode. If this is so then press **F5** to manually recalculate the new profit or, alternatively, select **Auto-Recalc** on Command list 5 and put the Worksheet into **Automatic mode**.

Having changed the single cost of an Outdoor Light you will wish to see the effect on the cost of a batch of 10 or 100. Still in window #1 use the cursor key to scroll the Worksheet to display the **Costs Per 10** column. At the same time you will notice that the other two sheets in the other two windows scroll as well giving the appropriate displays in their windows. That is the effect of the **Link** command.

To **Unlink** the windows use the **Unlink** command. At the prompt requesting the window number to be unlinked either enter a number to unlink that window or simply press **enter** to unlink them all.

Chapter 8 : Graphs

Objectives

When you have completed this Section you will be able to :

- Understand the use of a Worksheet to define the parameters of a Graph
- Appreciate the various stages necessary to define a Graph
- Generate a Graph
- View a Graph
- Appreciate the various Graph types available within SMART

Introduction

It is possible within SMART to use the numerical data contained within a Worksheet to act as the data for constructing a **Graph**. This is an extremely useful facility since any message imparted by a set of figures is far more effectively transmitted when it is accompanied by a Graph that displays the general features of the figures. There are a number of possible graph types available within SMART but we shall just consider two in detail here. We shall construct a **Bar Chart** for the four weekly sales of each of the Salespersons and a **Pie Chart** for the total month's sales.

The Bar Chart

To construct any graph there are three processes that must be completed.

1. The data for the graph, contained in the appropriate Worksheet, must be either **Loaded** or **Activated**.

2. The **Graph Definition** file must be created by defining the parameters for the graph.

3. The graph is then **Generated** using both the data on the Worksheet and the information in the **Graph Definition** file.

Once the graph has been generated it is saved to disk and is available for **Viewing** at any later time.

1. Load The Worksheet

Load the Worksheet SALES

The following display appears. Your numerical entries may be different but that does not matter. If yours are different then leave them as they are.

	1	2	3	4	5	6
1	Sales Summary By Week And By Period					ABC Suppl;ies
2						
3	SALESPERSON	WEEK 1	WEEK 2	WEEK 3	WEEK 4	TOTAL(£)
4						
5	Angela	123.45	200.00	300.00	400.00	1023.45
6	Brian	1003.04	800.00	700.00	200.00	2703.04
7	Clara	578.11	400.00	600.00	700.00	2278.11
8	David	990.25	600.00	900.00	800.00	3290.25
9	Erica	1125.69	1200.00	1000.00	900.00	4225.69
10	Felix	774.65	800.00	600.00	500.00	2674.65
11		------------	------------	------------	------------	--------------
12	TOTAL	4595.19	4000.00	4100.00	3500.00	16195.19
13		=======	=======	=======	=======	========

2. The Graph Definition

In Command mode move to Command list 2 where you will see the Graphics command:

PROMPT	ENTER
	G: Graphics
Select option: Define Edit Generate Matrix-Print Plot Slideshow Undefine View	D: Define
Enter graphics definition filename:	SALES

We shall now be required to enter information into three screens:

The General Graph Definition Screen

```
┌─────────────────────────────────────────────────────────────────┐
│                    General Graph Definition                     │
├─────────────────────────────────────────────────────────────────┤
│   Graph Definition File name:    SALES                          │
│                                                                 │
│              Main Title                  Color   Size   Font    │
│                                                                 │
│   Weekly Sales------------------------     1-     L      2      │
│   ----------------------------------       -      -      -      │
│   ----------------------------------       -      -      -      │
│                                                                 │
│              Footnote                    Color   Font           │
│                                                                 │
│   ABC Supplies (Month 5)------------       1-     5             │
│   ----------------------------------       -      -             │
│   ----------------------------------       -      -             │
│                                                                 │
│   Graph border:  Yes  No                                        │
│                                                                 │
│   Page border:   Yes  No                                        │
│                                                                 │
│   Graph type: Bar/Line  Pie  Hi-Lo  Histogram  XY-Graph         │
└─────────────────────────────────────────────────────────────────┘
```

F6 Define Block   F10 Finished   Escape to cancel
graphics define SALES
Worksheet: SALES   Loc: r1c1   FN: 0   Font: Standard
GRAPHICS - define, generate, print, plot, view or edit a graph

Select **Yes** for both **Graph** and **Page border** and select **Bar/Line** for **Graph type** - in all three cases move the highlight with the space bar and then use the cursor keys to move down to the next question.

Notice the options we have selected. Color 1 is the default color, Size L is Large and Fonts 2 and 5 are both Roman - 5 being in italics. So far we have defined the title, the footnotes and the type of graph that we want. Next we have to define the **Graph Definition Screen** for the **Bar/Line** option.

The Bar/Line Graph Definition Screen

As soon as the **Graph type** option is selected press **enter**. The following screen is then displayed requesting information pertinent to the Bar/Line graph:

```
┌─────────────────────────────────────────────────────────────────┐
│                    Bar / Line Graph Definition                   │
├─────────────────────────────────────────────────────────────────┤
│   Data block:              Legend         Type  Pattern  Color  │
│                                                                 │
│      r5:10c2----------     Week 1-------   B      1-      1    │
│      r5:10c3----------     Week 2-------   B      2-      1    │
│      r5:10c4----------     Week 3-------   B      3-      1    │
│      r5:10c5----------     Week 4-------   B      4-      1    │
│      ---------------       -----------     -      -       -    │
│      ---------------       -----------     -      -       -    │
│                                                                 │
│   X-Axis title block: -----------------                         │
│              X-Axis title                                       │
│                                               Color     Font    │
│   Weekly Sales-----------------------          1-        2-    │
│                                                                 │
│              Y-Axis title                     Color     Font    │
│   Value---------------------------------       1-        2-    │
│                                                                 │
│   Options:  No   Yes                                            │
└─────────────────────────────────────────────────────────────────┘
```

F6 Define Block   F10 Finished   Escape to cancel
graphics define SALES
Worksheet: SALES   Loc: r1c1   FN: 0   Font: Standard
GRAPHICS - define, generate, print, plot, view or edit a graph

The data block can be inserted directly from the keyboard but if you are unsure of the exact block address the information can be entered by **pointing** at the block using **F6** - try it.

Type **B** is a simple bar and for each week there will be four bars per salesperson - each bar side by side. To distinguish one bar from another each will be shaded with a different pattern - there are 14 to chose from.

The X-Axis title could also be obtained from the Worksheet by selecting a block of information. Instead, here we prefer to annotate the axes as shown.

For **Options** select **Yes** after which the Bar/Line Options Definition screen appears.

Bar/Line Options Definition

The **Options Definition** permits a number of enhancements to be defined.

```
┌─────────────────────────────────────────────────────────────┐
│                    Bar / Line Graph Options                 │
├─────────────────────────────────────────────────────────────┤
│ Bar dimension: 2-dimension 3-dimension Line                 │
│ Bar orientation: Vertical Horizontal                        │
│ Values on top of bars: None Horizontal Vertical             │
│ Legend position: None Bottom 1 2 3 4                        │
│ Point type: Dots Symbols                                    │
│                                                             │
│ Divisions:   Color   Font    Tics/Div                       │
│   X-Axis      ---    ---     ---                            │
│   Y-Axis      ---    ---     ---                            │
│                                                             │
│ Grids:  (y/n)  Color   Style                                │
│   X-Axis  –    ---     ---                                  │
│   Y-Axis  –    ---     ---                                  │
│                                                             │
│ Scaling   Type   Minimum   Maximum   Increment              │
│   Y-Axis   ---   ------    ------    ------                 │
└─────────────────────────────────────────────────────────────┘
```
F6 Define Block   F10 Finished   Escape to cancel
graphics define SALES
Worksheet: SALES   Loc: r1c1   FN: 0   Font: Standard
GRAPHICS - define, generate, print, plot, view or edit a graph

On this screen select a **3-dimensional**, **Vertical** bar chart with **no values - None -** on the bars and with the **Legend** at the **Bottom**. Point type is **Dots** and the other options are left empty.

We have now completed the **Graph Definition File** and when you press **F10** the information is saved to disk and you are returned to the Worksheet display and Command list 2.

3. Generating the Graph

Having defined all the parameters necessary to draw the graph we are now in a position to **Generate** the graph. Select the following commands on Command list 2:

PROMPT	ENTER
	G: Graphics
Select option: Define Edit Generate Matrix-Print Slideshow Undefine View	G: Generate
Enter graphics definition filename:	SALES
Select option: Black/White Color	B: Black/White
To save screen, enter screen name:	SALES

Now you will see the graph drawn on the screen. Notice that the **Footnotes** do not appear - they only appear when the graph is printed. As soon as the graph is drawn it is cleared from the screen but as it has been saved in a screen file it can be viewed at leisure by using the **Graphics View** option. Try it.

Graphics View

When you select to **View** a previously generated and saved graph, then the viewing can be preceded by one of three options:

> **Curtain**: A striped curtain appears on the screen and slowly rises to reveal the graph behind it
>
> **Fade-in**: The graph appears drawn in a random fashion giving the effect of a fade-in.
>
> **Instant**: The graph just appears complete.

Printing a Graph

There are two methods of obtaining a hard copy of the graph. Firstly, using the **Graphics Matrix-Print** option sends the graph to your printer. Secondly, using the **Graphics Plot** sends it to your plotter.

Using **Matrix-Print** takes some time. The following prompt appears:

> **Drawing to printer buffer, pass 1 of 2**

The graph is printed in two stages.

There are three further options that follow the **Graphics** selection:

> **Undefine**: This is used to erase a graph definition file from the disk.
>
> **Slideshow**: This relates to Project Processing where graphs can be made to be displayed automatically. We shall discuss this in a later Section of the book.

Edit: Using the **Graphics Edit** option any previously drawn graph saved to disk can be edited. Also, using this command, graphics screens can be drawn without any reference to graphical data stored in a Worksheet. Indeed, **Graphics Edit** is a very useful facility to have and deserves a detailed discussion in its own right. This we do in the following Chapter.

The Pie Chart

To complete this Chapter we shall create a **Pie Chart** from the accumulated month's sales figure on the SALES Worksheet. Each portion of the pie will then correspond to the portion of a particular salesperson's sales accumulated over the complete month. Make sure that the SALES Worksheet is still loaded, select Command list 2 and enter the following:

PROMPT	ENTER
	G: Graphics
Select option: Define Edit Generate Matrix-Print Plot Slideshow Undefine View	D: Define
Enter graphics definition filename:	TOTSALES

We shall now be required to enter information into the three screens that complete the Graph Definition File.

Graph Definition

Graph Definition File Name - TOTSALES   (Already entered)

		Color	Size	Font
Main Title	SALES BY PERSON	1	L	2
	--------------------------	1	L	2

		Color	Font	
Footnotes	--------------------------	1	5	
	Current Month to Date	1	5	
	--------------------------	1	5	

Graph Border   Yes

Page Border   Yes

Graph Type   Pie

Pie Chart Definition

Legend/Label	Color	Pattern	Explode (y/n)
Angela	1	1	Y
Brian	1	2	N
Clara	1	3	N

David	1	4	N
Erica	1	5	N
Felix	1	6	N

Data Block: r5:10c6   This can be entered by pointing. Press F6 and use F2 to Drop the Anchor.

Options   Yes

Pie Chart Options

Pie type   3-Dimensional

Slice Labels   Text

Legend Type   Text

Sort slices   No

Number of slices to omit   0

Press **F10** to complete this procedure.

You have now Defined the Graph. All that remains to be done is to **Generate** the Graph from the definition file - save it under TOTSALES - and then to **View** and **Matrix-Print** it. This is left to you.

Chapter 9 : The Graphics Edit Mode

Objectives

The purpose of this Chapter is to demonstrate the facility within SMART for creating graphic screens without the need for data stored in a Worksheet.

Introduction

In the previous Chapter we considered the creation of graphs - plots of one set of data against another set of data. There are a number of different types of such graphs available within SMART and, in addition, there is a facility for creating a graphic picture without recourse to information stored in a Worksheet.

Graphic Pictures

A graphic picture is a screen display that is created when the SMART Spreadsheet is in **Graphics Edit** mode. This is achieved from Command list 2:

PROMPT	ENTER
	G: Graphics
Select option: Define Edit Generate Matrix-Print Slideshow Undefine View	E: Edit
Enter graph filename:	enter

This results in the following screen display:

```
┌─────────────────────────────────────────────────┐
│                                                 │
│                                                 │
│                                                 │
│                                                 │
│   F2  Edit      F10  Finished    Escape to cancel │
└─────────────────────────────────────────────────┘
```

Press **F2** to activate the screen editor. The screen now appears as:

```
┌─────────────────────────────────────────────────┐
│                                                 │
│                                                 │
│                       +                         │
│                                                 │
│                                                 │
│   <E>rase  <L>ine  <S>et  <T>ext  <Esc>         │
└─────────────────────────────────────────────────┘
```

In the centre of the window is a cross. This is the graphics cursor and is used to locate the position of a line or a letter that you enter onto the screen. Before we look at the various drawing options that are available we must first consider the movement of the cursor.

Movement of the Cursor

The cursor can move around the graphics screen either a single pixel at a time or five pixels at a time. A **pixel** is a single 'dot' on the screen.

Single Pixel Movement

UP	PgUp
DOWN	PgDn
LEFT	Ctrl + Left Arrow
RIGHT	Ctrl + Right Arrow

Five Pixel Movement

UP	Up Arrow
DOWN	Down Arrow
LEFT	Left Arrow
RIGHT	Right Arrow

Lines

The <L>ine option permits straight lines to be drawn on the screen. Place the cursor at the start of the line, press **L**, move the cursor to the end of the line and press **enter**.

Text

The <T>ext option permits text to be placed anywhere on the screen. Press **T**, type in the text (it appears at the bottom of the screen) and press **enter** when the text is complete. Move the cursor to the location you desire for the text (the text moves with you) and when you are satisfied press **enter** again. This sets the text in place.

Set

The <S>et option permits **Color, Font, Orientation** and **Path** to be set.

Color And Font: To set colour press C and select a number for the colour desired. To set font press **F** and again, select a number for the font desired.

Orientation: The **Orientation** dictates whether text is printed left to right (select **Up**), top to bottom (select **Right**), bottom to top (select **Left**) or upside down (select **Down**).

Path: The **Path** refers to the direction in which letters follow their predecessor when being typed in. The two options are **1** for **Down** and **2** for **Right**.

Erase

<E>rase permits pixels to be cleared from the screen display.

Editing Existing Graph Files

Not only is the Graphics Editor available for drawing graphs it can also be used for amending previously drawn graphs that have been generated from tabulated data. To give you some practice with the Graphics Edit Mode edit the Bar Chart SALES by erasing the annotation **Weekly Sales** along the horizontal axis and then entering the names of each Salesperson against their respective sets of bars.

Chapter 10 : Reports

Objectives

When you have completed this Section you will be able to :

- Understand the principles of a Report generated from a Worksheet
- Define the various Report Definition Parameters
- Define the various Page Definition Parameters
- Print a Report
- Appreciate the various Report Options

Introduction

The principle of the Spreadsheet Report is that it will selectively duplicate the contents of a Worksheet. Just as the Worksheet consists of labelled rows and columns along with a rectangular array of data so the Report will consist of labelled rows and columns and a rectangular array of data. The difference between the two is that the Report contains in it only those rows and columns that you specify. The following diagram illustrates the relationship:

Worksheet

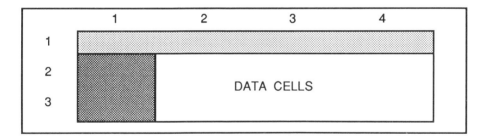

Report

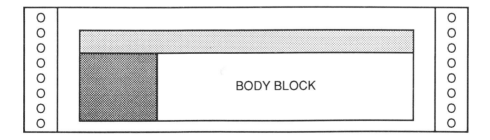

Report Headings and Body

The Report headings are of two types:

> **The Fixed Horizontal Title Blocks**: The Headings for the Report come from selected Headings of the Worksheet.
>
> **The Fixed Vertical Title Blocks**: The Labels for the Report come from selected Labels of the Worksheet.
>
> **The Body**: The body of the Report comes from selected areas of the body of the Worksheet - the data cells.

To produce a Report there are three stages that must be completed:

1. The information to be included in the Report will be located on a Worksheet and this Worksheet must be either Activated or Loaded.

2. The parameters that define the Report must be saved in a Report Definition File.

3. The Report is printed by referring to both the Worksheet containing the information and the Report Definition file.

Load the Worksheet

To demonstrate the principles behind report generation, we shall create a report that takes the Salesperson's names and cumulative monthly figures to form the Worksheet SALES.

Load the Worksheet SALES and, in Command mode, move to Command list 1.

The Report Definition

The Report Definition is in three parts:

> A. Defining the Headings and Labels of the Report
> B. Defining the Body of the Report
> C. Defining the Page onto which the Report will be printed.

A. Defining the Headings and Labels

PROMPT	ENTER
	R: Report

Select option: Define Print Preset Template
                        Undefine   **D: Define**
Enter report definition filename: **MSALES**

This is then followed by the **Report Definition Screen:**

Headings and Footings

Heading

Choose Justification to be Center

Line 1: SALES FOR MONTH
Line 2: ---------------

Blank lines after heading 2.

Footing

Line 1: ---------------
Line 2: Past Month Only
Line 3: ---------------

Blank lines before footing 3.

Fixed Horizontal Title Blocks

Group 1: r3c1;r3c6

There are two title blocks here. They can be identified by pointing. When **r3c1** has been **pointed** to, enter a **semicolon** and repeat the process to enter **r3c6**.

Separating these two blocks by a semicolon ensures that they will be printed side by side. Had the semicolon been a **Comma** the blocks would have been printed one below the other.

It is possible to have up to three Groups in a Report - here we shall have only one. Each Group starts printing on a new page.

Fixed Vertical Title Blocks

Group 1: r5:10c1   Again obtained by **pointing**.

B. Defining the Body of the Report

Report Body Blocks

Group 1: r5:10c2;r5:10c6 - **pointing** again.

C. Defining the Page

Having defined the Report we must now define the Page onto which the Report will be printed.

Set the following on the Page Definition Screen :

Date	Alpha-Date
Lines to enclose report	Yes
Page numbers	Right
Start page number	1
Spacing	Single
Continuous printing	No
Lines per inch	6
Characters per inch	10
Form length	66
Form width	80
All margins/indent	1

Printing the Report

Ready your printer, select Command list 1 and enter the following :

PROMPT	ENTER
	R: Report
Select option: Normal Enhanced	N: Normal
Enter report definition filename:	MSALES Report name
Select option: disk Printer	P: Printer
Enter number of copies:	1
Enter new sheet and enter any key:	

The Report is then printed.

SALES FOR MONTH
-------------------------   1 January 1980

SALESPERSON	WEEK 1	TOTAL
Angela	123.45	623.45
Brian	1,003.04	2,503.04
Clara	578.11	1,578.11
David	990.25	2,490.25
Erica	1,125.69	3,325.69
Felix	774.65	2,174.65

Past Month Only

1

Further Report Options

Preset: Permits the default Report Definition to be changed. After changing the default all further reports follow the new default definition.

Template: Prints the Report and Page Definitions that have been established for a report.

Undefine: Erases a Report definition from Disk.

Chapter 11 : The Remember Mode

Objectives

When you have finished this Section you will be able to :

- Appreciate the programmability of the SMART Spreadsheet
- Generate a simple program using the Remember Mode

Introduction

All of the SMART Spreadsheet Commands are capable of being written into a Text-File and executed sequentially. This method of generating an executable program can be done in two different ways.

Directly Written Programs

The coding for an executable program within the SMART Spreadsheet can be written in much the same way as writing a program in any other high-level language. To achieve this level of competence is beyond the scope of this book and will not be dealt with here.

The Remember Mode

The SMART System can be put into Remember Mode so that any Commands that are activated are **Remembered** and listed sequentially in a text file. This will then constitute a program that can be executed at any time so duplicating all the Command selections made previously.

PROFITS

After we had created the three Worksheets we demonstrated how the connection between them operated by changing numbers in the COSTS and PRICES Worksheets and Recalculating to show the resulting effect on the PROFITS Worksheet. Instead of having to remember the procedure every time we use it we shall perform it in Remember Mode and generate a simple program that can be used to demonstrate this connectivity.

In Command mode, move to Command list 5 and enter the following:

210   *Chapter 11: The Remember Mode*

PROMPT	ENTER
	R: Remember
Select option: Compile Delete Edit Finish Help Print Start	S: Start
Enter project filename:	PROFITS

The **Remember Mode** is now switched on. Now load the three Worksheets into three windows and arrange the COSTS, PRICES and PROFITS Worksheets so that as you enter data into COSTS or PRICES and Recalculate you will be able to see the effect in PROFITS.

As soon as this is complete and you are actually ready to enter data press **F10** to terminate the entry of data. We must now reverse the procedure to Unload All the Worksheets and Close twice to close all the Windows. What you have just done is to set the stage for the **What ... If ...** profit projection. We shall now see how that stage can be set automatically. We must now turn off the Remember Mode.

PROMPT	ENTER
	R :Remember
Select option: Compile Delete Edit Finish Help Print Start	F: Finish
Enter project file name:	PROFITS

Now let us look at the program that has been written.

PROMPT	ENTER
	R: Remember
Select option: Compile Delete Edit Finish Help Print Start	E: Edit
Enter project file name:	PROFITS

The listing then appears in the Project Editor Window:

@r1c3 split vertical
@r1c2 goto 2
@r1c2 split vertical
@r1c1 goto 1
load COSTS
@r1c1 titles fix columns 1
@r1c2 goto 2
load PRICES
@r1c2 goto 3
load PROFITS
link 1 2 3
@r1c2 goto 1

**@r6c2 cursor Enter projected value
unload all
close
close**

Look at the listing - it duplicates everything that you did to perform data entry into the PROFITS File. Press **Esc** to quit this display and we shall now **Execute** this program.

Executing the Project

The command to **Execute** a project is also located on Command list 5.

PROMPT	ENTER
	E: Execute
Enter project file name:	PROFITS

And so you see the sequence of commands hitherto entered manually now performed automatically.

To obtain a hard copy of this program use the **Remember Print** sequence of commands.

Chapter 12 : Additional Commands

Objectives

When you have completed this Section you will have been introduced to the following Commands not used so far in this Section:

- Blank
- Find
- Sort
- Fill
- Index
- Write, Send and Read
- Macro
- Parameters

Introduction

There are a number of Commands that have appeared in this Section due to our selection of Confidence Level 3 that have not been specifically mentioned in the body of this Section. These are listed here with a brief description of each command.

Command list 1   Quick Key

Blank   Alt-B

    Used to empty the contents of a cell or block of cells.

Find   F3

    Finds a specified item of data within a Worksheet.

Command list 2   Quick Key

Sort   NONE

    Sorts a block of data according to the values or text contained in a specific row or column.

214 *Chapter 12: Additional Commands*

Command list 3   Quick Key

Fill   NONE

Used to Fill a block of cells with incremented or decremented values.

Command list 4   Quick Key

Index   Alt-A

Lists all currently active Worksheets in memory.

Macro   NONE

Macro permits the redefinition of almost any key on the keyboard to output a series of alternative characters. A Macro key definition can consist of up to two full lines of characters and can be used to define your own personal Quick-Keys.

Parameters   NONE

Parameters permits the setting of default items that control the operation of the SMART Spreadsheet.

Write, Send and Read

These commands form the subject matter of Section 5.

There are three commands that have not been mentioned. These are **Text-Editor**, **Input-Screen** and **F-Calculator** and they are covered later in the book.

Section 4 : The Wordprocessor

This Section consists of a description of the SMART Wordprocessor. The intention of this Section is to develop further the introductory ideas of the Wordprocessor discussed in the Overview Section.

When you have completed this Section you will have been exposed to the Wordprocessor Module and will be able to **Create, Edit, Spellcheck** and **Print** a Document. You will also be able to **Link** documents together and be able to use the **Mail-Merge** facility. Finally you will have been exposed to the programming facility of the Wordprocessor in preparation for a further Section dealing specifically with Project Processing.

This course is divided into seven Chapters :

- **Editing a Document**
- **Document Layout and Handling**
- **Spellchecking a Document**
- **Printing a Document**
- **Handling Multiple Documents**
- **The Mail-Merge Facility**
- **The Remember Mode**

Chapter 1 : Editing A Document

Objectives

When you have completed this Section you will be able to :

- Insert, Replace, Copy, Move, Delete and Undelete text
- Scroll through a document
- Find a specific word, Goto and Replace text
- Draw boxes and lines and insert Graphics into the document
- Sort lists of text into alphabetical order
- Insert Footnotes into a document
- Embolden and Underscore text and change Fonts within a document
- Start a new Page

Introduction

By now it is assumed that you are fairly familiar with the structure of the SMART System and that you can move around from Module to Module quite happily. In Chapter 5 of Section 1 we covered a substantial part of the Wordprocessor Module so we shall not review the basic features of the Wordprocessor here. Instead we shall immediately embark upon the editing of the document LETTER that was produced in the last Section.

The Document LETTER

ABC Supplies have a very enthusiastic Sales Manager and it was she who initiated the Sales Competition. What follows is a letter that the Sales Manager has written to all the members of the Sales Department. The letter has been typed in rough draft and now requires editing.

The letter is as follows :

    ABC Supplies   **Sales Memo To All Sales Personnel**

    <u>**SUBJECT : Sales Figures And Competition Result**</u>

    I should like to congratulate all the members of our Sales Team who have maintained their sales record consistently over the past two or three months.

218   *Chapter 1: Editing A Document*

Now that the Company has settled down into its new selling procedures I feel that it is time to start making that extra effort that will make all the difference between continuing as we are and becoming a leading supplier in the region we serve. To spur you all on to higher sales levels the management has decided to run a Sales Competition. This competition will be based on your sales performance figures accumulated every week for each of our three-week Company Periods. At the end of each period the top salesperson will be awarded a free gift of substantial value.

If this competition proves to be successful - by which I mean our sales figures increase - then the competition will be reviewed to make it even more attractive

Thank you all once again for your continuing effort and I wish you all success in the future.

Sincerely

Jane Doe

Sales Manager

Before we proceed into the rest of this Chapter, enter this text just as it appears into the SMART Wordprocessor if you do not already have it on disk. If you do have it stored on disk then load it into memory. Refer to Chapter 4 of Section 1 if you need to correct any errors and cannot remember how.

Replace

Reading through the Memo the Sales Manager has decided that the phrase **sales performance** should be used instead of the single word **sales**. We can replace the latter by the former whenever the latter occurs by using the **Replace** Command. Select Command List 1 and enter the following :

PROMPT	ENTER
	R: Replace
Enter search text [" "]	sales
Enter replacement text [" "]	sales performance
Enter replacement options ["F"]	CIW:

The letters **CIW** refer to Conditional, Ignore case, Whole words only - see below.

The replacement options are:

F: Forwards. A search is made forwards from where the cursor currently resides.

B: Backwards. A search is made backwards from where the cursor currently resides

G: Global. Searches the entire text regardless of the cursor's position.

C: Conditional replacement. A prompt is given to request whether a replacement is to be made at each occurrence of the text to be replaced.

I: Ignore case. Searches for text regardless of case.

W: Whole word. Searches only for whole words and does not replace when the word to be replaced is within a longer word.

Immediately the replacement is effected by the cursor moving through the document and stopping at each occurrence of the word **sales**. The option to change it to **sales performance** is then given.

Scroll

Because the entire memo does not fit on one screen we must **Scroll** it up and down the screen in order to review it all. We can **Scroll** as we have done before by using the cursor keys. Alternatively, we can use an automatic **Scroll**.

Place the cursor at the very top of the document, select Command List 1 and enter the following :

PROMPT	**ENTER**
	S: Scroll
Select option: Up Down	D: Down
Enter scroll rate (1 is slowest, 10 is fastest):	5

The screen now scrolls a line at a time.

Find/Goto

If you wish to find a particular word or phrase within the memo then we can use the Command **Find**.

Select Command List 1 and enter the following :

PROMPT	ENTER
	F: Find
Enter search text [" "]	gift
Enter search option [" "]	GIW

The cursor then moves through the document and comes to rest immediately after the word **gift** in the last sentence of the second paragraph of the memo.

A similar facility is afforded by **Goto**. Select Command List 1 and enter the following :

PROMPT	ENTER
	G: Goto
Enter window, page, line column or marker:	**L10: Line 10**

The document then scrolls until line 10 is at the top of the screen.

Bold, Underscore and Font

There are a few minor changes we wish to make in the appearance of the memo. These concern the use of Commands on Command List 2. The first one concerns the use of emboldening text. Select the Command List 2 and enter the following :

PROMPT	ENTER
	B: Bold
Select option: Insert Remove	**I: Insert**
Select option: Block Character Document Line Paragraph	
Remainder Sentence Word	**B: Block**

Now point to the block. Place the cursor on the **S** of **SUBJECT** and press **F2**. Move the cursor to the paragraph marker at the end of the word **Competition** and press either **F10** or **Enter**.

This completes the process and the words **SUBJECT ....** will now print out in bold typeface. On a color monitor this is evidenced by the fact that they now appear in white on the screen.

We also wish to underscore the Subject of the memo. Select Command list 2 place the cursor on the **S** of **SUBJECT** and enter the following:

PROMPT   **ENTER**

                                                    U: Underscore
Select option: Insert Remove   I: Insert
Select option: Block Character Document Line Paragraph
              Remainder Sentence Word   P: Paragraph

The fact that you have succeeded is evidenced by the prompt **FN: 0BU** on the Status line which indicates **standard font with bold and underline**.

Finally we wish to add a script style signature to the letter. This is done by selecting a specific **Font**. Place the cursor on the **J** of the signature **Jane Doe**, select Command List 2 and enter the following

PROMPT   **ENTER**

                                                    F: Font
Select option: Change Select   S: Select
Enter font number: 9: The script font

Make sure that **Insert** is indicated on the Status line as being **OFF** and overtype **Jane Doe**. On a color monitor the text appears in **magenta** which indicates that when printed it will appear in the script font.

Footnotes

Many documents require footnotes. This facility is provided via Command list 3. Place the cursor at the letter **M** of **Memo** on the first line of the document, select Command List 3 and enter the following :

PROMPT   **ENTER**

                                                    F: Footnote
Select option: Insert Modify   I: Insert

The **Footnote** Definition Screen then appears in the Control Area. Type the lines to read :

```
| 0|||||||||L |||||||||2 |||||||||3 |||||||||4 |||||||||5 |||||||||R |||||
Enter text for footnote 1.        F10 Finished                 Insert:  ON
Line  1  -----------------------
Line  2 Date 31 March 89
Line  3  -----------------------
```

The number **1** appears next to the **M** in magenta to indicate that when the document is printed a **superscript 1** will appear there and a corresponding **footnote** will be printed at the end of the page. It is possible to have a number of footnotes and each are numbered automatically. The footnote does not appear on the screen unless you use the **Split Footnote** option from Command List 3.

Split

Select Command List 3 and enter the following :

PROMPT   **ENTER**

                                                              S: Split
Select option: Horizontal   Vertical   Footnote   F: Footnote
Enter line number or use Tab or cursor keys to select location.

Place the cursor about ten lines from the bottom of the screen and press **enter**. Immediately the screen splits and the numbered footnote appears in the bottom section of the screen

It may be, of course that you find that there is not enough room on the page for all the text and all the footnotes that you wish to be present. In this case it is possible to **Break** the page at any line you wish to form a new page. The Command for this is **Newpage**.

Position the cursor at the line below the name **Jane Doe**, select Command List 2 and enter the following :

PROMPT   **ENTER**

                                                              N: Newpage
Select option: Insert Remove   I: Insert

Immediately a new page is formed. If you wish to have a visible prompt on the screen for the boundary between pages then you must use the Visible toggle. Move to Command list 2 and select the following;

PROMPT	ENTER
	V: Visible
Select option: Newpage Paragraph-Marks Tabs	N: Newpage

Ordinarily, by default, the Newpage markers, the Paragraph markers and the Tab markers are Visible when you type your document. If for some reason you do not wish to have any of these displayed then the Visible Command can be used to switch them ON and OFF.

There are many times when text enclosed within a box can make a document more attractive to the eye. The **Draw** Command is available to permit lines and boxes to be drawn for inclusion into the document. What we shall do is draw a box to contain the word **MEMORANDUM** at the top of the memo.

Place the cursor at the top left-hand corner of the memo, make sure that you are in Command Mode, select Command list 3 and enter the following :

PROMPT	ENTER
	D: Draw

The document disappears and you are now in **Draw Mode** and the Control Area displays a number of options

```
 0|||||||||L|||||||||2|||||||||3|||||||||4|||||||||5|||||||||R|||||||||
F2 Load          F4 Draw box/line        F6 Font select
F3 Save          F5 Clear screen         F10 Finished
Document (none) Pg: 1 Ln: 1 Ps: 10 FN: 0 Font: Standard   Insert: ON
DRAW - draw boxes, lines or grids in graphic fonts
```

Move the cursor to **Ln 1 Ps 28** and enter the following:

224   *Chapter 1: Editing A Document*

PROMPT	ENTER
	F 4 (press F4)
Select line type: Single Double Heavy Block	D: double
Select corner type: Square Round	R: Round

Now move the cursor down 4 lines and to the right 13 spaces. You should then have the following display

```
              qFFFFFFFFFFFe
              v           v
              v           v
              v           v
              zFFFFFFFFFFFe
```

What is happening is that the system is using letters of the alphabet to denote different types of lines. When you print out the document you will have double lines and rounded corners. Having completed the box press **enter** followed by **F10**.

At this point you are brought back to the document, only this time the box is there. Put the Wordprocessor into Enter Mode, move the cursor into the box, make sure that **Insert** is **OFF** and type into the middle of the box the word **MEMORANDUM**.

Graphics

A further way to enhance a document is to insert pictures and graphs. We can do this using the **Graphics** Command.

Go to the top of the second page of the memo, make sure that you are in Command Mode, select Command List 4 and enter the following :

PROMPT	ENTER
	G: Graphics
Select option: Insert Remove View	I: Insert
Enter graph name:	TOTSALES

This is the name of the graph already on the disk created within the Spreadsheet Module and which shows the relative total sales for each of the last four months.

| Select option: Large Medium Small | M: Medium |

Select option: Left-Justified Right-Justified   L: Left-justified

A **shaded line** now appears in the appropriate area of the document. Move to Entry Mode and press **enter** a number of times and you will see the area reserved for the graph displayed as a **shaded block** with the name of the graphics file in the centre. The graph is not displayed on the monitor but it can be viewed using **Graphics View**. However, when the document is printed it will be visible.

Compute

The graph is based on the last month's sales figures that are recorded in the Spreadsheet. In order to make the graph more sensible, the Sales Manager intends to enter the actual sales information from which the graph was generated. These figures are:

> 1234.00
> 5987.00
> 3945.00
> 6904.00

These figures were entered by the Sales Manager after rummaging through a sheaf of papers on her desk. To complete the presentation the Sales manager wants to total these figures. To do this move to Command list 2 and select the **Compute** command.

PROMPT   **ENTER**

                                                             C: Compute
Select option: Formula Sum   S: Sum
<cursor keys> F2 drop new anchor F3 inspect F10 or ENTER end block

Use the cursor keys to mark the block of figures and press **enter**. This has **computed** the **sum** and has stored the result in memory. Now enter Entry Mode and move the cursor to the position where the total is to appear and then press **Ctrl C** and the total appears.

This completes our coverage of the editing facilities of our memo. What we now wish to consider concerns the various means whereby we can affect the layout of the document as it will appear when it is printed and this we do in the next Chapter.

Chapter 2 : Document Layout and Handling

Objectives

When you have completed this Section you will be able to :

- Reformat sections of or an entire document
- Set Tabs, Margins and Justification for a document
- Adjust the screen display by deleting the Border, by Painting the screen, by deleting the Ruler and by changing the Display to Monochrome
- Change the Name of a document
- Password protect a document
- Access the Directory to display files currently resident on the disk
- Access the Index to display files that are currently active
- Use the Files Command to manipulate disk files

Introduction

During the course of document construction it may be desirable to reformat either the entire document or just part of it. This we shall now do with the second paragraph of our memo.

Reformat

Place the cursor anywhere inside the second paragraph, make sure that you are in Command Mode. Select Command List 2 and enter the following:

PROMPT	ENTER
	R: Reformat
Select option: Document Paragraph Remainder	
	P: Paragraph
Select option: Normal Left-Justified Right-Justified Centered Same	
	N: Normal

Normal means both left- and right-justified.

228   *Chapter 2: Document Layout and Handling*

Enter new left margin or use Tab or cursor keys to move to column

Move the cursor to column **9** and press enter to set the left margin.

Enter new right margin or use Tab or cursor keys to move to column

Move the cursor to column **60** and press enter to set the right margin.

Enter new indent (ENTER for no change)	**Enter: No change**
Enter new spacing (ENTER for no change)	**Enter: No change**

(blank lines between text lines - can be 1 to 8)

Immediately you will see the newly formatted paragraph appear as a narrower block of text within the memo.

The **spacing** option refers to the number of blank lines between paragraphs - it is possible to have from 0 to 7. There is also a **Spacing** command on Command list 2 which can be used to change the spacing for newly entered paragraphs.

Tabs

We can also reset the **TABS**.

Select Command List 2 and enter the following :

PROMPT	**ENTER**
	T: Tabs
Select option: Normal Decimal	N: Normal

Decimal is used for tabbing on a decimal point.

The following display appears in the Control Area :

```
        F3  Set       F5  Left 10     F9  Clear all
        F4  Unset     F6  Right 10    F10 Finish
```

These options are self-explanatory. We do not wish to change the tab settings so we shall press **Esc** and **escape** from this Command. Remember that if you have erroneously entered a

Command, pressing **Esc** will allow you to leave it prematurely.

In addition to these document layout facilities there are also various screen display features that can be used to enhance the appearance of your document as it appears on the screen.

Border, Paint, Ruler and Display

> **Command list 3: Border** This Command turns the Document Window **Border** display ON and OFF. This can be very useful if you have a screen with multiple windows (we shall see this later on) and you do not wish to have the screen cluttered up with borders around each window.
>
> **Command list 3: Paint** This Command permits you to change the colour display of the screen. It is possible to change both the background and the foreground colours. It is also possible to change the **Painting** of a particular block of text. Try it.
>
> **Command list 3: Ruler** This Command can be used to switch the display of the **Ruler** ON and OFF.
>
> **Command list 5: Display** This Command permits the display of the entire screen to be in either Monochrome or Colour. Try it.

Newname

Having changed our document from its original form we shall now save it under a different name. We can either do this by selecting the **Save** Command on Command List 4 and giving the document a new name or, alternatively, we can simply rename the document using **Newname**.

Select Command List 3 and enter the following :

PROMPT	ENTER
	N: Newname
Enter new document filename:	MEMO

The document **LETTER** has now been renamed **MEMO**.

We are now going to create a new document called NAMES. This document will consist of a collection of Christian names in the form of a list. Before we actually start typing in the names we shall set up the page by identifying our **Indents** and **Margins**. We shall also change the **Justification** from the default setting. Before we start we must ensure that there is no document currently residing in memory. Select Command List 4 and enter the following:

PROMPT	ENTER
	U: Unload
Save modified document first (y/n):	Y: Yes

Immediately the current document disappears. If there was more than one document in memory then SMART would have asked for the name of the document. You could then enter the name or the word All. Entering the latter will then clear All Documents from memory.

Margin

Now make sure that you are in Command Mode. Select Command List 2 and enter the following :

PROMPT	ENTER
	M: Margin
Select option: Left Right Temp-Release	L: Left

Move the cursor to column 20 and press **enter**. This sets the left margin. We repeat this procedure to set the right margin.

	M: Margin
Select option: Left Right Temp-Release	R: Right

Move the cursor to column 40 and press **enter**. This sets the right margin.

We now have a page that is only 20 characters wide.

Justify

Select Command List 2 and enter the following :

PROMPT	ENTER
	J: Justify
Select option: Normal Left-Justified Right-Justified Centered	L: Left-Justified

Now, anything that is typed in will be justified to the left but **ragged edged** on the right.

We are now ready to enter a list of Christian names. Enter in the five names of the ABC Supplies' salesforce under the list title **Names** in the following order:

> **Names**
> **Felix**
> **Clara**
> **Erica**
> **Angela**
> **David**
> **Brian**

When you have done that you will see that the names are not alphabetically listed. Let's put them in alphabetical order.

Text-Sort

Make sure that you are on Command Mode, select Command List 4 and enter the following :

PROMPT	ENTER
	T: Text-Sort
Select option: Ascending Descending	A: Ascending

Now we must **point** to the list to be sorted. Place the cursor at the beginning of the first name on the list:

F2 : Drop the Anchor

Move the cursor to the end of the list.

Press F10

The list is then sorted alphabetically. We now wish to **Save** the new document to disk. Still on Command list 4 select:

PROMPT	ENTER
	S: Save
Enter document filename:	NAMES

Document Handling

Marker

There are many times when a specific paragraph needs to be referred to. Perhaps it is a contract between two companies and it contains many clauses. If such is the case then to help locate specific clauses in a long document **Markers** can be placed at strategic points in the document. Then when a particular clause is required the **Goto Marker** command sequence will locate the desired clause immediately. This is clearly better than scrolling through the entire document.

The **Marker** Command is located on Command list 3 and we shall now demonstrate its use by placing a marker on our document NAMES. Place the cursor on the **D** of the name **David** and enter the following:

PROMPT	ENTER
	M: Marker
Select option: Directory Set Unset View	S: Set
Enter marker name:	M01

The **Marker** is then set. Every marker name must start with a letter and can contain up to 60 characters but only the first three will be used to distinguish one marker from another. To view the record of all the markers in a document enter the following:

PROMPT	ENTER
	M: Marker
Select option: Directory Set Unset View	D: Directory

A menu of all the markers set is displayed. Now enter the following:

PROMPT	ENTER
	M: Marker
Select option: Directory Set Unset View	V: View

The entire document is now scrolled through, stopping at each marker in turn with the message

> Marker is <marker name>
> ENTER to go to next marker

To see how specific sections of a document can be located using markers move to Command list 1 and select the **Goto** command.

PROMPT	ENTER
	G: Goto
Enter window, page, line, column or marker	M01

The cursor now instantly moves to the location of the marker named **M01**. Note, do avoid using **P, L** or **C** as the first letter of the marker name as this will confuse your intentions when using the **Goto** command.

There are a number of other commands that facilitate the handling of documents and these we shall now consider in turn.

Password

A Document can be protected by assigning a Password to it. The **Password** is then requested whenever the file is accessed with **Load**, **Print** or **Read**.

PROMPT	ENTER
	P: Password
Select option: Attach Remove	A: Attach
Enter password	ABCD
Protect current document with the password "ABCD"	Y: Yes

When the Password is so Attached then the document must be **Saved** to effect the password protection. If the Document is changed into a text-file this password is not retained though, of course, you will need to know the password to effect the change. To effect the password enter the following:

PROMPT   **ENTER**

                                                                  U: Unload

Save modified document first (y/n):   Y: Yes

Directory

This Command allows you to view the files that are available on the disk. Try it, select Command List 4, press **D** followed by **enter**.

Index

This Command displays all currently active Documents and Text files. Try it, select Command list 4, press **I** followed by **enter**.

File

This Command facilitates disk file handling. It permits files to be **Copied**, **Erased** or **Renamed**. It also allows you to change the current **Data Path**.

Chapter 3 : Spellchecking A Document

Objectives

When you have read this Section you will be able to :

- Understand the facilities offered by the **Spellchecker**
- Check a document or part of a document for spelling errors and amend it

Introduction

The **Spellchecker** is a facility that permits all or part of a document to be checked for spelling errors. Any errors that are detected can then be amended either by reference to a **Dictionary** or by simple editing.

Dictionary

Load the document MEMO into memory, ensure that you are in Command Mode and move to Command list 2 and select the following sequence of commands;

PROMPT	ENTER
	D: Dictionary
Select option: Custom Hyphenate Options Spell-Check	S: Spell-Check
Select option: Block Document Line Paragraph Remainder Sentence Word	D: Document
Select option: File screen	S: Screen

The Wordprocessor now reviews every word in the document by comparing it with words stored in a **Dictionary** stored on disk. If an error is located then the suspect word is highlighted and a number of possible options appear.

```
|0|||||||||L|||||||||2|||||||||3|||||||||4|||||||||5|||||||||R|||||||||
```
Enter replacement text:
Word misspelled, Bad capitalisation, No suggested spellings
F2 Replace all   F3 Ignore   F4 Ignore all   F5 Custom   F6 Delete
Words: 245   Corrections: 10

In this display the Spell-Checker has located a word that is misspelled and starts a sentence without a capital letter. It is also informing you that it has no suggestion as to how the word should be spelled after referring to its dictionary. The function keys are:

- **F2** Replace all occurrences of this misspelling with an entered text
- **F3** Ignore the misspelling and look for the next misspelled word
- **F4** Ignore this and all future misspelling of this kind
- **F5** It may be that the word is correctly spelled but it is not in the Dictionary. Pressing F5 will ensure that it is placed in the dictionary for future use.
- **F6** Delete the word

When the check is complete, a log of words checked and corrections made is displayed:

SPELL CHECK SUMMARY	
Number of words checked:	300
Number of corrections made:	15
Number of words added to Custom Dictionary:	0

If the option **File** had been selected instead of screen then a disk file would have been Spell-Checked without it being loaded into memory. At the end of this a Spell-Check Summary would be produced indicating the number of words checked and the number of corrections made.

Dictionary Custom

The option **Dictionary Custom** will permit a customised dictionary to be created. Many times you will use words that are not contained within the dictionaries resident within the SMART System. There are two ways around this. You can either **add** words to the current dictionary or you can **create** your own dictionary. Every dictionary falls into one of three categories:

American English French

and SMART provides one of each. If you wish to create your own dictionary then you must first select which of the three options you wish. If you choose **English** then any dictionary you create will also be in this category.

When using the Spell-Checker facility it is possible to make use of up to **five** dictionaries provided they all fall within the same category. This option is made available via the **Dictionary Options** selection.

Dictionary Hyphenation

Dictionary hyphenation adds hyphenation to the existing document without changing the margins, indentation or spacing.

PROMPT	ENTER
	D: Dictionary
Select option: Custom Hyphenate Options	
Spell-Check	H: Hyphenate
Select option: Document Paragraph Remainder	D: Document

The document will then be reformatted with hyphenation added where appropriate.

Chapter 4: Printing a Document

Objectives

When you have completed this Section you will be able to :

- Print multiple copies of all or part of a document to either the Printer or the Disk
- Obtain a hard copy of the Printer Options settings
- Change the Printer Options settings for either all documents or just the current document

Introduction

The **Print** Command permits both a document to be printed and the general control information for the layout of a document to be set.

Print

Move to Command list 1 and enter the following:

PROMPT	ENTER
	P: Print
Select option: Normal Enhanced Options Preset Template:	N: Normal
Select option: Printer Disk:	P: Printer
Enter number of copies:	1
Enter start page number:	1
Enter end page number:	. enter

The memorandum will now be printed - when you press **enter** in response to the last question the document is printed in its entirety. Notice that the graph is absent as is the special font for the signature. To print these we must use **Print Enhanced** mode. Try it. You will find there is a delay between ending the printing of the first page and the starting of the printing of the graph. This is quite normal - after all the graph has to be reduced in scale to fit the letter. This process is signalled by the word **Scaling** . . . on the Status Line.

We should take a closer look at those options presented to us when we first selected **P** for **Print**.

> **Normal** This will print any document containing ASCII characters. This option prints using the fonts and print attributes normally available with the printer. For most printers this will include underscoring and boldfacing.
>
> **Enhanced** This option prints a document on a printer that supports graphics. It will also print special fonts available within the SMART Wordprocessor. It prints the entire document in graphics mode and is therefore slower than the Normal option. If a document contains a graph then this mode must be used.
>
> **Options** This selection permits the various format options such as headings and footings to be amended from their default values.
>
> **Preset** This option allows you to view, edit and set the standard print template which is the list of settings for the control of the printer.
>
> **Template** A printed copy of the print template is produced from this selection. This template is a list of the printer control settings.

Print Template

This option prints the **Print Option Settings** currently set for document printing.

Select Command List 1 and enter the following :

PROMPT	ENTER
	P: Print
Select option: Enhanced Normal Options Preset	
Template:	T: Template
Select option: Current-Document Preset	C: Current-Document

The settings are then printed on the printer. Look at the print-out and you will see the settings that are installed for the current document.

```
Print heading on:          ALL-PAGES
Use secondary headings:          NO
Print footing on:          ALL-PAGES
        Form length:      66
        Form width:       80
        Top margins:       4
        Bottom margins:    6
        Text lines:       56
        Text width:       80
        Left indents:      0
        Right indents:     0
        After header:      0
        Before footer:     0
        Date:       SHORT-ALPHA
        Enclose text:     NO
        Page #:        ARABIC
```

These settings may be different from the default settings, a printout of which can be obtained by selecting the option **Preset**. These parameters are available for resetting using the **Print Options** sequence of Commands.

Print Options

This sequence of Commands allows you to change the currently set print **Parameters** for the current document only. The options consist of :

Headings Headings can be defined and set to be printed on **All Pages**, **First Page Only** or **All But First Page**. It is possible to have Primary Headings for all pages or just odd pages and Secondary Headings for even pages.

Footings Footings can be set in the same manner as Headings.

Date Style Can be chosen from **Short** or **Long Alphanumeric** or simply **Numeric**.

Page Numbers These can be set at **Arabic**, or **Roman**.

There are also a number of **Control Codes** listed in the SMART Manual that permit control of the placement of information on the document. We shall not deal with those here.

Additional Options

These include lines to enclose the document, the number to use for the first page of the document, the number of lines per inch, the number of characters per inch and the number of lines per page.

Chapter 5 :   Handling Multiple Documents

Objectives

When you have completed this Section you will be able to :

- Split the screen into multiple windows
- Load different documents into different windows
- Zoom into any particular window
- Transfer information from one document to another

Introduction

It is possible to **split** the Document Window into separate **windows** and each window can contain its own document. There is a maximum of 32 windows possible at any one time. They can be created by **Splitting Vertically** and/or **Splitting Horizontally**. We move from window to window by using the **Goto** Command on Command List 1. We have already seen an application of this when we used the **Split Footnote** Command.

Windows

Ensure that the document MEMO is loaded, move to Command list 3 and select the following commands:

PROMPT	ENTER
	S: Split
Select option: Footnote Horizontal Vertical	V: Vertical

Enter column number or use Tab and cursor keys to select location:

Move the cursor to about midway across the screen and press **enter:**

Leave new window empty? (y/n):   Y: Yes

You are now faced with a screen split into two windows, one of which contains the MEMO and the other empty.

To move into the second window select Command List 1 and enter the following :

PROMPT   **ENTER**

                                                                  G: Goto

Enter window, page, line, column or marker: 2

And the cursor is now in window 2. Select Command List 4 and **Load** in the document called NAMES.

Now you see the two documents side by side.

Zoom

Select Command list 3 and press **Z** for **Zoom**. Immediately the screen fills with the contents of window 2 - you have **zoomed** into window 2. Pressing **Z** again restores the two window display. **Zoom** is a toggle that **zooms** into and out of a window.

Transferring Information Between Documents

We can now demonstrate how to **Copy** parts of one document into another document. Make sure that you are in window 2 where the NAMES file is displayed. Place the cursor on the **N** of **Names**, select Command List 1 and enter the following commands:

PROMPT   **ENTER**

                                                                  C: Copy

Select option: Block Line Paragraph Remainder
                 Sentence Word   W: Word

Nothing appears to have happened but in fact the **Word Names** has been copied into the **Copy buffer**. Now Goto Window 1, select Command List 3 and enter the following;

PROMPT   **ENTER**

                                                                  Z: Zoom

Place the cursor at the very end of the document on the **diamond** prompt. Select Command List 1 and enter
                                                                       I: Insert

Immediately the word **Names** appears.

Close

Having performed the desired **Copy** the document in Window 2 is no longer required, nor are the two windows. To revert back to the single window select the following commands from Command list 1:

PROMPT	ENTER
	Z: Zoom
	G: Goto
Enter window, page, line, column or marker:	2
	C: Close

Immediately the second window is closed and its contents **Unloaded**. Please note that a **Zoomed** window must be **un-Zoomed** to display the **Split** screen before it can be **Closed**.

By using windows in this way information contained on different documents can be transferred using **Move** or copied using **Copy** from one document to another.

We are not going to require **Names** at the end of our MEMO so get rid of it by using the **Delete** command. We put it there just to demonstrate the facility.

Chapter 6 : The Mail-Merge Facility

Objectives

When you have completed this Section you will be able to:

- Understand the differences between a Document File and a Text File
- Change a Document File into a Text File and vice versa
- Merge two documents together to produce a personalised memo

Introduction

The **Mail-Merge** facility is so-called because it permits a standard form letter to be produced that contains personalised names and addresses. Two documents are joined together at the printing stage and information from one is inserted into the other.

Text-File

We are now going to cause the two documents MEMO and NAMES to be **Merged** together. We shall personalise the memo by addressing it to particular individuals. The names of these individuals are contained in the document called NAMES. We shall assume that following on from the last Chapter the document MEMO is loaded into window 1 and the document NAMES is resident in window 2.

The first step in this process is to indicate where in the MEMO the names are to go. On the first line that reads **Memo To:** we shall insert the name of the addressee. So we amend

Memo To All Sales Personnel

to read
Memo To: <<Name>>

The brackets << and >> are inserted by using **Ctrl-J** for << and **Ctrl-K** for >>. If you look at your keyboard you will see that **J** and **K** are directly above and a little to the left of < and >.

This insertion will tell the system that it has to look elsewhere to find the **Name**. Where the system will look is in a **Text-File**. The document that we have created called NAMES that is currently in window 2 is not a text-file but a **Document**. A Text-File is a file that contains only ASCII Characters whereas our Document contains special characters such as margin settings etc. Fortunately we do not have to create another file. Instead we change the **Type** of file.

Goto Window 2 and select Command List 4.

Now press C for Change-Type

and a message appears on the Status Line to indicate that the file is now a **text file**. So far so good. Now we must arrange the NAMES file so that it is in a state to be **Read** for **Merging** with the MEMO. We must change the file so that the first line reads :

"Names"

where the double quotes are visible. Then each name following must also be enclosed in double quotes. Do this now.

The finished Text-File will then look like the following:

"Names"
"Angela"
"Brian"
"Clara"
"David"
"Erica"
"Felix"

Notice that there is no blank line between **"Names"** and the first name. When this is complete **Save** the **Text-File** called NAMES and **Unload** it.

Select Command List 3 and press C for **Close**. Immediately the second window disappears. The screen is no longer **Split**.

Merge

We are now ready to print our memo that has been personalised by **Merging** with a NAMES text file.

Select Command List 4 and enter the following :

PROMPT	ENTER
	M: Merge
Select option: File Screen:	File
Select option: Normal EnhancedE:	Enhanced
Enter filename:	NAMES

Notice that this name does not appear in the pop-up box of Document names. This is because it is not a Document but a Text-File.

The printer will now produce a personalised copy of the MEMO, one for each member of the Department.

If the Sales Manager had written the MEMO so that the individual's last month's sales could also be inserted then the Document MEMO would have to be appropriately annotated with << and >> and the Text File would have a heading for each type of insertion. For example;

```
        "Names"      "Amount"
        "Angela"      623.45
        "Brian"      2503.04
        "Clara"      1578.11
        "David"      2490.25
        "Erica"      3325.69
        "Felix"      2174.65
```

Had we selected the option **Merge Screen** then as each memo was printed we could have entered the name to be inserted at the keyboard.

Chapter 7 : The Remember Mode

Objectives

When you have completed this Section you will be able to :

- Appreciate the existence of the Programmability of the SMART Wordprocessor
- Generate a simple program using the Remember Mode

Introduction

All of the SMART Wordprocessor Commands are capable of being written into a Text-File and executed sequentially. This method of generating an executable program can be done in two different ways.

Directly Written Programs

The coding for an executable program within the SMART Wordprocessor can be written in much the same way as writing a program in any other high-level language. To achieve this level of competence is beyond the scope of this Chapter and will not be dealt with here. Instead it will be left to a later Section.

The Remember Mode

The SMART System can be put into **Remember Mode** so that any Commands that are activated are **remembered** and listed sequentially in a text file. This will then constitute an executable program that can be run at any time so duplicating all the Command selections made previously.

The program we shall generate will be the sequence of commands that **inserts a graph** into the MEMO and then issues a **Merge print** command.

252   *Chapter 7: The Remember Mode*

Graphics Insert and Mail Merge

Within the Command Mode move to Command list 5 and enter the following sequence of commands:

PROMPT	ENTER
	R: Remember
Select option: Compile Delete Edit Finished Help Print Start	S: Start
Enter project filename:	MEMO

The Wordprocessor is now in **Remember Mode** and every command issued from here on in will be remembered until the Remember Mode is turned off.

Now execute the **Graphic Insert** and **Mail-Merge** procedures as follows:

List	Command	Explanation
4	Unload All	Clear memory of all documents
4	Load MEMO	Load the MEMO document into memory
2	Graphics Insert TOTSALES Small Right-Justified	Insert a small copy of the Pie Chart graph on the right hand side at the start of the second paragraph
4	Merge/File/Normal/Enhanced/NAMES	Print the MEMO document merged with the NAMES text file in the enhanced mode

When all the documents have been printed we must turn **off** the **Remember Mode**. Move to Command list 5 and enter the following :

PROMPT	ENTER
	R: Remember
Select option: Compile Delete Edit Finished Help Print Start	F: Finished

SmartWare: A Beginner's Guide   Section 4   253

Now let us look at the program we have written. Still in Command list 5 enter the following:

PROMPT	ENTER
	R: Remeber
Select option: Compile Delete Edit Finished Help Print Start	E: Edit
Enter project filename:	MEMO

The following lines of code are displayed in the **Project Editor Screen:**

```
load MEMO
graphics insert TOTSALES small right-justified
merge file enhanced NAMES
```

The listing duplicates exactly everything that you did to perform the **Mail-Merge**.

Executing the Project

Press **Esc** to quit this display, **Unload** the Document MEMO and we shall now **Execute** this program.

From Command list 5 enter the following:

PROMPT	ENTER
	E: Execute
Enter project filename:	MEMO

and the entire sequence of commands is now executed automatically. To obtain a hard copy of the program listing use **Remember Print**.

Section 5 : The SMART System : Integration

This Section consists of a description of the various features that permit the transmission of information from one Module to another within the SMART System.

When you have completed this Section you will be able to transfer information between any pair of the **Data-Manager, Spreadsheet** and **Wordprocessor** Modules.

This Section is divided into three Chapters:

- **Integration**
- **Write and Read**
- **Send and Xlate**

Chapter 1 : Integration

Objectives

When you have completed this Chapter you will be able to:

- Appreciate what is meant by the term 'integration' with the SMART System
- Appreciate how information to be transferred from a Module is placed in a holding file ready for onward transmission to another Module
- Appreciate the existence of different file types that can be accommodated within the SMART System

Introduction

The SMART System possesses the versatile and crucial feature of **modular integration**. As you have seen so far the system is designed on a **modular** pattern. Each of the modules that make up the system are designed to either act alone as we have seen or act in concert as we shall soon see. This latter aspect is what is meant by the term **integration**. Information can pass freely between modules so that, for example, information contained within the Data-Manager can be gathered together, passed to the Spreadsheet and analysed within the Spreadsheet without ever leaving the SMART System.

There are three commands that are intrinsic to the concept of integration, these are **Write**, **Send** and **Read**. We shall consider each one of them in turn. But first it will be instructive to stand aside from ABC Supplies for a while and take a look at what exactly happens when information is transferred between modules.

Information Transfer

Any information contained within a given module that is required to be transferred to another module must first pass through an intermediate stage. The information in the original module is collated and **written** into a special disk file. The contents of this disk file can then be **read** by any other module.

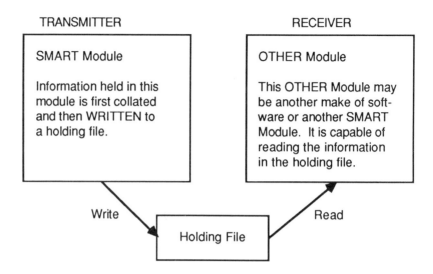

File Types

To facilitate this ability to transfer information between two modules there are a number of different file type options available.

ASCII: An ASCII file - American Symbolic Code for Information Interchange - is a file where text is contained within double quotes whereas numbers are not. Fields are separated by commas and each record is terminated with a **carriage return** followed by a **line feed**. The end of the file is marked with a **Ctrl-Z**. A typical example of this format is

"ABC Supplies",123.45,19,"text"

The ASCII format can be used to transfer information that can be read not only by SMART Modules but by any other program that can read ASCII files. ASCII files can also be read from DOS.

DIF: A **DIF** file - Data Interchange Format - is used to transmit information from SMART to non-SMART Spreadsheet programs such as Visicalc.

M-SYLK: An **M-SYLK** file - Symbolic Link - is also used for Spreadsheet applications.

SMART: The SMART file option is used only for transmitting information between SMART Modules. Text fields are surrounded by **double quotes**, whereas numeric fields are not. A **space** separates each field and a record is terminated with a **carriage return** followed by a **line feed**. A **Ctrl Z** terminates the end of the file. Typical of the SMART format is as follows:

"ABC Supplies" 123.45 19 "text"

The SMART option can be used to transfer information from the Data-Manager to the Spreadsheet or the Wordprocessor via the **Merge** command.

TEXT: This option is similar to the SMART option without the double quotes around the text fields. A typical example is:

ABC Supplies 123.45 19 text

This option is used when the information is to be transmitted to a document or text file in the Wordprocessor Module.

3-DBASE: This option creates a dBase III file.

Document: **Document** format creates a file in the format of a SMART Wordprocessor document.

123: The 123 format creates a file that can be accessed by **Lotus 1-2-3 Release 1A**.

R2-123: The R2-123 format creates a file that can be accessed by **Lotus 1-2-3 Release 2**.

DCA: A DCA file - Document Content Architecture - can be converted into a SMART file format for use within the SMART System. This facility is available only within the Wordprocessor Module using the **X-Late** command.

Transmitting Information

Collated information can be written to a disk file by using either of the two commands **Write** or **Send**. We shall look at these in the next Chapter.

Chapter 2 : Write and Read

Objectives

When you have read this Chapter you will be able to:

- Write a summary of information held in the Data-Manager to disk
- Understand the Summary Definition Screen for a Row Summary
- Read the summary into a Worksheet in the Spreadsheet Module

Introduction

In this Chapter we shall consider the procedure that is followed when transmitting information between the SMART Data-Manager and the Spreadsheet. The entire discussion is centred around the **Write** and **Read** commands.

Write - the Format

The **Write** command is available in the Data-Manager, the Spreadsheet and the Wordprocessor Modules. In all three modules it is found on Command list 4 and in all three modules its effect is to produce a file on the disk that is readable from within any other module. We shall consider the Data-Manager module in particular.

The format of the ultimate disk file written from the Data-Manager is in the format of a **table** - organised rows and columns. The rows and columns are labelled with the contents of a particular **search** field.

Write and Read

We shall exemplify the **Write** command by writing information contained within the Data-Manager to a file in readiness for it to be read from within the Spreadsheet.

You will remember that ABC Supplies are running a competition amongst their sales personnel. Each month every salesperson's sales figures are accumulated in the spreadsheet over a four-month period. At the end of that period each salesperson's four months' sales are totalled and the salesperson with the greatest total wins a prize.

The sales information is contained within the Data-Manager but the totalling of the sales figures is done within the Spreadsheet. To make this an automatic procedure we must collate the information contained in the Data-Manager and transfer it to the Spreadsheet. To demonstrate this procedure we shall **Write** the names of the customers accompanied with their accumulated Total Value order figures from the Data-Manager ORDERS file to a holding disk file called PERSONS. When we have done this we shall move to the Spreadsheet Module and **Read** the information contained in PERSONS into a Worksheet.

Write

Enter the Data-Manager and load the ORDERS file. Move to Command list 4 and enter the following sequence of commands:

PROMPT	ENTER
	W: Write
Select option: All Summarized	A: All

The available fields are now displayed in a pop-up menu at the bottom of the display window.

F6 will select the current field

This prompt is requesting you to list every field that you wish to include in the information you are wishing to write to the disk. We wish to write the list of Customer Names and the Total Values from each record of the ORDER file so place the pointer against the field **Customer Name - [4]** and press **F6**, then move the pointer to the field **Total Value - [27]** and press **F6** again. Now press **enter** to complete the field selection. The following prompt now appears:

Select option: Ascii Dif M-Sylk Smart Text	S: Smart
Enter filename:	PERSONS

The SMART System now collates the names of all the customers along with the Total Values on each record contained in the ORDERS file. The information is then sent to the PERSONS file. This file can then be **Read** from within the Spreadsheet module thereby transferring all the names into a Worksheet.

Move to the Spreadsheet Module, enter Command Mode, move to Command list 4 and select the following sequence of commands:

PROMPT	ENTER
	R: Read
Select option: Dif Sylk Text 123 R2-123	T: Text
Enter filename	PERSONS

And there is the information. But we have made the wrong choice. When the names are read into the Spreadsheet you will find that what has happened is that the System has taken the contents of the [**Customer Names**] and [**Total Value**] fields in **every** ORDERS record. As a result every name is repeated as many times as there are records containing that name. This is no good - we only want a list of different names - each name having an accumulated sales figure associated with it. We must re-think the problem.

Let's try again.

PROMPT	ENTER
	W: Write
Select option: All Summarized	S: Summarized
Select option: Define Predefined Undefine	D: Define
Enter summary definition filename:	PERSONS
Select option: Column/Row Row	R: Row
Select option: Complete Partial	C: Complete

Now the Summary Definition Screen appears:

```
┌─ Summary Definition ────────────────────────────────────────┐
│                                                             │
│              COL FLD  ─────  ─────  ─────  ─────  ─────     │
│  ROW FLD                                                    │
│                                                             │
│  ──────      PRINT    ─────  ─────  ─────  ─────  ─────     │
│  SEARCH      PRINT   ┌──────────────────────────────────┐   │
│  ──────      ─────   │                                  │   │
│  ──────      ─────   │                                  │   │
│  ──────      ─────   │                                  │   │
│  ──────      ─────   │                                  │   │
│  ──────      ─────   │                                  │   │
│                      └──────────────────────────────────┘   │
├─────────────────────────────────────────────────────────────┤
│  F2 Match unique    F3 Mathch others    F4 Match all    F5 Count hits    F6 list fields │
│  F7 Insert slot     F8 Delete field     F10 Finished    PgUp (left)      PgDn (right)   │
│                                                             │
│  WRITE - writes information to another application          │
└─────────────────────────────────────────────────────────────┘
```

The Summary Definition Screen

What we want to do is to:

> Search each record and accumulate the Total Value against the Customer Name.

We do this as follows. Place the cursor on the **ROW FLD** line. Press **F6** and from the display of available fields select [**Salesperson**]. Now move the cursor to the first blank line below the word **SEARCH** and press **F2**. The word **UNIQUE** appears on this and the adjacent lines. This selection will cause the System to search each record and place the **Customer Name** in the left hand column. The choice of **Match Unique** - selected by pressing **F2** - ensures that no names are repeated.

Now place the cursor in the **COL FLD** space and press **F6**. Select the [**Amount**] field from those available. This selection will cause all **Total Values** to be added into the second column against the appropriate customer. The cursor is now in the next **COL FLD** along. Press **F5** - Count hits - this will give the total number of orders made by each customer.

```
┌─ Summary Definition ─────────────────────────────────────────┐
│                                                              │
│            COL FLD    Value    COUNT  ─────  ─────  ─────    │
│ ROW FLD                                                      │
│                                                              │
│ Name___    PRINT      Value    COUNT  ─────  ─────  ─────    │
│                     ┌─────────────────────────────────────┐  │
│ SEARCH     PRINT    │   1                                 │  │
│ UNIQUE     UNIQUE   │   1                                 │  │
│ ─────      ─────    │                                     │  │
│ ─────      ─────    │                                     │  │
│ ─────      ─────    │                                     │  │
│ ─────      ─────    │                                     │  │
│ ─────      ─────    │                                     │  │
│                     └─────────────────────────────────────┘  │
│ F2 Match unique   F3 Mathch others   F4 Match all   F5 Count hits   F6 list fields │
│ F7 Insert slot    F8 Delete field    F10 Finished   PgUp (left)     PgDn (right)   │
│                                                              │
│ WRITE - writes information to another application            │
└──────────────────────────────────────────────────────────────┘
```

Press **F10** to indicate that the Summary Definition is complete.

So far we have only **Defined** the Summary Definition. We must now use it. From Command list 4, enter the following:

PROMPT	ENTER
	W: Write
Select option: Define Predefined Undefine	P: Predefined
Enter summary definition filename:	PERSONS
Select option: Ascii Dif M-Sylk Smart Text 3-dBase	T: Text
Enter filename:	PERSONS

The Summary Definition is now enacted and the appropriate file is created.

Read

Now move to the Spreadsheet module, press **Esc** to enter Command Mode, move to Command list 4 and enter the following:

Chapter 2 : Write and Read

PROMPT

Select option: Dif Sylk Text 123 R2-123
Enter filename

ENTER

R: Read
T: Text
PERSONS

And the screen fills with the summarized information that has been gleaned from the Data-Manager.

Customer Name	Total Value	COUNT
xxxxxxxxxxx	xxx.xx	x
xxxxxxxxxxx	xxx.xx	x
xxxxxxxxxxx	xxx.xx	x
xxxxxxxxxxx	xxx.xx	x
xxxxxxxxxxx	xxx.xx	x
xxxxxxxxxxx	xxx.xx	x

Chapter 3 : Send and Xlate

Objectives

When you have read this Chapter you will be able to:

- Send information from the Spreadsheet to the Wordprocessor
- Appreciate the use of the Xlate command

Introduction

Just as the **Write** command is available in all three modules so is the **Send** command - this time found on Command list 5. The difference between **Write** and **Send** is that when **Send** is enacted the user follows the transmitted information and ends up in the module to which the information is being sent along with the information - there is no further need to **Read** the information into the module. We shall consider information being sent from the Spreadsheet to the Wordprocessor.

Send - the Format

The **Send** format is identical to the **Write** format. The information transmitted is stored in the holding file in the form of a table complete with row and column labels. The Sales Manager of ABC Supplies is planning to send a letter to each of the sales personnel to thank them for their past efforts and to encourage them to greater heights of sales performance. To assist in putting the message across, the Sales Manager has decided that the letter must contain a summarized table of sales figures for the past month. These are currently available in the Spreadsheet in a Worksheet called SALES. We wish to select information form this table and **Send** it to the Wordprocessor.

Send

Load the Worksheet SALES and move to Command list 5. Select the following sequence of commands:

PROMPT	ENTER
	S: Send
Select option: Communications Data-Manager	
Wordprocessor	W: Wordprocessor
Select option: Document Graphics Both	D: Document
Enter name or block reference:	LETTER

You will remember we called the particular block of information relating to the last month's sales LETTER. We did this because we knew that we would need it in a letter at some later stage. We are now at that later stage.

Enter project file for next application: enter

We shall be talking about **Project Files** in the next Section of the book - for now we do not have a project file so we just press **enter**.

After a few moments we find that we have left the Spreadsheet and have entered the Wordprocessor and there before our eyes is the information that we were looking at in the Spreadsheet. Magic!

Xlate

Whilst we are in the Wordprocessor a brief mention of the **Xlate** command is appropriate. The purpose of the **Xlate** command is to translate a document written in Document Content Architecture - **DCA** - format into a format that can be read by SMART, and vice versa.

PROMPT	ENTER
	X: Xlate
Select option: Dca Smart Edit	D: Dca
Enter filename	XXXX

This is the **DCA** filename

Enter filename   YYYY

This is the filename of the end product - a file readable by SMART. If we had chosen S for **SMART** instead of **D** for **DCA** then a **SMART** Document would have been converted into **DCA** format.

Section 6 : Project Processing

This Section contains a description of Project Processing within the SMART System. The intention of this Section is to develop further the introductory ideas of Project Processing introduced in the previous Chapters dealing with the respective Modules contained within the SMART Suite.

When you have completed this Section you will be familiar with all the aspects of **project creation, integration** and **execution**. Whilst you will not be an expert in the application of Project Processing, you will have been exposed to sufficient detail to make you competent to initiate your own projects. Expertise will then come from use and your own imagination.

This Section is divided into twelve Chapters :

- **Introduction to Project Processing**
- **Creating Projects**
- **Project Variables**
- **Project Commands**
- **Project Data Files**
- **Project Menus**
- **The Principles of Project Construction**
- **The System Project**
- **The Data-Manager Projects**
- **The Spreadsheet Projects**
- **The Wordprocessor Projects**
- **Implementation and Maintenance**

Chapter 1 : Introduction to Project Processing

Objectives

When you have completed this Chapter you will be acquainted with

- The existence of the SMART Programming Language
- The existence of Project Files within each Module

Introduction

Project Processing refers to the creating and execution of **Project Files**. A Project File is a collection of commands which perform some predetermined activity. The available commands consist of all the Commands that we have been introduced to in the various SMART Modules plus a few specific Project Commands. The entire collection of SMART Commands constitute the **SMART Programming Language**.

The SMART Programming Language

The SMART Programming Language is a comprehensive set of Commands that permits the building of systems capable of interacting with the user via a **menu**, making decisions, manipulating **variables** as well as performing all the tasks hitherto used in the various Modules. It also makes full use of the SMART System formulae capabilities to manipulate **text, number, time** and **date** information. By using the SMART Programming Language we create a which is referred to as a Project File.

Project Files

A Project File consists of a sequence of commands, each of which are executed sequentially as soon as the Project is **executed**. The Project File exists in two forms, the **readable** form and the **compiled** form. The readable form consists of a **text-file** of commands that can be displayed on the screen. In this way the Project File can be built and edited. The compiled form is the readable form converted into an executable file - **a file that can be read and understood by the computer**. When we build a Project File we create the readable form. The SMART System itself then creates the compiled form.

Project File Extensions

All Project Files have a **name** which includes an **extension**. For example, the Project File called **SALES** could have an extension **PF3**. This means that the **DOS** name is of the form:

SALES.PF3

To every Project there are three possible files :

> The readable file has an extension   **PFn**
> The compiled File has an extension   **Rfn**

and if the Project File has been edited there is also a backup File with an extension:

BFn

In each of these extensions the value of **n** denotes the application in which the Project is written :

> 0 Main Menu (SMART System)
> 1 Spreadsheet
> 2 Wordprocessor
> 3 Data-Manager
> 6 Communications

In the next Section we shall concern ourselves with the creating of a Project File.

Chapter 2 :   Creating Projects

Objectives

When you have completed this Section you will be able to :

- Use the Remember Command
- Use the Project Editor
- Move around the Project Editor Window
- Edit a Project
- Exit the Project Editor
- Use the SMART Wordprocessor as a Project Editor

Introduction

Just as every Fairy Tale begins with "Once upon a time ..." so the creation of every Project begins with
Remember

The Remember Command

This command is found on Command List 5 of each of the SMART Modules and Command List 3 of the SMART System Main Menu.

Selecting **Remember** displays the following further options in the Control Area :

Compile   Delete   Edit   Finish   Help   Print   Start

We ended each Section dealing with a SMART Module by creating a Project File using the **Remember Start** and **Remember Finish** sequence of Commands This produced a Project File that we later viewed on the screen using **Remember Edit**. Had we wished for a printed copy of the readable Project File then we would use **Remember Print**. Should we wish to delete a Project File from the Disk we would use **Remember Delete**. The sequence **Remember Help** automatically displays all the information available relating to the Remember command.
The process of building a Project File using **Remember Start** followed by a sequence of

manually selected commands and terminated by **Remember Finish** will not be discussed in this Section. It has been adequately dealt with in the other Sections where it was introduced purely to show the SMART Programmable facilities. It is not a recommended way of constructing useable Projects of any size though it can be useful whenever a particular visual effect is required to be instituted within a Project or as an aid to constructing a sequence of commands. Instead we shall concentrate on the use of the **Project Editor**.

The Project Editor

The Project Editor is accessed from Command list 5 by selecting the following sequence of commands:

PROMPT	ENTER
	R: Remember
Select option: Compile Delete Edit Finished Help Print Start	E: Edit
Enter project filename:	XXXX

Immediately the screen fills with the Project Editor Window which is headed by **Project File Editor**.

```
┌─ Project File Editor ─────────────────────────────────┐
│                                                       │
│                                                       │
│                                                       │
│                                                       │
│                                                       │
│                                                       │
│                                                       │
└───────────────────────────────────────────────────────┘
F1 Help     F3 Find      F5 Replace      F7 Insert line     F9 Repeat
F2 Calc     F4 Goto      F6 List field   F8 Delete line     F10 Finish
                                    Line:  1   Column:  1    Insert: ON
REMEMBER - create a new project file or modify an existing file
```

If the Project you have just named does not exist then the Window is empty and ready for the

Project to be built. If the Project does exist then it appears in the Window ready to be edited or added to.

In the Control Area the effects of pressing the function keys **F1 - F10** are described and these are self-explanatory. On the Status Line are two indicators telling you on which line and column the cursor is located. A further indicator shows whether the **Insert Mode** is ON or **OFF**.

Moving Around the Project Editor Window

The following list of key-strokes permit movement around the Window :

Arrow Keys: Move the cursor one space in the direction of the arrow

Home: Move the cursor to the top of the screen

Ctrl Home: Move the cursor to the first page of the project

End: Move the cursor to the end of the screen

Ctrl End: Move the cursor to the last page of the project

Tab: Move the cursor FIVE spaces right

Shift Tab: Move the cursor FIVE spaces left

Ctrl L Arrow: Move cursor to the leftmost column of the current line

Ctrl R Arrow: Move cursor the rightmost column of the current line

PgUp : Display the previous page of the project

PgDn: Display the next page of the project.

Editing a Project

Commands are entered into the Project via the keyboard. The commands are entered in multiple lines, each line having a capacity of up to 255 characters. Having entered commands it is almost certain that you will need to **edit** them. The following is a list of edit functions that are available in addition to those described on the Status Line:

> **Ins**: Toggle the insert/overstrike mode
>
> **Del**: Delete the character under the cursor
>
> **Backspace**: Delete the character to the left of the cursor
>
> **Alt F3**: Read a Text-File stored on disk and insert it into the Project Editor
>
> **Alt F2** : Clear all information from the Project Editor
>
> **Ctrl Y**: Delete the current line without placing it in the Delete Buffer. This is as opposed to F8 which does place it in the Delete Buffer so permitting its re-insertion via the F7 key.
>
> **Esc**: Exit the Project Editor and abandon all changes.

Exiting the Project Editor

To leave the Project Editor there are two routes :

> **F10**: This route saves the Project File and automatically generates the compiled form of the Project.
>
> **Esc**: This route abandons the Project and neither saves it nor compiles it.

The SMART Wordprocessor as a Project Editor

Because the readable form of the Project File is an ordinary Text-File it is possible to create a Project File using the SMART Wordprocessor. Refer to Section 4 regarding the writing of Text-Files in SMART. The comprehensive editing facilities of the Wordprocessor make this a very versatile option.

Having created the Text-File in the Wordprocessor it will have to be compiled so that it can be executed by SMART. This is facilitated by using the **Remember Compile** sequence of commands. Having selected these commands you will be asked whether you wish **Line-Numbers** or **No-Line-Numbers**.

Line-Numbers: These are necessary if you wish to use the **Singlestep On** or **Quiet Off** options. We shall discuss these later.

Note: When you compile a Text-File you must compile it within the application Module to which it refers.

Chapter 3 : Project Variables

Objectives

When you have completed this Section you will be able to :

- Understand the differences between the three types of Project Variable
- Assign values to a Project Variable

Introduction

A **variable** is a defined **name** to which **data** can be assigned. Furthermore, this **data** can be changed - the **name** can be reassigned another **datum** - hence the use of the word **variable**.

Variables

Within SMART there are three types of variable:

Standard Project Variables
User-Defined Project Variables
Parameter Variables

Standard Project Variables

There are four Standard Project Variables available. Their **names** and **types of data** they can be assigned are :

Name	Data Type
TEXT1	Alphanumeric
TEXT2	Alphanumeric
VALUE1	Numeric
VALUE2	Numeric

These variables would be used whenever you wished to ensure that the data they store is of a particular type.

User-Defined Project Variables

It is possible within SMART to define your own variables. The names of these variables can contain any characters other than a space provided they are **preceded** by a $ sign. For example,

$name, $USER, $VARIABLE

are valid **user variable names**. There can be up to **80** characters in a name but only the first **10** characters are used by SMART to identify the variable.

User-Defined variables can be assigned data of either type.

Parameter Variables

The third category of variable is the Parameter Variable of which there are **ten** available. Their **names** are :

%0, %1, ... up to %9

These variables can be assigned data of either type and they **must** be used whenever variables are required within a **command format**. We shall say more about this later.

Note : All Project variables retain their values when moving from one Project to another and from one Module to another

Assigning Data to Variables

Within the SMART Programming Language is the Command **Let**. This Command is used to **assign data to variables**. For example,

Let VALUE1 = 25.4	Numeric
Let TEXT2 = "abc"	Alphanumeric
Let $name = 4.3	Numeric
Let $name = "one"	Alphanumeric
Let %5 = 0.987	Numeric
Let %4 = "INCOME"	Alphanumeric

Notice that alphanumeric data is always enclosed within **double quotes** - this means, of course, that "123" is alphanumeric and **not** numeric.

It is also possible to assign to variables the values of other variables, for example :

>**Let %7 = TEXT1**
>**Let $VARIABLE = VALUE2**
>**Let TEXT2 = $name**

The word **Let** is **optional**.

>**%7 = TEXT1**

is as equally valid as

>**Let %7 = TEXT1**

When Let is included in the command line it makes the command more easily understood.

Chapter 4 : Project Commands

Objectives

When you have completed this Section you will be able to :

- Recognise the various commands available within the Project Processing capability of the SMART System

Introduction

In addition to the commands that are available within each Module of SMART there are a number of commands that are available for Project Processing that are executable from within all Modules. These are referred to as **Project Commands**. The Project Commands and a brief explanation of their effects are given below :

Display Commands

Beep: Displays a message and beeps a stated number of times.

Message: Displays a message and suspends execution until a key is pressed.

Wait: Displays a message and suspends execution for stated number of seconds.

Control Commands

Command: Accesses DOS and optionally executes a DOS Command.

End: Terminates execution of the current Project.

Quit: Terminates execution of all Project Files and returns to the Operating System.

Stop: Terminates execution of all project Files and returns to the current Module.

Suspend: Pauses execution and returns program control to the user.

Execute: Executes another Project File then returns to the current Project File.

Transfer: Executes another Project File but does not return to the current Project File.

Decision Commands

If: Checks a logical expression to find out if it is true or false. If it is true then a specified set of commands will be executed. If it is false then an alternative set of specified commands will be executed.

While: Repetitively executes a specified set of commands while a certain condition is true. As soon as this condition becomes false the specified set of commands is no longer executed.

Sub-Routine Commands

A sub-routine consists of a block of Commands within a Project that can be executed specifically on command. The execution of a sub-routine interrupts the normal sequential execution of commands.

Procedure: Marks the beginning of a set of commands that are executed when the procedure, or sub-routine, is commanded to be executed.

Call: Executes a named procedure.

Return: Marks the end of a procedure. During execution this command returns execution to the command following the Call Command that caused the execution of the procedure.

Label: Marks a specific place in a Project.

Jump: Causes execution to jump to the specified Label.

Break: Exits a While loop.

Continue: Returns to the beginning of a While loop and re-evaluates the logical expression.

Variable Assignment Commands

Unless specifically stated the following commands can be used with any of the three types of project Variable.

Input: Displays a message and suspends execution until data is entered at the keyboard. Entry is terminated by pressing enter.

Let: Assigns data to a variable.

Parameters: Displays a message and suspends execution until data is entered at the keyboard. The data can only be assigned to a Project variable. Entry is terminated by pressing enter.

Clear: Clears user defined variables from memory.

Screen Commands

Menu: Permits the construction of a custom designed screen for menu display.

Repaint: Removes a menu display and regenerates the SMART Screen display.

Repaint Off: Turns off the automatic repainting of the SMART Screen display during Project Execution.

Repaint On: Turns on the automatic repainting of the SMART Screen display during Project Execution.

Project Execution Control Commands

Quiet On: Suppresses the Control Area display of the commands as they are executed.

Quiet Off: Permits the Commands to be displayed in the Control Area as and when they are executed.

Singlestep: Permits Project Execution to pause before executing a command. Singlestep On will cause a pause between the execution of two successive commands.

Comment: Enters descriptive information into the body of the Project listing that is not executed as a command.

Special Data-Manager Commands

Enter-Blank: Creates a new blank record.

Lock-Record: Locks the current record of the current file. This command is used whenever SMART is operating in a network.

Only-One: Follows the Update command and permits just one record to be updated.

Special Spreadsheet Commands

Cursor Down: Moves highlight down one cell.

Cursor Up: Moves highlight up one cell.

Cursor Left: Moves highlight left one cell.

Cursor Right: Moves highlight right one cell.

Cursor Text: Permits only text entry into a cell.

Cursor Value: Permits only numeric entry into a cell.

We shall review these commands in more detail as this Section progresses. They were listed here to give you an idea of the scope of the SMART Project Processing facilities.

Chapter 5 : Project Data Files

Objectives

When you have completed this Section you will be able to :

- Understand and use Project Data Files

Introduction

There are occasions during the execution of a Project when data is required to be stored on the Disk in a file that is different from all the usual Module Files. For example, suppose that you were building a LEGO house and you selected the pieces that you needed before starting the construction. The pieces that you selected would depend upon which model of house you were going to build. Consequently, you would not devise a **standard box** to store all possible selections. Instead you would, for any specific selection, create enough space to store that collection. This could be where the Project Data File comes in. If the Data-Manager contains information on all the different types of LEGO blocks then we could make a selection from the Data-Manager and store our selection in a Data File.

A **Project Data File** is an ordinary Text File that can be created and handled during the execution of a Project. Typically, any file must be capable of being **Opened** and **Closed**. When a file is **Open** we must be able to **write** to it or to **read** from it. To facilitate these requirements there are five Commands in SMART for handling Project Data Files.

Fopen

Fopen is the command that will **Open** a file. The command must be followed by both a **File Name** and a **Logical File Number**. For example,

FOPEN "BOOK" AS 1

This sequence of commands will **Open** a Project Data File that is called **BOOK** and it will henceforth refer to it as **File number 1**. If **BOOK** does not already exist then it will be created at this time.

Fwrite

Fwrite is the command that will permit data to be **entered** into the File. This Command must be followed by both the **File Number** and the **data** to be written to the file. For example,

FWRITE 1 FROM "Chapter 5"

This sequence of Commands will **write** the **string** of characters **Chapter 5** followed by a **carriage return** and **a linefeed** into a file that has first been **Opened** and referred to as **File Number 1**. Since there are **9** characters in the string **Chapter 5** and **2** characters in a **carriage return + line feed** there are **11** spaces occupied in the file.

C	h	a	p	t	e	r		5	CR	LF
1	2	3	4	5	6	7	8	9	10	11

Fread

Fread is the command that will permit data to be **abstracted** from the File. This Command must be followed by both the **File Number** and the **user-defined variable** to which the data is to be assigned. For example,

FREAD 1 INTO $name

This sequence of commands will read the file that has been previously Opened and referred to as File Number 1. It will start reading a string of characters from the **beginning of the file** up to (but not including) the first carriage return it encounters. The string will then be assigned to the user-defined variable **$name**.

It is possible to specify the number of characters to be read. For example,

FREAD 1 LENGTH 4 INTO $name

will read only the string **Chap** (a string of length 4 characters) and assign that to **$name**.

Fclose

Fclose is the command that will **Close** a file that has been previously **Opened**. For example,

FCLOSE 1

will **Close File Number 1**. It is important to remember to Close all files after you have been using them otherwise the data they contain could become corrupted.

It is also important to realize that when you read from or write to a file you will do so from the beginning of the file **unless you specify** otherwise. We can specify where to start reading and writing by using the **Fseek** command.

Fseek

Fseek permits the reading from and writing to a file at a specific point in the file. For example,

FSEEK 1 3

will permit access to the **fourth character position** in the file that has previously been **Opened** and referred to as **File Number 1**. For example,

FOPEN "INVOICE" AS 3	Open a file called INVOICE and refer to it as File Number 3.
FWRITE 3 FROM "Grand Total"	Enter the string Grand Total + CR + LF into File 3.
FCLOSE 3	Close file number 3.
FOPEN "INVOICE" AS 1	Open the file called INVOICE and refer to it as file number 1.
FSEEK 1 6	Count inwards from the beginning of the file 6 characters and get ready to read or write at the seventh position.
FREAD 1 LENGTH 1 INTO $SLOT	Read 1 character and assign it to the user-defined variable $SLOT - it does in fact read the letter T.
FCLOSE 1	Close file number 1.

Chapter 6 : Project Menus

Objectives

When you have completed this Section you will be able to :

- Understand the various uses of the Menu command to customise a screen display

Introduction

During the execution of a Project the user will invariably have to interact with the program via the keyboard. Questions will be asked and selections will have to be made in response to **prompts** issued by both the SMART System and the Project. To ensure the smooth and coherent execution of the Project these prompts will have to be readily understood by the user. To facilitate the Project's **user-friendliness** the SMART System makes use of the **Menu** command.

The **Menu** command permits custom screens to be designed that both display information and cater for the inputting data via the keyboard. Because the SMART System is designed to be used with both Monochrome and Colour Monitors the use of the **Menu** command requires a knowledge of the colours that are available within SMART.

SMART Colours

SMART has two categories of colour: **Background** colour and **foreground** colour.

Background Colour

There are eight possible options each one coded with a number ranging from 0 to 7. They are :

```
0   Black
1   Blue
2   Green
3   Cyan
4   Red
```

292 *Chapter 6: Project Menus*

```
5  Magenta
6  Brown
7  White
```

Foreground Colour

There are sixteen possible options each one coded with a number ranging from **0** to **15**. The first **8** are identical to the Background colours. The second **8** are high intensity versions of the first 8. They are :

```
 8  Grey
 9  Light Blue
10  Light Green
11  Light Cyan
12  Light Red
13  Light Magenta
14  Yellow
15  High Intensity White
```

Menu Commands

In all the following Commands some or all of the following abbreviations are used :

```
(r)   Screen Row number.      This ranges from 0 to 79
(c)   Screen Column number.   This ranges from 0 to 23
(fg)  Foreground colour
(bg)  Background colour
```

Menu Clear (fg) (bg)

The entire Window is cleared and a border is painted around it. The Window is painted in the colour of (**bg**) and the border is painted in the colour of (**fg**). For example,

menu clear 1 2

Menu Clear (fg) (bg) No-Border

This is the same as Menu Clear except no border is drawn. For example,

menu clear 5 12 no-border

Menu Clear Box (r1) (c1) (r2) (c2) (fg) (bg)

The area of the Window specified is cleared and a border drawn around it.

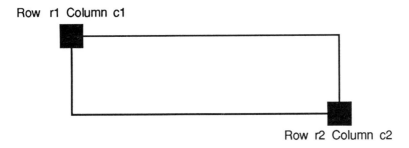

Menu Draw Box (r1) (c1) (r2) (c2) (fg) (bg)

This command is similar to Menu Clear Box except that the area specified inside the box is not cleared.

Menu Print (r) (c) (fg) (bg) (message)

The menu print command sequence is used to print information on the screen. For example,

> menu print 1 10 2 5 Hello there

Menu Input (r) (c) (fg) (bg) (length) (project variable)

Menu Input is used to locate the cursor at a particular position on the screen and to wait for a response at the keyboard. The response is of a maximum specified (length) and is assigned to the (project variable).

We shall see extensive use of the **menu** command in later Chapters.

Chapter 7 : Principles of Project Construction

Objectives

When you have completed this Section you will be able to :

- Appreciate the four phases involved in creating an Information System

Introduction

An Information System is a computer program that processes information. A typical example of such an Information System is the ORDERS file that we created in the Section dealing with the Data-Manager. Information can be entered into the ORDERS file and at a later time it can be processed to provide reports, analyses, graphs etc. Creating an Information System is a time consuming and, therefore, costly process. There are many ways of tackling the problem and most of them are inefficient and often ineffective. To minimize effort and time an Information System is designed using a well-defined sequence of tasks known as the **Information System Life Cycle.**

The Information System Life Cycle

The Life Cycle of an Information System has four stages. These are:

1. The Terms of Reference
2. Analysing the System
3. Designing the System
4. Implementing and Maintaining the System

The Terms of Reference

The Terms of Reference consist of a document in which the desired Information System is specified. This specification of the system is the initial process where the Client and System Designer define what the System will be expected to do. At this stage the primary concern is to define the overall needs of the Client. When these needs are clearly defined the Designer can then discuss the capabilities of the software. The purpose of this latter exercise is to allow the Client to review the needs in the light of capabilities of which he or she was hitherto unaware. It is most important that the specification be completely clear to both Client and Designer because radical changes at a later date can prove to be very costly. The situation that we shall consider is as follows:

You are the Designer and your Client is ABC Supplies Ltd. ABC Supplies already have a computerised Sales Competition System. To operate the System the user currently has to be aware of how the SMART Software System works. For example, the user must understand both the modular structure and the command structure so that information can be moved from one module to another. The management of ABC Supplies have decided to automate a large part of the Competition System so that a naive user can operate it. To enable this the following Terms of Reference have been arrived at:

> The Competition System should permit Sales Orders to be entered at different times during the course of a week.
>
> At the end of each week a Sales Summary in the form of a table is to be generated that displays the past four weeks' sales and the running total over the four-week period against individual Salespersons.
>
> At the end of every four-week period a Monthly Sales Summary is to be generated. This Summary will include a table and two graphs; a BAR Chart that displays each week's sales for each Salesperson and a PIE Chart that displays each Salesperson's share of the total monthly sales.
>
> Also, at the end of each four-week period the Top Salesperson will be identified and every Salesperson will be notified of the result of the competition in a personalised letter.

Designing the System

The next stage in the procedure is for you, the Designer, to interpret this specification by producing a report that describes the structure of the system from which it will eventually be designed.

The System Structure: The Competition System consists of a sequence of tasks that have to be performed to achieve the objectives of the system as laid down in the Terms of Reference. These tasks can be described as a sequence of modules, and the way the problem is attacked is to break the system down into a series of such modules in an organised manner. Starting with the entire System, it is broken down into smaller and smaller sub-modules until everything has been defined down to the smallest detail. This method is known as Top Down Design.

Top Down Design: Our design of the Sales Competition System consists of 3 Phases.

Phase 1: The System

ABC Supplies
Sales Competition
System

This is the simplest way to describe the entire system. It may seem trivial but we must start somewhere and this is the best place. We now break this system down into a series of modules.

Phase 2: System-to-Module Breakdown

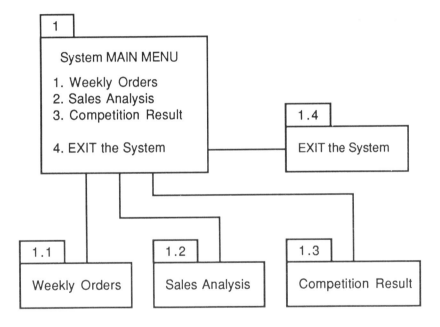

Here we see more clearly both what it is that the system is to achieve and how it will achieve it. On entry into the system the user will be presented with a menu of options. Notice the EXIT option - it is essential that escape routes be incorporated at all levels of the system's structure. Notice also the numbering of the modules. These numbers will serve as a useful reference during later phases in the system design.

The next phase is to break each individual module down into smaller component modules.

298 *Chapter 7: The Principles of Project Construction*

Phase 3: Module-to-Module Breakdown

The modules that need to be broken down further are those numbered 2, 3 and 4.

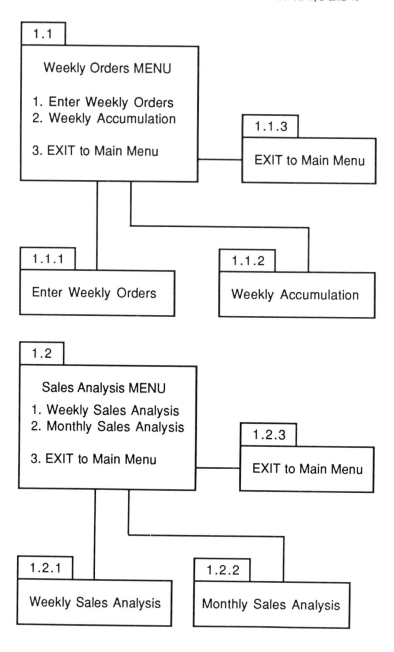

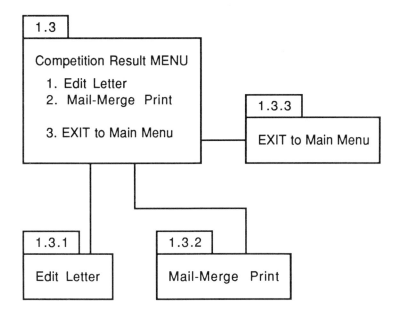

These diagrams display the structure of the problem and complete the design stage.

Developing the System

From the System Design we now proceed to develop the system. This development will consist of 4 further phases:

1. **Naming the Modules**
2. **Specifying the Action of the Modules**
3. **Pseudocoding the Modules**
4. **Constructing the Final System**

Phase 4: Naming the Modules

Each module will form a separate Project File and as such will require a name under which it will be stored on the disk. The names are as follows:

Project Filenames		Module Location
1:	MAINMENU	System
1.1:	MENUWO	Data-Manager
1.2:	MENUSA	Data-Manager

1.3:	MENUCR	Wordprocessor
1.4	SYSQUIT	System
1.1.1:	ORDERS	Data Manager
1.1.2:	WEEKLY	Data-Manager
1.*.3:	TOMAIN	Various
1.2.1:	WEEKSA	Spreadsheet
1.2.2:	MONTHSA	Spreadsheet and Wordprocessor
1.3.1:	LETTER	Wordprocessor
1.3.2:	PRINTOUT	Wordprocessor

The next phase consists of breaking down each module into its separate tasks.

Phase 5: Specifying the Action of the modules - Module-to-Task Breakdown

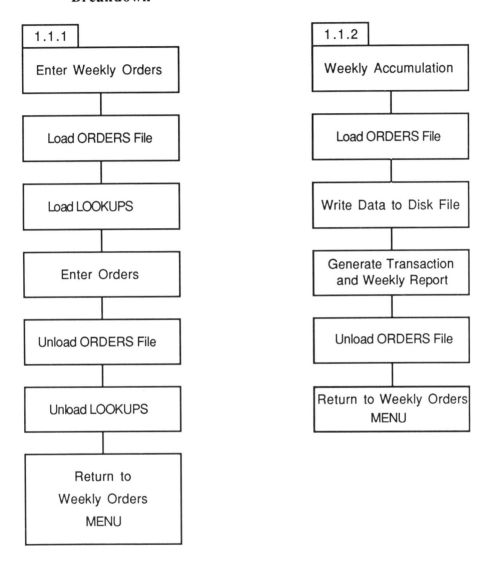

302 *Chapter 7: The Principles of Project Construction*

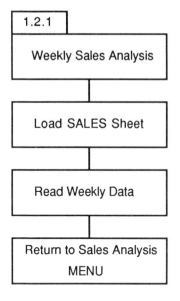
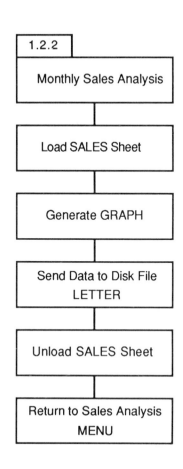

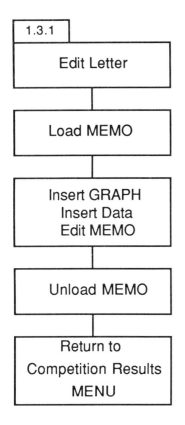 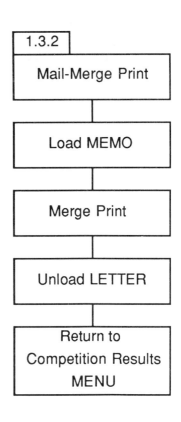

304 *Chapter 7: The Principles of Project Construction*

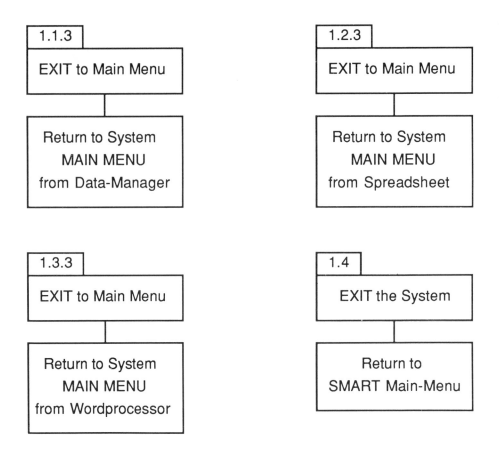

Phase 6: Pseudocoding the Modules

The next phase in the system development is to pseudocode each module. Pseudocode is 'pretend code' that is easily read by us but is not readable by the computer. The purpose of pseudocoding is to create a first try at a working program. A 'dry run' of this pseudocoded program can be performed by the system developer to ensure that it will work. Because the module-to-task breakdown adequately describes all the various tasks to be performed, the pseudocoding that we shall use will be very similar to this. The modules will not be listed in numerical order. Instead they will be grouped according to the System Module in which they operate.

Notice the COMMENT lines. Every project must be annotated so that its purpose can be ascertained by anyone else who reads it.

System Projects

There are just two projects operating from the System Main-Menu.

Module 1: System MAIN MENU

       Name: **MAINMENU**   Location: **SYSTEM**

```
COMMENT **********************
COMMENT * SYSTEM MAIN MENU *
COMMENT **********************

    print
        1. Enter weekly orders
        2. Produce sales analysis
        3. Deduce the competition winner

        4. EXIT the System

        Please enter your selection:

    input $selection
    test the value of $selection and route further execution
```

Module 1.4: EXIT the System

       Name: **SYSQUIT**   Location: **SYSTEM**

```
COMMENT *******************
COMMENT * EXIT THE SYSTEM *
COMMENT *******************

    goto DOS
```

Data-Manager Projects

There are four projects operating within the Data-Manager.

Module 1.1: Weekly Orders MENU

    Name: **MENUWO**   Location: **DATA-MANAGER**

COMMENT **************************
COMMENT * WEEKLY ORDERS MENU *
COMMENT **************************

    print
        1. Enter weekly orders
        2. Accumulate weekly orders

        3. EXIT to Main Menu

    Please enter your selection

    input $week
    test the value of $week and route further execution

Module 1.1.1: Enter Weekly Orders

    Name: **ORDERS**   Location: **DATA-MANAGER**

COMMENT **************************
COMMENT * ENTER WEEKLY ORDERS *
COMMENT **************************

    load ORDERS file
    load LOOKUPS
        enter orders
    unload ORDERS file
    remove LOOKUPS

    return to weekly orders menu

Module 1.1.2: Weekly Accumulation

    Name: **WEEKLY**   Location: **SPREADSHEET**

COMMENT **************************
COMMENT * WEEKLY ACCUMULATION *
COMMENT **************************

    load ORDERS file
    load CUSTOMER file
    perform TRANSACTION between ORDERS and CUSTOMER file
        write data to disk file
    unload ORDERS file
    return to weekly orders menu

Spreadsheet Projects

There are four projects operating within the Spreadsheet.

Module 1.2: Sales Analysis MENU

    Name: **MENUSA**   Location: **DATA-MANAGER**

COMMENT *************************
COMMENT * SALES ANALYSIS MENU *
COMMENT *************************

    print
        1. Analyse weekly sales
        2. Analyse monthly sales

        3. EXIT to Main Menu
    Please enter your selection:

    input $sales
    test the value of $sales and route further execution

Module 1.2.1: Monthly Sales Analysis

    Name: **MONTHSA**   Location: **SPREADSHEET**

```
COMMENT *****************************
COMMENT * MONTHLY SALES ANALYSIS *
COMMENT *****************************

        load SALES worksheet
        generate GRAPH
        write data to LETTER on disk
        return to system main menu
```

Module 1.*.3: EXIT To Main Menu

    Name: **TOMAIN**   Location: **VARIOUS**

```
COMMENT **********************
COMMENT * EXIT TO MAIN MENU  *
COMMENT **********************

        goto system main menu
```

Wordprocessor Projects

There are four projects operating within the Wordprocessor.

Module 1.3: Competition Result MENU

    Name: **MENUCR**   Location: **WORDPROCESSOR**

```
COMMENT ********************************
COMMENT * COMPETITION RESULTS MENU *
COMMENT ********************************

        print
            1. Edit letter
            2. Print letter

            3. EXIT to Main Menu
```

Please enter your selection:

input $competition
test the value of $competition and route further execution

Module 1.3.1: Edit Letter

Name: **LETTER**   Location: **WORDPROCESSOR**

COMMENT ***************
COMMENT * EDIT LETTER *
COMMENT ***************
    goto wordprocessor
    load MEMO document
    read data into MEMO
    read GRAPH into MEMO
        edit
    unload MEMO
    return to system menu

Module 1.3.2: Mail-Merge Print

Name: **PRINTOUT**   Location: **WORDPROCESSOR**

COMMENT ********************
COMMENT * MAIL-MERGE PRINT *
COMMENT ********************
    load MEMO document
        merge print
    unload MEMO
    return to system main menu

You will by now be aware of how involved the process of creating an Information system can become. It is just for this very reason that a systematic method is used in its development.

The final phase in the development of the project concerns the actual coding of each individual project.

Phase 7: Constructing the Final System

To construct the final system we have two possible options. We can write the pseudocoded modules using the Text-Editor. Having done this we can then move to Remember Edit mode and replace the pseudocode with actual code. Alternatively, we can move directly to Remember Edit mode and code each module from the hard copy of the pseudocoded modules.

To demonstrate the mechanics of actually writing Projects within each module we shall consider each SMART Module in turn in the following four Chapters.

Chapter 8 : The System Main Menu

Objectives

When you have completed this Chapter you will be able to:

- Create project files within the System Main Menu
- Run a project from the Introductory Screen

Introduction

We have seen from the last Chapter that the ABC Supplies Competition System will be run from the System Main Menu as displayed on the Introductory Screen. We shall have two project modules here:

> The Main System Menu : MAINMENU
> The System EXIT : SYSQUIT

The Main System Menu

From Command list 3 on the Introductory Screen enter the following sequence of commands:

PROMPT	ENTER
	R: Remember
Select option: Compile Delete Edit Finish Help Print Start:	E: Edit
Enter project filename:	MAINMENU

You are now faced with the **Project Editor** screen. This is where the project will be coded. Enter in the following code:

```
COMMENT ******************************
COMMENT * SET THE SCREEN FOR DISPLAY *
COMMENT ******************************

         repaint on
```

312 Chapter 8: The System Main Menu

```
COMMENT *********************************
COMMENT * PRINT THE MENU INFORMATION   *
COMMENT *********************************

        menu clear 10 1
        menu print 1 3 10 1 ABC Supplies
        menu print 1 65 10 1 SYSTEM MENU
        menu print 3 26 10 1 ORDER ENTRY, SALES ANALYSIS
        menu print 4 38 10 1 AND
        menu print 5 31 10 1 COMPETITION SYSTEM
        menu print 9 28 10 1 1. Weekly Orders
        menu print 10 28 10 1 2. Sales Analysis
        menu print 11 28 10 1 3. Competition Winner
        menu print 13 28 10 1 4. EXIT the System
        menu print 16 28 10 1 Please enter your selection

COMMENT *********************************
COMMENT * PREPARE FOR KEYBOARD INPUT *
COMMENT *********************************

        LABEL INPUT menu input 16 57 10 1 1 $mainmenu

COMMENT *********************************
COMMENT * ISSUE DELAY WARNING TO USER   *
COMMENT *********************************

        menu clear box 18 32 20 46 10 1
        menu print 19 34 15 1 PLEASE WAIT

COMMENT *********************************
COMMENT * TURN OFF SCREEN DISPLAY SET *
COMMENT *********************************

        repaint off

COMMENT ******************************************************
COMMENT * TEST INPUT & DIRECT FLOW OF FUTURE EXECUTION *
COMMENT ******************************************************

        %1=$mainmenu
        if %1=1 then jump data-manager project-file MENUWO
        if %1=2 then jump spreadsheet project-file MENUSA
        if %1=3 then jump wordprocessor project-file MENUCR
```

> **if %1=4 then execute SYSQUIT**
>
> **JUMP INPUT**

When this is complete it must be **Compiled** to create a file that the computer can read and obey. This is an automatic process at this stage. Press **F10** and the prompt:

> **Compiling ...**

appears in the Command Area. When the project has been compiled it is then ready to use.

PROMPT	ENTER
	E: Execute
Enter project filename:	MAINMENU

Immediately the following screen appears:

```
┌─ ABC Supplies ─────────────────── SYSTEM MENU ─┐
│                                                │
│           ORDER ENTRY, SALES ANALYSIS          │
│                      AND                       │
│              COMPETITION SYSTEM                │
│                                                │
│              1. Weekly Orders                  │
│              2. Sales Analysis                 │
│              3. Competition Winner             │
│                                                │
│              4. EXIT the System                │
│                                                │
│          Please enter your selection: -        │
│                                                │
└────────────────────────────────────────────────┘
```

Make sure that you can correlate the coding you have just entered with the screen display before you.

When the user presses a key then the value of that key is assigned to the variable **$mainmenu**. After this a message appears at the bottom of the Display Window:

> Please wait ...

The purpose of this message is to assure the user that all is well. There will be a time lag between the user entering a number at the keyboard and the next screen display. Without the message a user may think that something has gone wrong.

The progam then assigns the value of **$mainmenu** to the **parameter variable** **%1**. This value is then tested using the if ... then statements. If **%1** has a value **1, 2** or **3** then the flow of execution is to another project-file in another module. If **%1 =4** the the computer is instructed to **execute** a project file from the System Main Menu called **SYSQUIT**. This we shall code next.

If the input at the keyboard happened to be none of these four numbers then all four tests would fail and execution would move to the:

JUMP INPUT

command. This instructs the computer to re-start execution from the line:

LABEL INPUT

When it does this it merely returns back to the 'waiting for input' stage. Try it.

Next we give the coding for **SYSQUIT**.

```
COMMENT ***************************
COMMENT * EXIT THE SMART SYSTEM *
COMMENT ***************************

      quit
```

Wasn't that hard? This command causes the computer to quit the SMART System and return the user to **DOS**. Whilst we are developing the complete system we shall continually return to this menu from various other modules. The only way out of the project will then be to input **4** and leave SMART altogether. This can be very frustrating, continually leaving and re-entering the SMART System. To avoid this frustration replace the **quit** by **stop** in **SYSQUIT**. Then execution of **SYSQUIT** will then leave you in SMART. Only when the system is completely developed need you replace the **stop** by **quit**.

Chapter 9 : The Data-Manager

Objectives

When you have completed this Chapter you will be able to:

- Create project files in the Data-Manager
- Run project files from the Data-Manager

Introduction

As we saw from the Project Module **MAINMENU** the link between the Project Module **MAINMENU** and the Data-Manager is the Project Module **MENUWO**. We shall now code this along with the other three modules in the Data-Manager - **ORDERS**, **WEEKLY** and **TOMAIN**.

The Data-Manager MENU

From Command list 5 in the Data-Manager enter the following sequence of commands:

PROMPT	ENTER
	R: Remember
Select option: Compile Delete Edit Finish Help Print Start:	E: Edit
Enter project filename:	MENUWO

You are now faced with the **Project Editor** screen. Enter in the following coding:

```
COMMENT ***********************
COMMENT * LABEL THE FIRST LINE *
COMMENT ***********************

        LABEL START

COMMENT *******************************
COMMENT * SET THE SCREEN FOR DISPLAY *
COMMENT *******************************

        repaint on
```

316 *Chapter 9: Project Processing - The Data-Manager*

```
COMMENT ********************************
COMMENT * PRINT THE MENU INFORMATION  *
COMMENT ********************************

        menu clear 10 1
        menu print 1 3 10 1 ABC Supplies
        menu print 1 65 10 1 ORDERS MENU
        menu print 3 32 10 1 WEEKLY ORDERS
        menu print 8 25 10 1 1. Enter Weekly Orders
        menu print 9 25 10 1 2. Accumulate Weekly Orders
        menu print 11 25 10 1 3. EXIT to Main Menu
        menu print 13 25 10 1 Please enter your selection:

COMMENT ********************************
COMMENT * PREPARE FOR KEYBOARD INPUT *
COMMENT ********************************

        menu input 13 54 10 1 1 $weekly

COMMENT ********************************
COMMENT * ISSUE DELAY WARNING TO USER *
COMMENT ********************************

        menu clear box 18 32 20 46 10 1
        menu print 19 34 15 1 PLEASE WAIT

COMMENT ********************************
COMMENT * TURN OFF SCREEN DISPLAY SET *
COMMENT ********************************

        repaint off

COMMENT **************************************
COMMENT * TEST INPUT & DIRECT FLOW OF EXECUTION *
COMMENT **************************************

        %2=$weekly
        if %2=1 then execute ORDERS
        if %2=2 then execute WEEKLY
        if %2=3 then execute TOMAIN

        JUMP START
```

Press **F10** to complete and then **Execute** to ensure the coding is correct. If it is then press

F10 and move to the **Main Menu** - **Execute** the project **MAINMENU** and select the option **1** to end up with the screen display of **MENUWO** in the Data-Manager. Are you beginning to see how the system operates?

Now we shall code the Project Module **ORDERS** - you will remember we already have this coding from Section 2. We shall reproduce it here with **COMMENTS** added.

ORDERS

```
COMMENT ****************************
COMMENT * SPLIT WINDOW 1 INTO TWO *
COMMENT ****************************

        split vertical 2 38

COMMENT ******************************************
COMMENT * LOAD ORDERS AND ORDER ON KEY [1]  *
COMMENT ******************************************

        load ORDERS screen ORDERS order key [1]

COMMENT ****************************
COMMENT * SPLIT WINDOW 2 INTO TWO *
COMMENT ****************************

        goto window 2 split vertical 2 59

COMMENT ***********************************************
COMMENT * LOAD CUSTOMERS AND ORDER ON KEY [1]  *
COMMENT ***********************************************

        load CUSTOMER screen customer order key [1]

COMMENT ******************************************************
COMMENT * LOAD STOCK INTO WINDOW 3 & ORDER ON KEY [1]  *
COMMENT ******************************************************

        goto window 3
        load STOCK screen STOCK
        order key [1]
```

COMMENT **************************
COMMENT * LOAD ALL FOUR LOOKUPS *
COMMENT **************************

       lookup load ORDCUST
       lookup load ORDSTOC1
       lookup load ORDSTOC2
       lookup load ORDSTOC3
       lookup load ORDSTOC4

COMMENT ********************************
COMMENT * SET THE SCREEN FOR DISPLAY *
COMMENT ********************************

       repaint on

COMMENT *******************************
COMMENT * ZOOM INTO ORDERS RECORDS *
COMMENT *******************************

       goto window 1 zoom

COMMENT **
COMMENT * ENTER INFORMATION INTO ORDERS RECORDS *
COMMENT **

       enter

COMMENT ****************************
COMMENT * ZOOM OUT OF WINDOW 1 *
COMMENT ****************************

       zoom

COMMENT ***************************************
COMMENT * TURN OFF THE SCREEN DISPLAY SET *
COMMENT ***************************************

       repaint off

```
COMMENT ********************************
COMMENT * ISSUE DELAY WARNING TO USER *
COMMENT ********************************

        menu clear 10 1
        menu clear box 10 32 12 46 10 1
        menu print 11 34 15 1 PLEASE WAIT

COMMENT ****************************************************
COMMENT * UNLOAD FILES, CLOSE WINDOWS, REMOVE LOOKUPS *
COMMENT ****************************************************

        unload all
        close
        close
        lookup remove ORDCUST
        lookup remove ORDSTOC1
        lookup remove ORDSTOC2
        lookup remove ORDSTOC3
        lookup remove ORDSTOC4
```

WEEKLY

Next we shall code the Data-Manager Project Module **WEEKLY**:

```
COMMENT ********************************
COMMENT * SET THE SCREEN FOR DISPLAY *
COMMENT ********************************

        repaint off

COMMENT ********************************
COMMENT * ISSUE DELAY WARNING TO USER *
COMMENT ********************************

        menu clear 10 1
        menu clear box 10 32 12 46 10 1
        menu print 11 34 15 1 PLEASE WAIT
```

```
COMMENT ***************************
COMMENT * SPLIT WINDOW 1 INTO TWO *
COMMENT ***************************

     split vertical 2 39

COMMENT *********************************************************
COMMENT * LOAD ORDERS INTO WINDOW 1 & ORDER ON KEY [3]  *
COMMENT *********************************************************

     load ORDERS screen ORDERS order key [3]

COMMENT *********************************************************
COMMENT * LOAD CUSTOMERS TO WINDOW 2, ORDER ON KEY [1] *
COMMENT *********************************************************

     goto window 2 load CUSTOMER screen customer order key [1]

COMMENT *********************************************************
COMMENT * TRANSFER [11] TO [10], SET [10] = 0 IN ALL RECORDS *
COMMENT *********************************************************

     LABEL TRANSFER

     %1 = record
     rec-number [10] = [11]
     [11] = 0
     goto record next
     %2 = record rec-number
     if %1 = %2 then JUMP OUT
     JUMP TRANSFER

COMMENT *****************
COMMENT * INSERT LABEL  *
COMMENT *****************

     LABEL OUT

COMMENT ********************************
COMMENT * ORDER CUSTOMERS ON KEY [1] *
COMMENT ********************************

     order key [1]
```

```
COMMENT ***********************************************
COMMENT * TRANSACT FROM ORDERS TO CUSTOMERS  *
COMMENT ***********************************************

        transactions predefined TOTVALUE no-audit

COMMENT *******************************
COMMENT * ORDER CUSTOMERS ON KEY [1] *
COMMENT *******************************

        order key [1]


COMMENT ****************************
COMMENT * WRITE SUMMARY TO DISK *
COMMENT ****************************

        write summarized predefined WEEK text WEEK

COMMENT **************************************
COMMENT * UNLOAD ALL AND CLOSE WINDOW 2 *
COMMENT **************************************

        unload all close
```

This coding does not require much further explanation as it was covered in depth in Section 2. There are some minor changes such as **transaction name** and **holding file name** and the only major changes are the sections of code dealing with the transfer of information between fields in the CUSTOMERS file and the nature of the **summary** sent to **WEEK**. We shall look at these a little more closely.

Transfer of Information

We wish to place the total of this month's sales in field **ThisMonthSales** - [11] - of the CUSTOMER file but we do not wish to lose the record of the current contents of [11]. To do this we assign the contents of [11] to [10] and then set [10] to **zero** in each record. Having done this we **Transact** the individual **Total Value** of each record in the ORDER file into the CUSTOMERS file by **addition**. This updates the CUSTOMER file to the end of the four week period. Next we wish to summarize this information in the CUSTOMER file for later analysis in the Spreadsheet.

LABEL TRANSFER
%1 = record rec-number   This assigns the record number to %1.

[10] = [11]   This transfers the contents of **[11]** to **[10]**. That is, LastMonthSales now takes on the value of ThisMonthSales.

[11] = 0   Sets ThisMonthSales to zero.

goto record next   If you 'goto record next' from the last record in the file
file
%2 = record rec-number   you stay in the last record of the file. When this
if %1 = %2 then JUMP OUT   happens, execution moves out of this block of coding and moves to LABEL OUT.

JUMP TRANSFER

TOMAIN

Finally, we must code the Data-Manager Project Module **TOMAIN**. This is as follows:

```
COMMENT ***************************************************
COMMENT * LEAVE DATA-MANAGER & RETURN TO MAINMENU *
COMMENT ***************************************************
```

    jump main-menu project-file MAINMENU

Chapter 10 : The Spreadsheet

Objectives

When you have completed this Chapter you will be able to:

- Create a project file within the Spreadsheet Module
- Execute a project file from the Spreadsheet

Introduction

There are three Project Modules in the Spreadsheet, **WEEKSA**, **MONTHSA** and **TOMAIN**.

WEEKSA

At the end of every week the summarized information written to disk file WEEK from the Data-Manager will be read into the Spreadsheet to update the SALES Worksheet. The information in WEEK consists of the week's total sales by each Salesperson and is in the form of two columns - the first the name of the Salesperson and the second the amount of weekly sales made. This information will be inserted in the **WEEK 4** column of SALES. We do not wish to lose the information currently in **WEEK4** as this will now be relevant to **WEEK 3**. As a result we must **Move WEEK 4 to WEEK 3, WEEK 3 to WEEK 2** and **WEEK 2 to WEEK1**. When this is done the Worksheet is printed out for the use of the Sales Manager. The coding follows:

```
COMMENT *************************
COMMENT * LOAD WORKSHEET SALES *
COMMENT *************************

        load SALES

COMMENT *************************
COMMENT * MOVE WEEK2 TO WEEK 1 *
COMMENT *************************

        @r5c4 move block r5:10c3 to r5c2
```

```
COMMENT **************************
COMMENT * MOVE WEEK 3 TO WEEK 2 *
COMMENT **************************

        @r5c3 move block r5:10c4 to r5c3

COMMENT **************************
COMMENT * MOVE WEEK 4 TO WEEK 3 *
COMMENT **************************

        @r5c2 move block r5:10c5 to r5c4

COMMENT *******************************
COMMENT * AT R1C1 READ IN WEEK SHEET *
COMMENT *******************************

        @r1c1 read text WEEK

COMMENT ************************************************
COMMENT * WRITE COLUMN 2 OF WEEK INTO WEEK 4 OF SALES *
COMMENT ************************************************

        @r1c1 goto SALES @r5c5 copy from WEEK.r2:7c2 to r5:10c5

COMMENT **********************************
COMMENT * RECALCULATE THE WORKSHEET *
COMMENT **********************************

        recalc

COMMENT **********************************
COMMENT * SAVE UPDATED COPY OF SALES *
COMMENT **********************************

        save SALES

COMMENT **********************************
COMMENT * PRINT ENTIRE UPDATED SHEET *
COMMENT **********************************

        print text worksheet printer normal copies 1
```

```
COMMENT ********************
COMMENT * UNLOAD ALL FILES  *
COMMENT ********************

        unload all
```

MONTHSA

At the end of each four-week period the Sales Manager produces a personalised circular memo that contains:

>   a pie chart of the month's sales
>   a table of monthly sales against salesperson
>   an indication of the winner of that period's prize

This is performed in the Project Module **MONTHSA** whose coding follows:

```
COMMENT ***************************
COMMENT * LOAD WORKSHEET SALES   *
COMMENT ***************************

        @r1c1 load SALES

COMMENT ************************************
COMMENT * GENERATE A PREDEFINED GRAPH *
COMMENT ************************************

        graphics generate TOTSALES black/white screen TOTSALES

COMMENT ************************************
COMMENT * DELETE THE TOP 4 ROWS OF SALES *
COMMENT ************************************

        @r1c1 delete rows 4

COMMENT *************************
COMMENT * DELETE COLUMNS 2 TO 5 *
COMMENT *************************

        @r1c2 delete columns 4
```

```
COMMENT ****************************
COMMENT * DELETE THE BOTTOM 3 ROWS *
COMMENT ****************************

        @r7c2 delete rows 3

COMMENT ********************************************************
COMMENT * SORT THE TWO REMAINING COLUMNS ON COLUMN 2 *
COMMENT ********************************************************

        @r1c1 sort r1:6c1:2 descending using column 2

COMMENT ***************************
COMMENT * ANNOTATE TOP ENTRY *
COMMENT ***************************

        @r1c3 enter text !!! This Month's Winner !!!

COMMENT *******************************
COMMENT * WRITE WORKSHEET TO DISK *
COMMENT *******************************

        write worksheet text file LETTER

COMMENT *********************************
COMMENT * UNLOAD BUT NOT SAVE SHEET *
COMMENT *********************************

        unload
```

The action of this is to trim down the SALES Worksheet until the only information remaining consists of the sales personnel names and their monthly sales figures. These are then sorted in descending order on the sales figures. The top name then has the highest sales figure and is, therefore, the winner of that period's prize. This information is saved in the text file LETTER for later insertion into the memo within the Wordprocessor.

The final Project Module is **TOMAIN** and this is identical to the **TOMAIN** project-file in the Data-Manager.

Chapter 11 : The Wordprocessor

Objectives

When you have read this Chapter you will be able to:

- Create project files within the Wordprocessor
- Execute a project file from within the Wordprocessor

Introduction

There are three Project Modules in the Wordprocessor, **EDIT**, **PRINT** and **TOMAIN**. The final stage in the periodic competition run by ABC Supplies is completed by the printing of a personalised memo to all the sales personnel. This is accomplished by the Project Module **PRINT**. Before printing the memo it has to be edited. A graph has to be inserted and a table of sales figures indicating who has won the competition for this period. This is performed within the Project Module **EDIT**.

EDIT

The coding for this module now follows:

```
COMMENT **************************
COMMENT * LOAD DOCUMENT MEMO     *
COMMENT **************************

        load MEMO

COMMENT ****************************************
COMMENT * INSERT PIE CHART AT MARKER MA1       *
COMMENT ****************************************

        goto ma1 graphics insert TOTSALES small right-justified
```

328   *Chapter 11: The Wordprocessor*

```
COMMENT ***********************************
COMMENT * INSERT TABLE AT MARKER MA2  *
COMMENT ***********************************

        goto ma2 read letter

COMMENT ***********************************************
COMMENT * SAVE MEMO AS NEWMEMO AND UNLOAD *
COMMENT ***********************************************

        save NEWMEMO unload
```

PRINT

The coding for **PRINT** follows:

```
COMMENT *******************************
COMMENT * TURN OFF SCREEN DISPLAY *
COMMENT *******************************

        repaint off

COMMENT ***********************************
COMMENT * ISSUE DELAY WARNING TO USER *
COMMENT ***********************************

        menu clear 10 1
        menu clear box 10 32 12 46 10 1
        menu print 11 34 15 1 PLEASE WAIT

COMMENT *********************************
COMMENT * LOAD DOCUMENT NEWMEMO  *
COMMENT *********************************

        load NEWMEMO

COMMENT *************************************************
COMMENT * PRINT THE PERSONALISED CIRCULAR *
COMMENT *************************************************

        merge file normal NAMES
```

The third and final Project Module in the Wordprocessor is **TOMAIN** and this is identical to the **TOMAIN** Project Modules in both the Data-Manager and the Spreadsheet.

Chapter 12 : Implementation And Maintenance

Objectives

When you have completed this Chapter you will be able to:

- Appreciate what is necessary to implement the complete project
- Appreciate the role of maintenance in the life cycle of an Information System

Introduction

Before the Competition System can be implemented it has to be tested. Before it can be tested all the necessary files have to be in place and available for use. Many of the files we have already created as we progressed through the pages of this book. A number of files have yet to be created by you.

Implementation

What follows is a list of all those files necessary to implement the ABC Supplies Sales Competition System:

File	Description
ORDERS	A file of orders
CUSTOMER	A file of customers
STOCK	A file of stock
ORDCUST	A lookup between ORDERS and CUSTOMER
ORDSTOC1	A lookup between ORDERS and STOCK
ORDSTOC2	A lookup between ORDERS and STOCK
ORDSTOC3	A lookup between ORDERS and STOCK
ORDSTOC4	A lookup between ORDERS and STOCK
TOTVALUE	A transaction between ORDERS and CUSTOMER
WEEK	A summary of information in CUSTOMERS
SALES	A spreadsheet of sales

TOTSALES	A graphics definition using SALES
MEMO	A document suitable marked with ma1 and ma2
NAMES	A text file of sales personnel names

Maintenance

Maintenance of an Information system continues during the entire lifetime of the system until it is replaced by an alternative system. Maintenance involves modifying the system to add new features as well as correcting any errors that have gone unnoticed during the testing and implementation phase.

There are lots of features that could be added to this system. It could be used, for example, as the basis for a Sales Order Processing system. This would require the generation of INVOICES and the ability to update the STOCK file. Both the CUSTOMER file and the NAMES text file need to be updateable. All these features can be added fairly straightforwardly provided you follow the sequence of design and development phases described here.

Section 7 : The Communications Module

This Section consists of a discussion of the SMART Communications module. It is not to be read as definitive but rather as a guide to what the Communications package can offer. There are five chapters in this Section. They are:

- **Computer Communication**
- **The SMART Communications Module**
- **Establishing Contact as Originator**
- **Eatablishing Contact in Answer Mode**
- **The SMART Communication Commands**

Chapter 1 : Computer Communications

Objectives

When you have read this Chapter you will be able to:

- Appreciate the role of remote communication
- Understand the need for a Communications Program
- Appreciate the two major functions of the SMART Communications Module

Introduction

We all communicate with each other. We communicate by talking, by being silent, by the way we stand and by the way we gesticulate. When we communicate we transfer information from ourselves to another person. This is what computers do. Computers are involved with transmitting information from one location to another. We communicate to the computer by typing information into the keyboard. The computer communicates to us by printing characters on the monitor screen or at the printer. The computer communicates with its own component parts down electrical pathways called **buses**. The computer communicates with a disk drive down a **bus**. The computer communicates with its own memory store down a **bus**. So really, communication is what computers are all about. So much so that computers can communicate to other computers.

Computer-to-Computer Communications

Two computers can communicate with each other by being physically connected together by a wire or fibre optic cable. They can also communicate with each other without the physical connection by using radio waves. A computer in the USA can communicate with a computer in Europe by using a satellite radio link. What this Section is about is how we arrange for two remote computers to 'talk to each other'.

Talking to Each Other

When two computers talk to each other they can perform one of two major functions:

- One acts as a terminal to the other. We call this **terminal emulation**.
- One transmits and/or receives files to and from the other. We call this **file transfer**.

Terminal Emulation

When one computer emulates a terminal it is capable of making the connection between itself and the remote computer. It usually does this by using a device called a **modem** that permits the computer to dial the remote computer and establish contact when the remote computer **answers** the phone. Terminal emulation also permits information received to be selectively **captured** and stored in a disk file for later use.

File Transfer

Once communication has been established between two computers then files can be transferred from one to the other.

In summary, by using a Communication Program two or more computers can share their resources. These resources include storage of information on remote disks and software installed on one computer and used by another computer. Clearly, to facilitate all this, a Communication Program is needed.

The SMART Communications Module

The SMART Communications Module is a Communications Program that permits your computer to talk to another computer. Before we look at the SMART Communications Module in detail we must become familiar with a number of important communications terms.

> **Originate Mode** Originate Mode refers to the state of the computer wishing to establish contact with a remote computer. Such a computer in Originate Mode is called the **originating computer**. The contact is made by **dialling** the remote computer down a telephone line. For this to succeed the remote computer must be in **Answer Mode**.

> **Answer Mode** This is the mode of the remote computer answering the call made by the computer wishing to establish contact. During answer mode all information received at the remote computer is **echoed** on the screen - it is printed on the screen as it is received.

Carrier The Carrier is an audible tone that signals the remote computer to maintain the contact. The Carrier must be present whenever information interchange takes place.

Logging On Logging On refers to the processes performed at one computer to gain access to another computer. Usually logging on requires using your name and a password to identify yourself and your authority to use the resources of the remote computer. Logging on is done after contact has been established between the two computers.

Transmit and Receive When one computer sends information to another computer it is said to be **transmitting**. When it is capturing information from another computer it is said to be **receiving**.

Capture and Buffer A **Buffer** is a section of the computer's memory used to store incoming information. To permit this information to be placed in the buffer the computer must be in **Capture Mode**. A computer in Capture Mode will receive information and send it to the screen, a buffer or to a disk file. Information sent to the screen is lost as soon as it scrolls off the screen but information in a buffer or on a disk is retained until it is intentionally cleared.

Communications Settings The Communications Settings consist of the values of all the parameters necessary to maintain communications between two computers. These settings form a **protocol** or agreement between the two computers regarding the methods to be used to transmit information between them. Rather than enter all the appropriate settings every time a contact is to be made they are stored in a disk file called **a Profile**.

Duplex and Filter If your computer is in contact with another computer then characters typed at your keyboard will or will not be echoed on your screen. If they are echoed on your screen then your computer is said to be operating **Half Duplex Mode**. If they are not so echoed then your computer is in **Full Duplex Mode**. Usually the originating computer is in Full duplex and the answering computer is in Half Duplex. A **Filter** is a group of keyboard characters that cannot be used. Two filters can be defined. The Terminal Filter designates which characters are displayed on the screen and the Capture Filter determines which characters are not to be retained when received.

XMODEM XMODEM is an industry standard protocol of information transfer between two computers.

Chapter 2 : The Communications Module

Objectives

When you have completed this Chapter you will be able to:

- Recognise the various screens associated with the Communications Module
- Establish the Communications Settings

Introduction

When the SMART Communications Module is entered from the Introductory screen the first screen displayed is the **Status Screen**. When contact has been successfully established between two computers then interaction takes place with another screen, the **Terminal Screen**.

The Status Screen

Selecting C for **Communications** from the Introductory Screen results in the following display:

Chapter 2: The Communications Module

```
                        Originate Mode
            Name:      Smart Default settings
            Number:    -- None --
```

Modem Parameters		Settings	
Modem:	1	Capture Filters:	Off
Port:	Serial - 1	Terminal Filters:	Off
Speed:	300	Keyboard:	Default
Data-length:	8	Emulation:	None
Parity:	NONE	Attention Key:	Escape
Stop-bits:	1	Switch Key:	F3
Duplex:	Full	Break Key:	Alt-B

Command list 1: **Answer** Capture Dial Hangup Receive Settings Transmit

Capture   None
ANSWER - answer phone after waiting for it to ring   Null

This is the display of the current Communications Settings. They are:

Modem: When two computers talk to each other they send information along cables. If those cables join onto the telephone system so that the information flows down the telephone network a **modem** will be required. The modem translates the information transmitted by the computer into a signal that can be carried by the telephone cabling system. The computer at the other end of the line will also possess a modem to re-translate the signal back into computer-readable form. If the two computers are simply connected to each other with a **serial** cable then no modem is required and option 1 signifies this - the **Null Modem**.

Port: This signifies which serial port will be used - there is a choice of **Serial-1** or **Serial-2**.

Speed: The **Speed** setting determines how fast the information will be transmitted. The options are:

   110, 300, 600, 1200, 2400, 4800, 9600

Data-length: Information is transmitted in a sequence of **characters**, each character being composed of a sequence of **bits** - 0s or 1s. The **Data-length** fixes the number of bits that combine together to form a character. The options are 5, 6, 7 or 8.

Parity: Parity is a form of error checking to ensure that the character sent is the character received.

Stop-bits: Stop-bits are inserted at the end of each character to inform the receiving computer when the bits have defined the character. The options are 1.5, 1 or 2

Duplex: This defines which computer is responsible for echoing the typed characters. The options are Full and Half.

The Terminal Screen

```
Command list 1: Answer Capture Dial Hangup Receive Settings Transmit

Capture None
ANSWER - answer phone after waiting for it to ring
```

The terminal screen is obtained from the Settings Screen by pressing the Switch Key - usually defined in the Settings Screen as **F3**. The screen described above is the terminal screen in Command Mode. There is an alternative screen which is the terminal screen in Terminal Mode. Switching back and forth between these two screens is done using the **Attention** key - usually defined as the **Esc** key.

Terminal Mode : Terminal mode permits you to type characters that will be sent to the other computer. It also permits you to receive characters from the other computer.

Command Mode : In Command Mode the typed characters are interpreted as commands rather than as characters to be sent to another computer. It is in Command

Mode that you communicate to your computer.

Establishing the Communication Settings

The Settings are established by selecting the **Settings** command on Command list 1.

PROMPT	ENTER
	S: Settings
Select option: Edit Load Save	E: Edit

The following screen appears:

```
┌─ Communications Profile ─────────────────────────┐
│   Name or Prompt:   Smart Default settings       │
│   Mode: Originate  Answer                        │
│   Add Linefeeds:   Yes  No                       │
│   Autowrap:  Yes  No                             │
│   Select Emulation Type:   1                     │
│       1) Dumb Terminal                           │
│       2) Ansi Terminal                           │
│       3) VT100\102                               │
│       4) VT52                                    │
│   Keyboard definition file:                      │
│   Mask incoming data to seven bits:   Yes  No    │
│   Enable xon/xoff:   Yes  No                     │
│   Tab spacing:  8                                │
│   Terminal-Filter on:  Yes  No                   │
│   Capture Filter on:  Yes  No                    │
│   Dead time limit (seconds):   360               │
└──────────────────────────────────────────────────┘
```

F1 Help   F2 Edit text   F3 Blank text   F10 Finished
settings edit
Capture: none
SETTINGS - edit, load or save Communications settings

There are four pages of information required to define the settings and you can review them by pressing **PgUp** and **PgDn**. We shall not spend any more time discussing the settings, save to say that their values depend on both your computer and the computer you are communicating with. It is not the intention of this Section to convert you into a communications expert. The purpose of the Section is to expose you to the various considerations involved when two computers communicate and how SMART accomodates them. For a full description of the settings you are referred to the SMART System Manual.

Chapter 3 : Establishing Contact As Originator

Objectives

When you have completed this Chapter you will be able to:

- Appreciate how to make a communications connection to a remote computer
- Appreciate the methods used whereby information is transferred from one computer to another
- Close down the communications link

Introduction

When all the appropriate Settings have been defined and your computer is in the correct state for establishing contact with a remote computer the first thing to do is to **ring the other computer up and wait for an answer.**

Making a Call

To establish contact with a remote computer via a telephone line your computer must be in **Terminal Mode** with the Command list displayed. To enable this from the Settings Screen press **F3**. This will put you in Terminal Mode. If Command list 1 is not displayed then press **Esc** after which it will be. On Command list 1 enter the follwing sequence of commands:

PROMPT	ENTER
	D: Dial
Select option: Carrier Voice	C: Carrier
Enter number:	XXX XXX XXXX

The Carrier option tells the computer to expect a carrier signal after dialling the number. After dialling the number a countdown timer starts to count off the seconds. The number of seconds of countdown is set in the Communication Profile. This gives the time allowed for the remote computer to **answer the phone**. If no answer is received then the command is terminated so long as you have set the number of re-dials to zero. Otherwise the computer re-dials the remote computer up to the set number of times.

The Voice option permits the user to speak on the phone prior to making the connection. After speaking, the remote computer operator will place the handset into a modem unit and the sender will then **Goto Carrier** after which the two computers are connected.

Entering Commands

When contact is established, information can be sent to the remote computer either from a data file stored on your disk or from you via the keyboard. If the information is from you via the keyboard the Terminal Screen must be in Terminal Mode. If you wish to send information from a file you must instruct your computer to do this. To issue instructions to your own computer from the Terminal Screen you must be in Command Mode. Commands are then issued in the usual way by selecting options from lists of availble commands.

If you wished to use a program that was stored on the remote computer you would have to use instructions appropriate to the remote computer. In this case you would issue the commands in Terminal Mode.

Capture Mode

It may be that you wish to download information held on the remote computer into your computer. In this case you must be in Capture mode. To put your computer in Capture Mode from the Terminal Screen move to Command Mode and select the following from command list 1:

PROMPT   **ENTER**

                                                                    C: Capture

Select option: Buffer File Printer

We shall look at each of these three options in turn.

> **Buffer:** This option enters the received characters into an internal memory store called a Buffer. Selecting Buffer presents the following options:
>
> **Select option: Begin Clear End Save View**
>
> Clearly **Begin** and **End** form the start and finish of reception. **View** permits the Buffer contents to be viewed on the screen and **Save** will save the buffer contents in a named file. **Clear** will empty the buffer.
>
> **Printer:** Again this choice is followed by a **Begin** or **End** selection. Choosing this

option sends all received information straight to the printer.

File: Selecting **File Begin** request a filename to be given. Once given, the received information is sent directly to the file. **File End** terminates the reception.

Transmitting Files

As well as Capturing files from a remote computer it is possible to **Transmit** the other way. The **Transmit** command is found on Command list 1:

PROMPT   ENTER
                                          T: Transmit
Select option: Text-File   XMODEM

> **Text Files**: Text files should contain only standard ASCII characters. All SMART Worksheets, database files, document files or definition files should not be transmitted using this option.
>
> **XMODEM Protocol**: The XMODEM Protocol sends files in blocks of 128 characters after which it is checked for errors. If errors are detected in a block the block is re-transmitted. If errors are still detected after 10 attempts the transmission is aborted.

Hangup

When all information transfer is complete the **Hangup** command is used to break the communication link - the phone is **hung up**.

Chapter 4: Establishing Contact In Answer Mode

Objectives

When you have completed this Chapter you will be able to:

- Appreciate how the Answer Mode operates
- Appreciate the Remote Command Mode and the safeguards that can be imposed on unauthorised access to the answering machine

Introduction

So far we have been concerned with the procedures involved in originating a communications link. We now consider the other side of the picture, namely, how we respond to another originator attempting to communicate with us.

Answer Mode

For our computer to respond to another computer that is attempting to establish a communications link, our computer must be in **Answer Mode**. This is achieved from the Terminal Screen in Command Mode on command list 1:

PROMPT	ENTER
	A: Answer

The system of linked computers is then automatically put into Half Duplex Mode so that the caller can see on the screen what is typed at the keyboard. In Answer Mode the answering computer waits for the phone to ring. When the phone starts to ring it will wait for a predefined number of rings before **picking up** the phone and establishing the communiations contact. If the phone stops ringing before the set number of rings, the answering computer resets the ring counter and waits for the next call.

Remote Command Mode

The **Remote Command Mode** is initiated by the caller to the answering computer by issuing a **Ctrl-C** command whist in Terminal Mode. In this mode the originating computer can execute certain commands on the answering computer. This could be potentially hazardous as the caller could erase or corrupt files on the answering computer. To safeguard against this there are two protective measures taken.

Password Protection

When the answering computer receives the **Ctrl-C** command from the caller it checks to see if there are any passwords that limit access. There are four levels of possible password protection.

Connect-Only: This is the lowest level of access permitted. It permits access to the caller but denies the use of Remote Commands.

Transmit-Only: This next level of access allows the caller to transmit files in Text or XMODEM format.

Receive-Only : The third level of access permits the caller to receive files.

Receive/Transmit: The highest level of access permits both reception and transmission of files.

Resticted Commands

Once Remote Command mode has been granted the caller is issued with the prompt:

Command:

The commands that the originator can execute on the answering computer are restricted. The following commands are available:

Command	Access Level
Transmit Text-File <filename>	T & R, R-O
Transmit XMODEM <filename>	T & R, R-O
Receive Text-File <filename>	T & R, T-O
Directory <specification>	T & R, T-O, R-O
Help	T & R, T-O, R-O

Chapter 5 : The Communication Commands

Objectives

When you have completed this Chapter you will be able to:

- Appreciate the use of those commands not already discussed.

Introduction

We shall only consider those commands that are generic to the Communications module that have not been so far considered. Those that are not generic have already been adequately covered in the earlier parts of the book.

Setting Communications Parameters

Profile: A **Profile** is a file that contains a predefined collection of Settings. Using the Profile command on Command list 2, a new profile can be defined or an old profile can be deleted.

Duplex: **Duplex** on Command list 2 is used to switch the Duplex Mode between Full and Half.

Filters: The **Filters** command on Command list 3 permits the definition of a capture filter table and a terminal filter table. These filter tables are used to filter out any unwanted characters so that they do not appear on the screen or enter into a buffer.

Format: Format, on Command list 2, defines the rules to translate a received data file into fields and records (for use in the Data-Manager) or into rows and columns (for use in the Spreadsheet).

Keyboard: The **Keyboard** command permits keys on the keyboard to be redefined whilst in Terminal Mode. This is used to emulate other terminal keyboards. The Keyboard command also allows the **Attention, Break** and **Switch** keys to be redefined to different keys.

Miscellaneous Commands

Transfer-Time: The **Transfer-Time** command on Command list 4 displays the estimated time needed to send a file at the currently set speed.

Output: **Output** sends a specified set of characters directly to the serial port configured as the modem port. It is primarily used with Project Processing as it allows an unattended computer to send text to the other system.

Match : On Command list 3, **Match** causes program execution to pause until a specific sequence of characters is received. It is a useful command for Project Processing and can be used to allow a password to be entered.

Get: **Get**, on Command list 3, is used to input a character or a line of characters received from the remote computer and store it in a project variable.

Absolute cell references 164
Activating commands 9
Active and inactive records 85
Alphanumeric 34
Answer mode 336, 347
Autohelp 26
Autohelp line 7

Bar chart 191
Beep 26, 283
Blank 64, 213
Bold 220
Border 150, 175
Break 284
Breakpoints 134
Browse 46, 91
Browsing a file 88
Buffer 337

Calculated field 82, 104
Call 284
Capture 337
Capture mode 344
Carrier 337
Cell addresses 53
Cell references 163
Cells 53
Clear 285
Close 245
Colnumbers 64, 175
Command 283
Command mode 53, 341
Comment 285
Communications module 333
Communications settings 342
Compute 225
Confidence 49
Connect-only 348
Continue 284
Control area 7
Copy 59, 64
Copying formulas 163
Create 48
Creating files 32, 99
Cursor 286
Cursor control 55
Curtain 196
Customised screens 42

Data entry status 82
Data range 82
Data-length 340
Data-Manager 29, 79
Delete 48, 64, 73
Dairy displays 23
Dictionaries 236
Directory 49, 182
Display 150
Display window 7
Document editing 72
Documentation 14
Duplex 337

Edit 26, 64
Editing a document 217
End 283
Enter 48
Enter-blank 286
Entering data into records 40
Entering the SMART system 5
Entry mode 53

Entry status 102
Execute 49 284

F-Calculator 49
F10 Function key 9
Fade-in 196
Fclose 288
File 150
File transfer 336
File types 258
File-Specs 47, 49
Files and databases 29
Fill 65, 214
Filter 337
Find 26, 45, 149, 220
Font 220
Fonts 75
Footnotes 221
Fopen 287
Form report 137
Fread 288
Fseek 288
Fwrite 288

Get 350
Goto 220
Grand Total 134
Graphics 224
Graphics-Edit 199
Graphs 191

Hangup 345
Headings and footings 205
Help 11, 26, 48

If 284
Indent 70
Index 49, 65, 214
Information system life cycle 295
Input 285
Insert 60, 64, 73, 175
Instant 196
Integration 255
Interactive database 83
Intersect 121
Introductory screen 6

Jump 284
Justify 62, 65, 176

Key 49
Key fields 36, 88
Key organise 92
Key update 92
Keyboard 349

Label 284
Let 285
Link 150
Load 45, 63, 26, 76
Lock 182
Lock-record 286
Logging on 337
Lookup 109

Macro 151, 214
Mail-Merge 247
Making a call 344
Margins 70
Marker 232
Match 350

351

Matrix   171
Matrix-print   196
Menu   285, 292
Message   283
Modem   340
Module manuals   16
Move   64, 74, 175
Moving a block of cells   167

Name   182
Newname   65, 182
Not-intersect   122
Numeric precision   34

Only-one   286
Order   46, 49, 91
Originate mode   336
Output   27
Overview   3

Page layout   70
Paint   49, 64
Parameter variables   280
Parameters   49, 151, 214
Parity   341
Password   77, 181, 233
Password protection   82
Pie chart   197
Pointing   167
Port   340
Print   48
Print-Enhanced   240
Print-Template   240
Printing a worksheet   179
Procedure   284
Profile   349
Project commands   283
Project data files   287
Project editor   274
Project files   271
Project menus   291
Project Processing   269
Project variables   279
Pseudocoding   304
Purge   27

Query   94
Query clauses   98
Query options   96
Quiet   285
Quit   283

Read   151, 261
Receive   337
Receive-only   348
Reformat   65, 176, 227
Relating two files   118
Relations   117
Relative cell references   164
Remember mode   143, 209, 251
Remove   27
Repaint   285
Replace   98, 218
Reports   129, 203
Return   284
Rownumbers   64, 175
Ruler   77
Running total   35

Save   45, 49, 63, 76
Scroll   149, 219

Send   151, 267
Set   201
Singlestep   285
Slideshow   196
Sort   92, 213
Speed   340
Spellchecking   235
Spillover   62
Split   183, 222
Spreadsheet   51, 153
Standard project variables   279
Status line   7
Stop   283
Stop-bits   341
Subtract   122
SUM   59
Summary definition   264
Suspend   283
System commands   8
System design   296
System development   299
System manual   15
System structure   296

Table reports   129
Tabs   70, 228
Terminal emulation   336
Terminal mode   341
Terms of reference   295
Text-Editor   50
Text-File   247
Text-Format   176
Text-Sort   231
Time-Manager   17
Titles   64, 176
Top down design   296
Transactions   125
Transfer   284
Transfer-time   350
Transmit   337
Transmit-only   348

Undelete   73
Underscore   220
Union   123
Unlink   150
Unload   45, 49, 63, 76
Unlock   182
Update   45, 48
Use   27
User-defined project variables   280
Using the diary   19

Value-Format   65, 176
Variables   279

Wait   283
What ... if?   187
Where   98
While   284
Width   62, 65, 175
Windows   183
Wordprocessor   67, 215
Worksheet   52
Worksheet construction   57
Write   151, 261

Xlate   268
XMODEM   337

Zoom   244